THE TIMES

Guide to the European Parliament 1994

Edited by
Robert Morgan
The Times Political Staff

The Times

Published by Times Books
An imprint of HarperCollins*Publishers*
77-85 Fulham Palace Road
Hammersmith,
London W6 8JB

Acknowledgement
In compiling this guide, the Editor, *The Times* and Times Books wish to acknowledge their indebtedness for the assistance and co-operation given by the Directorate General of Information and Public Relations of the European Parliament based in Luxembourg, the staffs of the offices of the Parliament in the member states, particuarly in the United Kingdom, the secretariats and press officers of the political groups and offices of political parties in the United Kingdom.   REM

Compiled by
Wendy Showell and Steve Gibbs

Typesetting by
News International Newspapers Ltd
1 Virginia Street,
London E1 9XS

Printed in the UK by Butler and Tanner Ltd.,
Frome, Somerset.

British Library Cataloguing in Publication Data
"Times" Guide to the European Parliament.
— June 1994
I. Morgan, Robert
341.2424

ISBN 0 7230 0708 X

Contents

Foreword

By Dr Klaus Hänsch, President of the European Parliament

Parliament needs greater strength

Nothing will remain exactly as it has been for the last forty years. That is also true of the European Union.

It is not enough to hold on to the legacy of Jean Monnet and Robert Schuman. If we wish to preserve that legacy in the new Europe we must change it and develop it. Altiero Spinelli, whose memory still lives with us today, opened our eyes to that fact. But his proposals and visions must also grow into the new Europe.

The 1996 Intergovernmental Conference provides us with the next and perhaps last opportunity to achieve this. It must give the Union a form which will enable it to take up the challenges of the next decades. To this end, our Parliament must be fully entitled to put forward its ideas with all its weight from the preparatory stage onwards. There are three major areas in which this applies:

1. The European Union does not need more powers but greater parliamentary democracy. It needs a new balance between its institutions enabling it to act more effectively and to take decisions in a more democratic way.

In all 'normal' cases, from legislation as a whole to common initiatives under the common foreign and security policy and to the appointment of the President of the Commission, the Council and governments must now decide by a majority vote. And in all cases in which the Council can decide by a majority vote Parliament must be able to participate on an equal footing and with the same rights.

2. The reform must give the Union more depth so that it remains capable of taking action even with sixteen Member States. Only a deeper Union can absorb additional Member States without collapsing and dissolving.

3. The reform will succeed only if the national parliaments are also included in the discussions at an early stage. For that reason, at the appropriate time I will take the initiative and convene a conference of the national parliaments with the European Parliament in order to discuss the proposals prepared for the intergovernmental conference and to provide guidelines for its work.

In doing all this we are in no way trying to create a European superstate.

It is possible for the Union to remain a Union of Member States while at the same time becoming a citizens' Union.

Each of the nations of Europe will still be able to recognise in the future its own unmistakable features in the European Union. It has often been said, and remains true, that the diversity of Europe's peoples, cultures and traditions is not its weakness but its strength, provided that we succeed in uniting our forces, exercising our individual sovereignties together and replacing the old antagonism with a new spirit of co-operation.

Institutions are important, and the reform of institutions is important too. But we will not win the hearts and minds of the people with debates on institutional changes. We will only do this if our policies remove some of their fears and concerns, if we link the task of uniting Europe to their hopes and dreams.

4

Electors across Europe show anger with their governments

By Robert Morgan
The Times Political Staff

The elections to the European Parliament in June 1994 proved an overwhelming victory for Labour in Britain, but the outcome in continental Europe was far less clear. In almost every country there were marked anti-government votes with fringe and extreme parties picking up seats. The result was a somewhat muddied picture throughout the 12 union member states and although the Socialists emerged as the biggest group at Strasbourg, they still failed to get an overall majority.

It was only in Germany and Italy where the voters backed the ruling party. Chancellor Helmut Kohl's Christian Democrats defied dire predictions and trounced the opposition Social Democrats and his chief opponent in October's general election, Rudolf Scharping. The new Italian Prime Minister, Silvio Berlusconi, also emerged as a big winner, increasing his *Forza Italia's* vote by nearly 10 per cent over his general election tally earlier in the year. The vote consolidated his position as the new force in European politics.

The results in Britain, where the Conseravtives lost 14 seats, were seen as a condemnation of John Major's Government, but party officials were quick to point out that the results were better than many commentators and opinion polls had predicted. Although the British Liberal Democrats picked up their first two seats in the European Parliament, the overall result was disappointing for Paddy Ashdown's party.

Despite the success of the Labour Party in Britain, the tradition of using the Parliament as a cross-party pressure group to push for a federal Europe will fade a little inside the Socialist group. The German Socialists, among the most enthusiastically federalist, took a severe beating and the French socialists were decimated.

But the squad of centre-right MEPs elected in Spain, Danish Liberals, Belgians, Irish and Greeks of almost every hue will back Europe as before.

The voices arguing that European integration should be put into reverse will be a tiny fraction of the 567 people elected. The results, with the extreme right slipping in Germany and France and gaining only in Belgium, are symptoms of the confusion prevailing in Western Europe over what precisely the European Union is and where it should be going.

Although MEPs are hardly household names in Britain, the ruling Conservative Party lost most of those known outside Strasbourg. Sir Christopher Prout, the party's leader, lost in Herefordshire and Shropshire, and the man tipped to succeed him, Christopher Jackson, lost in East Kent. The Earl of Stockton, grandson of Harold Macmillan, the former British Prime Minister, was soundly beaten in Bristol and Edwina Currie, the former Conservative health minister, failed to capture Bedfordshire and Milton Keynes.

Probably the best-known of the Labour MEPs was making her first sortie into public life. Glenys Kinnock, wife of the former Labour leader, Neil Kinnock, not only captured South Wales East, but scored by far the highest number of votes. Three out of four voters in her constituency backed her. In Greece, Nana Mouskouri, the popular singer was returned on the New Democracy list.

The leader of the Labour MEPs, Pauline Green, had a massively increased majority in North London, and Phillip Whitehead, a Labour Party frontbencher in the Seventies, returned to public life from the television studio where he has been an award-winning producer.

Winnie Ewing, the long-serving Scottish Nationalist, known in Strasbourg as "Madame Ecosse", was again elected for the Highlands and Islands. She is joined for the first time by another Scottish National Party member, Allan Macartney. Ian Paisley and John Hume, the two Westminster MPs from Northern Ireland, continue with their dual mandates.

More than 269 million people were entitled to vote across the Union, but as in the past, turnout was disappointingly low with only a little over half the electorate bothering to turn out. In Britain just over one in three people (36.1 per cent) voted. Taken with the overwhelmingly national themes of the 12 campaigns, the turnout suggests that ordinary Europeans have yet to identify strongly with the Parliament or feel that they have a clear stake in the European Union's direction.

Voters had the choice of 10,000 candidates, and outside Britain, these made up 300 lists. Five hundred hopefuls put themselves up for the 84 British seats with a further 17 contesting the one three-member seat in Northern Ireland.

The Socialist Group, the Party of European Socialists (PES), will be able to muster around 200 votes with the European People's Party, made up mainly of Christian Democrats and including the 18 Conservatives from Britain, will be the next largest group with about 150 votes. The remaining seats are spread among the extreme right to the far left with many independent and non-affiliated MEPs.

In Britain, the result was seen as the biggest defeat suffered by the Conservatives in any election in modern times and probably this century. The swing from them to Labour was 5.5 per cent and the swing from them to the Liberal Democrats was 8.7 per cent. Although the Green vote collapsed compared 1989 when they polled 15 per cent, voting for them and other fringe groups, such as the Natural Law Party, seems to have saved some of the 18 seats the Tories managed to hold.

The pattern of voting across the country showed that Labour, for the first time since the 1960s, was able to pick up votes not only in its industrial heartlands, but in the shires and leafy suburbs, the traditional strongholds of the Conservatives. The electorate seemed to demonstrate that it had shrugged off its fear of voting Labour. The Conservatives did better in those seats with the highest turnout, indicating that more of their supporters than those of the other parties had stayed at home.

The Scottish Nationlists picked up a second seat and with about 30 per cent of the Scottish vote, claimed a breakthrough towards their goal of an independent Scotland within Europe.

Of the 518 MEPs in the outgoing parliament, only 242 were returned to the new, 567-seat Parliament. Italy returned 66 new members, France 56 and Germany 53. The United Kingdom elected 33 new members and 54 members of the old Parliament.

The lack of enthusiasm among Union voters was in stark contrast to the attitude in Austria. While the Euro-elections were being held in the 12 member states, more than 80 per cent of the Austrian electorate voted by two to one in a referendum in favour of their Government's application to join the union from January 1 1995.

Three other countries, Finland, Norway and Sweden, also intend to join on January 1 1995 and were scheduled to hold referendums in the autumn of 1994. In one of its last acts, the outgoing Parliament voted overwhelmingly in May 1994 in favour of their applications.

When the new Parliament assembled at Strasbourg in late July 1994, MEPs overwhelmingly endorsed Klaus Hänsch, the German Socialist, as its new President. He will take the chair of the Parliament for the next two-and-a-half years.

Herr Hänsch, who was born in Silesia just before the war, is committed to strengthening the role of the Parliament. His wide experience in international affairs will prove a useful asset as Parliament presses for a louder voice in the Inter-Governmental Conference scheduled for 1996.

The new President also wants to bring the work of the Parliament more closely to the European people. He describes himself as a European German and believes that it is not good enough that the public is reminded of the Parliament's existence only every five years when there are elections.

The only other contender for the presidency was Yves Galland, the French Liberal, but he could muster little support.

The appointment by the 12 governments of Jacques Santer, the Prime Minister of Luxembourg, as the new President of the Commission, angered many MEPs, particularly the Socialists who felt that Parliament should be the thirteenth voice at the table before such decisions are made. But after an acrimonious debate, Mr Santer's appointment was endorsed by 260 votes to 238.

He immediately underlined his determination to be a strong president of a strong commission committed to working in tandem with the Parliament.

Voters cautious about moves to greater integration

Peter Riddell, political columnist of *The Times*, says the election gave few pointers to closer European ties

The European elections of 1994 decided very little. Three-fifths of the members of the Parliament were new, but, paradoxically, the politics of Europe were little different from before. In theory, the elections were about the composition of a legislature covering all 12 member states. In practice, there were 12 different national campaigns, decided largely by domestic political factors. For all the links between the main socialist and centre-right groups, the national parties in various countries fought separate campaigns.

Moreover, insofar as European issues were raised during the campaign, as they were at times in Britain, they were more about the policies of the Government than about what members of the Strasbourg Parliament could, or should, do. It was an election about policy on the council of ministers than about votes by members of the Parliament.

Hence the results have diverse implications. Labour may have scooped up three quarters of the British seats in the Parliament. The Conservatives may have suffered their worst nationwide result in their history. And the Liberal Democrats may have won their first beachhead in Strasbourg. But, big though these changes were, their impact, both domestically and in the European Parliament, was less than might have been expected.

With one significant exception, the results were mainly a verdict on the domestic records of long-established governing parties, particularly in Britain (exaggerated by the impact of the first-past-the-post system) and Spain. In Greece, the vote of the ruling socialists fell back compared with last year's general election, while in Ireland the vote of the Fianna Fail-Labour coalition was much lower than at the 1992 election. In Denmark, the Social Democrats also suffered a big reverse. The two big exceptions are Germany, where Chancellor Helmut Kohl's Christian Democratic Union and its Bavarian allies in the Christian Social Union emerged well ahead of the Social Democrats, and Italy, where the newly elected *Forza Italia* led by Silvio Berlusconi improved on its share in the March election in face of continued disarray by the old parties.

The beneficiaries of Government unpopularity were the main Opposition parties in Britain and Spain, but elsewhere anti-establishment parties did well. Far-right groups gained in Belgium, though slipped back in France, Italy and Germany. Anit-Maastricht parties did very well in France (notably the Philippe de Villiers-Sir James Goldsmith group The Other Europe), Denmark, Spain and Greece.

But, in total, these anti-Maastricht parties are still small by comparison with the main socialist and centre-right groups (such as the European People's

Party). The broad left versus right balance changed little, though the right slipped back a little. More striking was a rise in the proportion of unaffiliated and independent members. It is hard to argue that the election delivered a clearcut verdict on the direction of Europe: rather there were a series of national verdicts, reflecting the confusion over the post-Maastricht shape of Europe. Neither those wanting faster progress towards integration nor those wanting a return of power to nation states can claim victory.

But, as the narrow results of the French and Danish referendums showed, voters in Europe are cautious about moving faster to integration. The Governments preparing for the 1996 conferencce on revising the Maastricht Treaty know they do not have *carte blanche* to push ahead regardless. The absence of a clear majority for any group in the new Parliament means that most measures will have to rely on a broad consensus between the Socialists and the European People's Party, though occasionally the Socialists may be able to form alliances with some of the smaller groups on the left. This is not a formula for dramatic action, especially when so many MEPs do not turn up. The Parliament may have greater powers under the Maastricht treaty: co-decision and veto on the appointment of the president and new members of the commission. But the initiative on policymaking will still lie with member governments.

However, it appeared to be business as usual shortly after the election when Chancellor Kohl and President Mitterrand proposed the nomination of Jean-Luc Dehaene, the Belgian Prime Minister, as the new president. Mr Dehaene is a skillful deal-maker, as must be anyone who survives at the top of Belgian coalition politics, but he appears, in style and views, a supporter of traditional European integration. This did not endear him to Britain, which alone pressed its opposition to the point of veto at the Corfu summit of European heads of government at the end of the Greek presidency in June 1994. Other countries were irritated by the Franco-German attempt to bounce through the appointment, but were willing to acquiesce.

The key tests about whether anything has changed will be not just the preparations for the 1996 inter-governmental conference but also the policy adopted on future Brussels regulations, opening-up the European Union to the east and moving towards the convergence criteria for economic and monetary union. On none of these was the outcome of the European elections conclusive.

The British Government argues that it is not isolated: that the views that John Major and Douglas Hurd put over during the election campaign and at the Corfu summit were more widely accepted. Britain can claim alliances, particularly with Germany, over issues such as deregulation and subsidiarity. But most important is how far the European Union develops together, or at different speeds. To some extent, the latter is already happening, with, for example, the Schengen agreement for a group of neighbouring countries. There are differences also on defence co-operation and the social chapter.

Under Mr Hurd's influence, that was elevated into the doctrine of a variable geometry Europe, described as a multi-track, multi-speed or multi-layered Europe. For Mr Hurd, it meant rejecting a detailed blueprint for the development of the European Union laid down in Brussels, and instead recognising a degree of national diversity. For Mr Major, it meant asserting the British national interest, and not always accepting the view of other European partners. These themes were highlighted by Mr Major during the campaign and struck a chord with most Tory supporters and MPs, especially after the later exercise of the British veto at Corfu. The Tory Euro-sceptics, who had so bitterly challenged the Government during the long passage of the Maastricht bill during 1992-3, were loud in their support of Mr Major. Even Baroness Thatcher made known her approval.

Although tactically this united the Tory party in the short term, even possibly until the general election, would it represent a viable long-term strategy? The Tory pro-Europeans were worried that the whole approach was too minimalist, too negative: that the use of the veto was not a matter for celebration, but rather for regret.

The central question remained economic and monetary union. The British Government officially maintained an agnostic position, stressing the opt-out negotiated by Mr Major in the Maastricht Treaty and the fact that any decision to participate would be taken by a future British Parliament. This formula was intended to embrace both those like Kenneth Clarke and John Gummer who believed that a single currency was a desirable long-term goal, whatever doubts they might have on timing, and committed opponents of monetary union like Michael Portillo. British ministers talked, and hoped, that the issue would go away, but, if or perhaps when, Germany and France moved towards a single currency, then any Conservative Government would face an agonising debate. The Euro-sceptics would argue that Britain could happily remain outside, while the pro-Europeans would favour joining to avoid being outside the central development of the European Union. The Government's monetary and fiscal policies were intended to ensure that Britain met the officially laid down convergence criteria on public borrowing, debt and inflation.

The European campaign was an easier ride for the Opposition parties in Britain. Labour capitalised on the Tories' domestic unpopularity and highlighted the British opt-outs to argue that Britain had lost influence with the rest of Europe. Yet Labour claimed that it would not go along with all proposals for closer integration. The Liberal Democrats were portrayed by the other two parties as the most pro-European and may have suffered a little electorally from that label.

But apart from the Tories' multi-track Europe theme, the campaign did little to alter British attitudes towards the rest of Europe. This was implicitly recognised after the elections were over by Tony Blair during his campaign for the Labour leadership. He challenged the Tories' judgment in adopting a more sceptical stance and said Labour, as "the thinking pro-European party", had to re-establish "support and understanding for the principles of European co-operation". The pro-European case, he said, had to be re-stated to take account of public doubts about the pace of integration.

Europe might again be a dividing factor between, as well as within, the main parties, though with the positions reversed.

Massive vote of confidence for the Labour Party

By Philip Webster
Political Editor of *The Times*

Early on May 12 1994 John Smith died, struck down by a heart attack, after less than two years as leader of the Labour Party.

It was an event that was to change the face of British politics, but its most immediate impact was on the European elections the following month.

Until Mr Smith's untimely death, that poll was always going to be regarded as a referendum on an unpopular British Government, and an even more unpopular Prime Minister.

After a torrid two years since his 1992 General Election victory, John Major was at a low political ebb. The battle over the Maastricht Treaty had riven an undisciplined Conservative parliamentary party; the Prime Minister had few friends in the predominantly Conservative media. A damaging row over changing the European Union's qualified majority voting system to take account of the imminent arrival of four new members further undermined his credibility.

Mr Smith, many thought, was poised to land the knockout blow, particularly after the disaster of local election night on May 5, when the Liberal Democrats made sweeping gains across the land and shared second place overall with the Tories, a long way behind Labour. Was June 9 going to be Mr Major's Waterloo?

The Smith tragedy changed everything. Rather than the, perhaps remote, possibility of a Conservative leadership election in the early summer, the political world was suddenly presented with the certainty of a Labour contest. There was little chance that the Conservatives would change their leader while Labour was without one; only a Tory wipeout on June 9 would have provoked the sort of panic that might have at last provided a role for the so called "men in grey suits", the Tory grandees dubiously supposed to have the power to ask a Prime Minister to stand down.

In the event the Conservatives did very badly, producing their worst national electoral performance of the century, and Labour triumphed. After a campaign truncated by a week because of a political truce in the aftermath of Mr Smith's death, Labour ended up winning 62 of the 84 seats in England, Scotland and Wales, and the Conservative tally slumped to 18.

The big surprise was the performance of the Liberal Democrats. They gained a foothold in the European Parliament by winning their first seats. But they managed only two, cheated of a third in Devon by the intervention of a rogue candidate calling himself a "Literal Democrat" who siphoned off 10,000 votes and let the Conservatives in. It was a bitter disappointment after hopes that they were on the verge of a breakthrough.

The Liberal Democrat share of the vote plummeted from 27 per cent in the local polls just a month before to 16 per cent. It was a fall that consoled the Conservatives — particularly those MPs in the South and South-east who had long been vulnerable to an advance from Paddy Ashdown's party.

Just 18 seats was an abysmal showing for the ruling party; but the expectations had been so low that it was tolerable. Mr Major was left to fight on. As the last results came in he called political correspondents to the garden of 10 Downing Street and told them straight. He would lead the Conservatives into the next General Election; if anyone wanted to challenge him they would find him waiting for them; and he would beat them.

As things turned out it would have been a cruel injustice if these particular elections had resulted in the demise of the Prime Minister.

Mr Major was generally reckoned by friend and foe to have done well. The old cliché about winning the campaign but losing the war appeared to have relevance here. In spite of the massive Tory divisions over Europe, Mr Major had taken the issue head-on.

While the Labour and Liberal Democrat battles concentrated heavily on domestic issues, trying to turn it into the referendum on the Government and Mr Major that they had sought, Mr Major spent the campaign hammering the message that the Conservatives were the true defenders of Britain's interests in Europe.

While some of the party's Euro-enthusiast wing were later to criticise the negative tone of the Tory efforts, it was a clear calculation of party strategists that the way to avoid disaster was to bring out the core Conservative vote. And if that meant pressing the patriotic and Eurosceptic buttons so be it.

Mr Major led from the front, making six regional tours and addressing four big rallies. He also chaired three national press conferences and gave about 20 interviews, mostly to the regional press. It was a sharp contrast to Margaret Thatcher's involvement in 1989; she restricted herself to one rally and two press conferences.

Mr Major's speeches set the tone of the campaign. From his first Bristol rally where he spoke of his spirits sinking just a little every time he left the country, and promised that he would never allow Britain to be swamped in a European superstate, the Prime Minister unashamedly wrapped himself in the flag. And he took the headlines.

A sudden onslaught on beggars in a regional newspaper interview was as surprising as it was out of character. He denounced down-and-outs as an eyesore who drove tourists and shoppers away; it was an offensive problem. It produced a predictable wave of outrage, but among Conservatives it seemed to strike a chord.

Moving on to Ellesmere Port, Cheshire, Mr Major delivered the speech that brought the campaign to life. His call for a "multi-track, multi-speed, multi-layered" Europe pleased the Eurosceptics — Lord Tebbit described it as "the best argument yet for voting Conservative at this election" — and worried the enthusiasts. Labour berated him for putting Britain into the "bicycle lane" and the Liberal Democrats of wanting a "drop-out Britain".

In fact, Mr Major was deploying a carefully thought-out strategy both to keep his party together and to appeal to traditional Tory voters. It had first been articulated by Douglas Hurd, the Foreign Secreary, in a speech to Scottish Tories.

But here, in the middle of the campaign and coming from the Prime Minister, it made a thunderous impact. The concept of a flexible Europe in which individual countries chose which institutions they wanted to join appeared to chime with public attitudes.

From the start of the campaign it was clear that all parties had perceived a more sceptical mood among the electorate.

The Liberal Democrats, traditionally the keenest pro-Europeans, notably toned down their support for a federal Europe in their manifesto. It contained few references to federalism and included a promise to seek popular assent through a referendum of any major constitutional changes to the structure of the European Union at the 1996 summit of European leaders.

It explicitly rejected a "centralised superstate — as secretive and inefficient as Britain's own bureaucracy in Westminster and Whitehall".

Labour, only a decade earlier, had entered a general election committed to pulling Britain out of the European Community but has since undergone a complete conversion. Margaret Beckett, its acting leader, explained the change as one that recognised the changes that had taken place in the world and reflected the wishes of British voters to stay within the EU. But at these elections it inserted a note of caution into its stance of backing for monetary union leading to a single currency. Now it emphasised more strongly than before the importance of the economies of the EU converging before a single currency could come into force and voiced doubts over when it could be achieved. For good measure Labour gave strong indications that it would offer a referendum before ever agreeing to a single currency.

Even so, Labour wore its general enthusiasm on its sleeve. The manifesto promised that Labour would move Britain from the margins to the centre where it would help to shape and direct Europe and foster economic and social benefits.

As one would have expected from a party that had been so torn apart over Europe, the Conservative Party took more time than its rivals over drawing up its manifesto. A committee chaired by the Foreign Secretary laboured long and hard, charting a way through the minefield of conflicting views to come up with a document that both sides could live with.

While underlining the party's commitment to Europe, it repeatedly declared opposition to the creation of a European super-state and said that the party wanted a decentralised Europe of nation states with less Brussels interference. Where almost everyone in the Tory party could agree was on a general statement of opposition to the Social Chapter. But most striking was the party's keenness to move the agenda away from domestic issues to Europe. Mr Major told voters in the foreword: "You will not be voting for Europe, Right or Wrong. You will be voting for Europe, Right or Left. To the right, more jobs, more prosperity in a wider union of free nations. To the left, more petty restrictions and longer dole queues."

It was a lively campaign, but one that only occasionally caught fire. Manifesto launch day set the tone with allegations from the Conservatives that Labour and the Liberal Democrats would put the national veto at risk. Labour hit back with claims that the Tories were telling a "tissue of lies" and had a passage in its manifesto promising that Labour would always keep the principle of unanimity for areas such as fiscal and budgetary policy, foreign and security issues to throw back at the Government. Michael Howard, the Home Secretary, later took the issue into his sphere by claiming that the Opposition policies on the veto would put immigration controls at risk. Predictably he was accused of playing the race card.

In truth, while the parties tried to be distinctive their underlying messages were similar. If you wanted a strong British voice at the centre of Europe all three parties told you to vote for them. If you wanted to keep a British veto over tax rates, foreign and defence policy and constitutional change you could quite happily vote for any of the three. If you wanted to put off a decision on the single currency indefinitely, again you could vote Labour or Conservative; the Liberal Democrats would go to monetary union when the rest of Europe did.

The beggars row gave the press an entertaining few days. There was the ritual dispute over whether the Government was planning further impositions of VAT. The only real hint of Tory trouble came when Kenneth Clarke, the Chancellor, and John Gummer, the Environment Secretary, pro-Europeans both, seemed to distance themselves from Mr Major's preoccupation with a multi-speed approach. Only two years before he had denounced the idea of a two-speed Europe. The Cabinet Eurosceptics were kept well out of the limelight. Peter Lilley, the Social Security Secretary, spent much of the campaign in Normandy.

But there were other things to keep the media amused. Much of the attention was focused on the still unofficial Labour leadership contest, and the question of whether Gordon Brown, the Shadow Chancellor, would stand aside for his friend Tony Blair, the Shadow Home Secretary. Eventually he did, but it was fun while it lasted. When it came to the final weekend of campaigning Euro-elections were a long way from the front of the nation's consciousness. The fiftieth anniversary of the D-Day landings were commemorated comprehensively by veterans, public, newspapers and television.

Meanwhile the polls steadily moved against the Government. In the end, however, it was the events unfolding in the Labour party that had the biggest bearing on the outcome of June 9.

When the voters set off for the polling stations Labour's internal election campaign had not officially begun. But for three weeks the media had told them that Mr Blair would be the next leader, and they appeared to believe it. Labour's strong showing, its best since 1966, was a testament not only to the legacy of John Smith, but to his predecessor Neil Kinnock, in helping to make Labour electable again.

It was also an advance vote of confidence in Mr Blair and the potential drawing power of a more outward-looking Labour Party under him. According to exit polls former Tories switched straight to Labour, rather than flirting with the Liberal Democrats, as they had done so often before. Ironically, had Mr Smith been alive Labour might have won just as many seats, but they might not have polled so well in the South. By doing that they helped to deprive the Liberal Democrats of more spectacular gains. No wonder they were accused of saving Mr Major's bacon.

Paisley claims support for hardline stand

By Nicholas Watt
Ireland Correspondent

The polarisation of Northern Ireland's politics was graphically illustrated by the European election results, with both sides claiming strong mandates from their respective communities. European issues played little part in the election which was effectively turned into a referendum on the Downing Street Declaration of December 1993.

The Rev Ian Paisley, the 68-year-old leader of the hardline Democratic Unionists, topped the poll for the fourth consecutive time and claimed overwhelming support for his party's uncompromising stance against the Anglo-Irish Declaration. He won 163,246 first preference votes or 29.2 per cent. Although this was down by 0.7 percentage points on his vote in the 1989 election, Mr Paisley portrayed himself as the standard bearer of Unionism because he pushed his share of the pro-Union vote to just over 50 per cent.

However, John Hume, leader of the Social Democratic and Labour Party, consolidated his position as leader of the nationalist community, and also claimed a powerful endorsement for his talks with Sinn Fein. Mr Hume, 57, scored the highest vote in his party's history when he won 161,992 first preference votes (28.9 per cent) which was up by 3.4 percentage points on his vote in 1989. Jim Nicholson, 49, the Ulster Unionist candidate, whose party has taken a more cautious approach to the Downing Street Declaration than Mr Paisley's thundering rejection, nudged his share up to 133,459 first preference votes (23.8 per cent) which was up by 1.6 percentage points on 1989.

Northern Ireland elects three MEPs by proportional representation from one constituency covering the whole Province. There were 17 candidates from parties which included Sinn Fein, Alliance, the Conservatives, and three groups campaigning for independence for the Province. Mr Paisley and Mr Hume won on the first round, while Mr Nicholson secured the third seat in the second round.

Within minutes of the declaration in Belfast Mr Paisley sought to capitalise on his victory. To roars of approval from his supporters he said: "The people of this Province will not have Dublin interference . . . We have won this election. We have now got to win the war." Referring to Mr Hume's vote, he said: "He has delivered Ulster into the hands of our enemy and given hope to the minority that they can trample over the majority. But they will never be able to do that."

Mr Paisley then strode out of the declaration hall and telephoned Downing Street on his mobile phone to demand a meeting with John Major. While officials in Downing Street were quick to consult their diaries in the light of Mr Paisley's win, they will almost certainly be less anxious about his warnings of the evils of allowing Dublin any say in the affairs of Northern Ireland. Officials know that

15

Mr Paisley's huge personal support invariably secures him first place in every European poll, but they never allow that to deflect them from working closely with the Irish Government and regarding the Ulster Unionist party as the voice of mainstream Unionism. The UUP has nine MPs at Westminster to the DUP's three, and John Major will be listening more carefully to James Molyneaux's measured tones than Mr Paisley's raucous language, not least because the Prime Minister has an informal parliamentary understanding with the UUP in times of crisis.

Although Mr Nicholson, of the UUP, failed to challenge Mr Paisley's resounding lead, his creditable performance was strong enough to ensure that his party will maintain its more cautious approach to the Anglo-Irish peace initiative. The party is deeply unhappy with many crucial aspects of the 1993 Downing Street Declaration, but feels that its interests are best served by adopting a less confrontational approach. There had been fears that if Mr Paisley had dramatically increased his vote at the expense of the UUP, Mr Molyneaux may have been forced to adopt Mr Paisley's strident tones.

However, Mr Nicholson pledged after the result to ensure that political progress is not slowed down. He said: "The increase in my vote indicates that people are not overly concerned about all the hype about the Downing Street Declaration. They want a steady process that Jim Molyneaux is involved in. They believe this is the best way for Unionism, rather than the confrontational-type politics that Dr Paisley has got involved in."

His comments underlined the tension between the two wings of Unionism which were exacerbated by the campaign. Mr Paisley was so determined to differentiate himself from the Ulster Unionists that at one point he infuriated his rivals by comparing Mr Molyneaux to Judas for betraying the Union.

If Mr Paisley was belligerent in victory, Mr Hume was composed after his historic result. Mr Hume, who tried to campaign on European issues, said his vote was a powerful message from people who wanted an end to violence. "We will continue our work with the peace process which threatens nobody," he said afterwards. "We want to work towards a total end to violence followed by dialogue to reach agreement between our people."

The Irish Government seized on Mr Hume's increased vote, which appeared to come from nationalists who had previously not bothered to turn out, as proof of widespread support for the Anglo-Irish peace initiative. However, Mr Hume's vote was ambiguous. Some of his support will have been anti-Sinn Fein while others will have voted for the SDLP because of Mr Hume's talks with Gerry Adams.

Sinn Fein will have been disappointed by its result. It increased only slightly its first preference votes to 55,215 (9.9 per cent) from 48,914 (9.2 per cent) in 1989 despite fielding three candidates to try to maximise its support. This was a long way behind the high point of 1984 when Danny Morrison, formerly the party's publicity director, won 91,476 first preference votes or 13.3 per cent. However, the party will have been encouraged when Sir Patrick Mayhew, the Northern Ireland Secretary, acknowledged after the election that Sinn Fein had an electoral mandate.

The Conservatives were dejected after the collapse in support for their candidate. Myrtle Boal won only 1 per cent of the vote compared with 4.8 per cent for the party's candidate in 1989. This was despite vigorous campaigning on her behalf by Sir Patrick and other leading Tories who flew over from London. Alliance also did badly. Mary Clark-Glass won just 4.1 per cent compared with 5.2 per cent for the party in 1989.

Established parties jolted by upsurge of the Greens

By Nicholas Watt, Ireland Correspondent

Ireland's established political parties were jolted by the dramatic success of the Greens who captured two seats in an election which led to the first signs of public strain in the Republic's 18-month-old coalition government. A strong protest vote coupled with feuding in some of the bigger parties allowed the Greens to make their biggest breakthrough in Ireland since the party was founded in 1982.

Fianna Fail, the senior coalition partner, did creditably well in the election by increasing its number of seats from six to seven. But Labour, its junior partner, only managed to retain its one seat, which led to calls from backbenchers for a more assertive voice in government. Fine Gael, the main opposition party, hoped that by retaining its four seats it would have killed off talk of its decline. However, the election provided a devastating blow to the small Progressive Democrats who lost their only seat in Munster.

The Republic of Ireland votes for 15 MEPs by proportional representation in four constituencies. Three are voted from a constituency covering Connacht and the three Ulster counties in the Republic, and four each are voted from Dublin, Leinster and Munster. The campaign was dominated by domestic issues and clashes between some of Ireland's best known political personalities — some within the same party — who were pitted against each other. European issues played little part despite the largesse from Brussels which has brought billions of pounds to the Republic. It is estimated that up to the end of the decade Ireland will receive IR£6.2 billion in EU structural and cohesion funds.

Dublin, which traditionally has a strong protest vote, provided the most dramatic result when Patricia McKenna, the little known Green candidate, topped the poll with 14.5 per cent of the vote ahead of heavyweight political figures. The Greens were given scant media coverage during the campaign, and they were usually bracketted with "Others" in opinion polls. But the Greens' opposition to the Thorp nuclear reprocessing plant at Sellafield across the Irish Sea and to nuclear weapons paid off. Ms McKenna's success was soon followed by a second victory when Nuala Ahern won the last seat in Leinster after a lengthy two-day count. She spent just IR£6,500 on her campaign and put her victory down to a wider range of policies and greater democracy within the party.

The Labour Party, led by Dick Spring, the deputy Prime Minister, withdrew into a series of post mortems after it managed to win just one seat in Dublin. Bernie Malone, the sitting Labour MEP, won the constituency's fourth seat at the end of a campaign which was overshadowed by her intense rivalry with Orla Guerin, who was promoted as the party's first candidate in Dublin. Ms Malone claimed that she was cold-shouldered by the party hierarchy, and said that her victory was a rebuff to the high-handed behaviour of the leadership.

The party's poor performance in Dublin was matched by its national poll. Although Labour's overall share of the vote at 11 per cent was up on the 9.6 per cent it won at the last European election in 1989, this was considerably down on the 19 per cent it won at the general election in 1992. Jim Kemmy, the party chairman, signalled growing signs of unease when he said that Labour's poor performance was due to a public perception that it was complacent in government.

Albert Reynolds, the Taoiseach and leader of Fianna Fail, was encouraged that his party gained a seat in Connacht/Ulster. However, the party failed to make the kind of breakthrough that will free it from the constraints of coalition government. Fianna Fail's jubilation in Connacht/Ulster was tempered by the fact that it won the seat from Neil Blaney who did not stand after winning the seat at the last election as an independent Fianna Fail candidate. Although Fianna Fail's overall share of the vote went up to 35 per cent (from 31.5 per cent in 1989) this was down on the 39 per cent it won at the general election of 1992. Its vote also fell by eight percentage points in Co Dublin, which is the key battleground in general elections.

However, party spirits were lifted by the resounding success of Senator Brian Crowley, the highly respected disabled candidate in Munster who campaigned from his wheelchair. He was the only candidate in the Republic to win a seat on the first count, and he polled nearly twice as many first preference votes as Gerry Collins, the second Fianna Fail candidate in Munster who is a former foreign minister.

Commentators directed most of their attention after the election to the virtual collapse of the Progressive Democrats. Des O'Malley, the party's founder and former leader, suffered the first defeat in his 26-year political career when Pat Cox, who resigned as the PD's deputy leader in May to stand as an independent candidate, beat him in Munster. The election confirmed that the party, which was compared to Britain's SDP after it broke away from Fianna Fail in 1985, is in terminal decline. Although its 6.5 per cent share of the overall vote was up on the 4.6 per cent it won at the general election of 1992, this was a dramatic decline on the 11.4 per cent the PDs won at the last European election.

The result was a damaging blow to Mary Harney, who succeeded Mr O'Malley as party leader in 1993. During the campaign she turned the election of Mr O'Malley into a vote confidence in her leadership. While there was no public threat to her position after the election, hopes of uniting the fractious party appeared poor. Many supporters of Mr Cox refused to resign from the party despite calls from Ms Harney to do the "honourable thing". The split was compounded when Mr Cox promised to resign his Dail seat in Cork South-Central when the new European Parliament met.

Fine Gael's performance showed that the party is still a long way from challenging Fianna Fail as the Republic's main party. It retained its four seats and increased its share of the national vote to 24.3 per cent compared with 24 per cent at the 1992 general election and 21.6 per cent at the last European election. John Bruton, the Fine Gael leader who nearly lost the leadership in February 1994, claimed that the result cemented his position.

Referendums on governments revealed chaotic pattern of voting

George Brock, European Editor of *The Times*, explains why voters were so complacent

In 1991, the leaders of the Socialist, Christian Democrat and Liberal groups in the European Parliament — by coincidence all Belgians at the time — asked the draftsmen of the Maastricht Treaty for a clause encouraging the creation of pan-European political parties. The text which emerged is an eloquent reminder of the optimism and the energy which then infused European integration. "Political parties at European level are important as a factor for integration within the Union," intones Article 138a. "They contribute to forming a European awareness and to expressing the political will of the citizens of the Union."

As we sat in the Parliament's vast glass palace in Brussels on the night of June 12 1994 watching a bank of screens carrying results programmes from across the Continent, Article 138a still looked like a dream and not a reality. Assembling in one electronic jigsaw the coloured graphs and droning pundits being broadcast from as far apart as Copenhagen, Dublin or Athens only underlined the differences and gulfs between the 12 political cultures. Every time since direct elections to the Parliament began, the overall turnout figure has fallen: 63 per cent of voters went to the European polls in 1979 and 15 years later the figure had slipped to 56.4 per cent. The average conceals huge variations. Three states (Belgium, Greece and Luxembourg) make voting compulsory and register turnouts above 90 per cent. This time Britain, Portugal, the Netherlands and Ireland sat at the bottom of the league with turnouts below 40 per cent.

The chaotic pattern of the results only stressed that each campaign had been a referendum on governments in power, many of them weak. The last European Parliament had been elected only weeks before Hungarian refugees began trickling across the borders of the Warsaw pact and starting the chain reaction which brought down the Berlin Wall. By 1994, that Parliament met against the background of a Europe changed almost out of recognition. Public reactions to the post-Cold War era and to the recession which took EU dole queues to almost 20 million fall into no clear pattern. Sitting governments survived the vote strongly in Germany and Italy. The right gained ground in Spain, Denmark and the Netherlands. The left did well in Greece, Portugal and Britain. Many small parties did well but the Greens fared badly in general. Pro-EU parties held the vast bulk of the votes in Germany while Euro-sceptics made striking gains in France.

The election campaign failed to express any sort of European political will for the simple reason that there no such thing. Politicians did not raise European issues except where they saw a clear domestic electoral advantage in doing so for the simple reason that few of them felt like taking risks. Two principal factors lie behind the fragmentation of the campaign.

The European Parliament has never been lucky with its timing. Not only was the last assembly elected just before the economic boom and stability of the 1989 world evaporated, but the 1994 election struck a cluster of domestic campaigns and pre-campaign manoevering. The first 10 months of 1994 mark one of the most intensive election seasons which Germany has ever witnessed: 19 votes in all, culminating in a general election in October. The low turnout in the Netherlands may in part be explained by voter exhaustion after both local and general elections only a few weeks before. In France, the European election was sandwiched between the year of a general election and the forthcoming presidential vote in spring 1995 which will elect François Mitterrand's successor. Italians were still recovering from the electoral earthquake which brought Silvio Berlusconi's *Forza Italia* to power when they were asked to vote again in June. Government ministers were neither in the mood nor the position to take risks by plunging into abstract Euro-issues of little obvious relevance to unemployment or other pressing items on national agendas.

One apparent exception to this stands out: Germany, where, Helmut Kohl, the most strongly pro-integration leader of all, did play up European solutions to German problems and scored well. But the strong presence of pan-European issues such as trans-national crime fighting, security and immigration only reflected something unique to German politics. In the EU's largest state, European issues are national political questions. An EU immigration policy is to a very large extent a policy about what will happen in Germany: that is where the bulk of asylum-seekers, immigrants and refugees go. The lengthy frontiers of the reunified Germany are being exploited by cross-borders criminals in ways probably unequalled elsewhere in the EU.

But even Chancellor Kohl sounded an uncertain note on the longer-term future of the EU and he reflected a mood which was the second factor splitting the campaign debate into so many pieces. It had been a mistake, Kohl admitted, to talk about a united states of Europe but he remained in favour of a federal Europe. Dominique Baudis, leader of the French centre-right government's list, caused a small stir by opening his campaign with a heretical announcement that he was not a federalist. Support for a French-flavoured federal Europe, an article of faith for the Parisian political class since the Second World War, has weakened steadily since the Maastricht treaty was signed.

French disenchantment is rooted in recent changes: dislike of German reunification and renewed diplomatic power, suspicion of the world trade liberalisation agreed at the end of 1993 and the sense that the bountiful days of the common agricultural policy are over. But the switch-off and suspicion went wider than France. The European Commission's own opinion polls clearly show that support for European integration began to cool well before the recession of 1991-4 began and the change seems to have begun after the Single European Act of 1987. Polls taken by newspapers during the 1994 campaign revealed that support for an eventual federal Europe was a minority view, although more people approve the general idea that integration should continue.

The message of the 1994 polls, both opinion surveys and the actual vote in June, is that no single view of Europe's future shape or structure prevails.

National governments reluctant to relinquish their powers

By George Brock, European Editor of *The Times*

The European Parliament lives in a permanent state of disappointment. Its members complain that national parliaments neither know nor care about their work. They moan that national governments conspire to deprive them of the pivotal position that is their due in the evolving European Union system. They feel neglected by the media, voters and their parent parties back home.

MEPs feel disgruntled because the promise of each "inter-governmental conference" which rewrites the Treaty of Rome is never quite fulfilled. The Parliament steadily acquires more power at each revision but never quite as much as its members think they need. The Maastricht negotiations of 1991 opened with high hopes but the states quickly made clear that they were not about to take a giant step towards a federal system. The disillusion and disinterest expressed by voters in several states when the treaty was ratified pushed the Parliament into the background.

But beneath the soured political mood on the surface, the Parliament has been steadily accumulating the capacity to armlock the EU's almost incomprehensibly complex system for making Union-wide law and to put the more powerful institutions of the European Commission and Council of Ministers under painful pressure. Maastricht made two innovatory concessions in the face of the Parliament's insistent pressure to hold the appointed members of the Commission and national governments accountable for what they do.

Starting with the Commission due to take office in January 1995, the newly-enlarged assembly of 567 MEPs must agree the governments' nominations of the new President and his fellow commissioners. Only the designated President can be rejected individually; the remaining members of the Commission must be accepted or rejected *en bloc.* The panic after the debacle at the EU summit in Corfu in June 1994 when the Union's leaders failed to decide on a successor to M Jacques Delors bears eloquent witness to the fear which the mere existence of this new power has provoked inside national governments.

Secondly, the Maastricht Treaty for the first time gave the Parliament a clear and unambiguous power of veto over certain categories of EU law. Given the European Commission's currently cautious mood and low rate of law-making, this weapon may not be wielded very often before the treaty is rewritten once more in 1996. But the power of what the treaty calls "co-decision", enshrined in Article 189B, marks a simple shift in the distribution of power which will affect decisions at all levels of the EU system.

The procedure involves three readings, a conciliation committee between the Parliament and the governments and requires an absolute majority of MEPs to reject a measure proposed. "Co-decision" covers: measures to ensure free movement of workers inside the EU, single market rules, education, culture, health, consumer protection and framework guidelines for trans-European networks (road, rail and telecommunications), research and development and environmental action.

Each change in the Parliament's procedures poses an old problem afresh. Can enough people understand the small print of the rules to make the machinery work? One senior EU official who has started to worry about the risk that the system might seize up calculates that the Union now has around 19 different ways of reaching a decision. The Parliament alone has between four and seven, depending on how you count them.

Followers of pure federalist doctrine, who believe that the Parliament should be the supreme political power in a proper federation, complain that the new clauses added by Maastricht were sops to keep MEPs quiet. National governments, they argue, never surrender real power unless forced to do so. The new powers conceded in 1991 but not used until 1994 concern second-rank subjects. The Parliament remains all but powerless on the "core" issues of monetary union, immigration and joint foreign policy.

But restricted in scope as they are, the Maastricht veto powers will give the Parliament real leverage for three reasons. First, for a straightforwardly political reason: the German government wants the Parliament to take a bigger role and to use the powers it has. Public pressure to make up the "democratic deficit" in the EU system continues to grow in Germany. The German government elected in October 1994 is likely to arrive at the Maastricht review conference in 1996 with a long list of requests to boost the Parliament's clout yet further. Those claims will be weakened if existing powers have not even been tested.

Secondly, the exercise of the new powers will reach into other parts of the EU system. MEPs have already begun to talk about wanting to share the right to initiate legislation which is now the sole preserve of the Commission. The threat that this demand will be pressed in 1996 may well affect what laws come forward and the way they are framed. The Commission, long accustomed to navigating its draft proposals through the obstacle course of ministerial councils, must now learn to combine that skill with parallel tactics in the Parliament.

Lastly, the areas in which the Parliament now wields a veto are the topics which often matter most to voters. As several opinion polls vividly demonstrated during the European election campaign, voters from Lisbon to Leipzig have lost interest in the grand designs for a Europe of the future and care more about education, health and consumer issues. The election of Mrs Pauline Green, first as leader of the British Labour Party MEPs and after the June 1994 poll as president of the whole Socialist Group, neatly symbolised how grassroots consumer issues can be turned into political power bases. Mrs Green made her name in the Parliament fighting over the intricacies of food labelling law.

Assessments of the Parliament's power based on treaty procedures alone fail to tell the whole story. Each Parliament gains or loses influence from the attitude of three sources of power which shape its role: voters, the European Commission and the national governments. The Commission and the governments remain as reluctant as ever to concede more power to the Parliament than they must. Whatever the Maastricht treaty may say on paper, the 1994 Parliament will be weakened by the fact that so few people turned out to vote for it.

Radical changes have made the Parliament unrecognisable

By Sir James Scott-Hopkins, former Conservative minister, MP and MEP, who retired in July 1994 after more than 30 years of close association with Europe.

Such have been the radical changes in the past few years that today the European Parliament is virtually unrecognisable from the early days of the Assembly. I tremble to contemplate the much turning in the grave of the Founding Fathers whose vision of the Community lay based in the Treaty of Paris way back in 1951.

While much of the development has been good and beneficial, we have been pushed into realms that not everyone is at all sure they want or why they are even necessary. What is certain, however, is that there has been continued peace in Europe — a factor that was of prime importance to the Fathers.

My excursions across the Channel go back to 1961 when, with Peter Kirk, I became a member of the Council of Europe, largely, I think, because I could speak French. We wondered what we had let ourselves in for, as it had little influence and was not allowed to make decisions.

Our presence was not exactly welcomed by de Gaulle, but then he made life difficult for everyone. It will be recalled that in the original Assembly of the six countries that being suspicious of Britain's intentions, he blocked our application for membership of the Community and was also absent for some eight months, because his power of veto was refused.

The Council of Europe still survives as a consultative body, but, despite having delegates from 22 countries stretching from Norway to Turkey, its voice is never heard.

Its demise came with the sowing of the true seeds of the Parliament as we know it today, by the establishment of the European Assembly in 1973. I so clearly remember that, as appointed members by Ted Heath, the Conservative Group received a standing ovation as it walked in. It was, indeed, an exceedingly warm introduction, compared to the virtual silence that had greeted the arrival of the Irish and Danes just minutes before.

Of course, the Socialists were not represented, because they were anti-Europe, though Roy Jenkins became President of the Commission following the 1975 referendum.

The Assembly days were happy and carefree — and Strasbourg is always delightful, whether in summer or winter. The debates were easy-going and the general atmosphere was one of a typical London club, due to the fact that we were restricted to expressing views as we had no decision-making powers. The hard work was still back in our national parliaments.

The first direct elections to the Parliament in 1979 altered all that and much of the fun disappeared, to be replaced by the cut and thrust of hard, brutal politics. The first decade was not easy. It coincided with economic difficulties, which

23

affected all industrial democracies, and the common agricultural policy, which saw the growth of food mountains and farm subsidies favouring the small French and German farmers, to mention just two of the problems we had to face.

There were differences, too, in perspective between us Conservatives and Downing Street. Mrs Thatcher, as she was then, rather took the view that we had "gone native". As the first leader of our MEPs I had a weekly informal meeting with her, a favour which gradually died out for my successors.

As one election followed another, we Conservative members of the European Democratic Group saw our representation gradually decline from 64 seats out of the 78 allotted to the United Kingdom in 1979 — we outnumbered the British Socialists by nearly four to one — to 34 in the last session. So in 1993 we decided to arm ourselves with a more formidable voice by linking up with the Christian Democrats and their allies to strengthen the Centre-Right Group. It meant that we now had 162 members and were the largest Group, apart from the Socialists, who had taken in 16 Italian Communists to bring their number up to 180.

Meanwhile, the Parliament's Budget Committee, of which I was vice-chairman, acquired the power to take joint decisions with the Council of Ministers. It resulted in some vicious rows with everyone shouting at each other when we failed to agree and there were often 200 to 300 amendments; now they number two or three.

Other dramatic changes have come since 1988, particularly with the advent of the Single Act, which removed a huge amount of legislation, such as customs duties and frontier controls, and with the accent being placed on much greater harmonisation between countries.

Since then the role of the Parliament has taken a tremendous step forward through the Maastricht Treaty. It now has the ability to amend or simply say "yes" or "no" to proposed legislation programmes and, if the Council fails to agree, especially in the fields of the environment, the budget, and agriculture, to continue talking until, at last, a compromise is reached with the final version coming before the Parliament for ratification.

That the Council had thus to face up to the Parliament's newly acquired force was clearly illustrated within days of the signing of the Treaty, when it had to concede victory by lifting the proposed ban on high-powered motor cycles, which would have had dire effects for British manufacturers.

Looking to the future, I am sure that serious consideration must be given to the Parliament becoming a full-time operation on similar lines to our Westminster House of Commons. Meeting once a month, with much of the work devolving upon committees, cannot be upheld and the situation will only worsen as the European Union enlarges with the admission of Austria, Norway, Sweden and Finland, apart from other countries knocking on the door.

Incidently, my view, too, is that for everyone's convenience and to reduce costs, the Parliament should meet in Brussels, despite the guaranteed violent objections by the French to moving from Strasbourg and their subsequent loss of high rents.

To emphasise a further point, it is currently ridiculous to restrict speakers in debates to one minute, because its is quite impossible to represent your electors with one pithy remark. While nobody wants lengthy, dreary speeches, Members should be capable in some five minutes, at the most, of being persuasive in opposing matters, the significance of which some may not even easily comprehend.

On a broader outlook, the task of the Parliament — and the Commission and the Council — must be to convince the citizens that Europe will never become a superstate or a bureaucratic monster, in which the autonomy of member states is dissolved.

The need is to assure them that the countries will remain free to develop in their own way, on the firmly-based principle of democracy, respect for human rights and an open market economy, except possibly in the spheres of defence, terrorism and crime, where united action is essential. The watchwords must be, to coin a phrase, "back to the basics" of the Founding Fathers.

Finally on a personal note, I find it intriguing, at the end of my span of 33 years association with Europe, during which talk of a common currency has seldom diminished, that my Euopean pension is to be paid in ECUs.

Parliament urged to play to its strengths

Pauline Green, President of the Party of European Socialists, examines the tasks for the next five years

The European Parliament has its strengths and its weaknesses. It also suffers from a number of handicaps that are not of its own making. The key in the next five years will be to play to its strengths and to try to eliminate those weaknesses and handicaps that can be eliminated.

Some weaknesses are inherent. The need to work in nine (and soon 12) languages means that EP debates will never have the cut and thrust of the House of Commons. The drama and theatre of Prime Minister's question time are lacking (though many would consider that to be an advantage). If a member tells a joke, laughter may follow in batches while the interpretation comes through in successive languages. Yet there is litle that can be done about this: one cannot say to the electorate of Portugal: "Vote for who you like as long as he or she speaks good English." Nor, for that matter, can one tell the electorate of Yorkshire to vote for who they like as long as the candidate speaks good French. Candidates will be selected by their parties and MEPs elected by the electorates on the basis of political criteria, not linguistic ability.

Where the EP does well is on real influence on the content of legislation, the nitty-gritty of parliamentary scrutiny, the shaping of the budget and the monitoring and questioning of the action of civil servants. Every year the European Parliament adopts thousands of amendments to draft European legislation, gradually reshaping the laws that affect us in many important areas: consumer protection, environmental standards, social legislation, equal opportunities, banking law, and so on. Through its budgetary powers, it redirects spending to priority areas, such as the structural funds which seek to improve economic and employment prospects in less prosperous regions.

Even before the Maastricht Treaty reinforced its powers, most EP amendments ended up on the statute book in the directives and regulations adopted by the Council of Ministers. With Maastricht, important areas of legislation fall under the "co-decision" procedure and are adopted jointly by Parliament and Council.

Parliament's influence on the content of legislation can only grow. In particular, the right to say "no" — to veto draft European legislation, to blow the whistle on behalf of our constituents — is likely to be crucial for the public perception of the Parliament. Judicious use of this power, weeding out unpopular proposals, will do more than anything else to put Parliament on the map.

This is in contrast to the situation in some national parliaments which act virtually as rubber stamps when it comes to adopting legislation proposed by their governments. In the United Kingdom, it is headline news if the Government does not get its way on a bill. In this respect the EP does better than many national parliaments.

Some of the EP's handicaps are caused by national governments, in whose hands the remedy lies. It is, after all, the national governments of the member states who have the power, under the treaty, to fix the seats of the institutions, and it is they who want Parliament to continue with the ludicrous system of spreading its activities over three countries.

In practice, most parliamentary work is carried out in Brussels, but once a month the whole show moves to Strasbourg for plenary sittings, and a large proportion of Parliament's secretariat is still based in yet another city, Luxembourg, some miles from any parliamentary activity.

Clearly, Brussels should be the single site of Parliament's activities, in close proximity to other institutions which Parliament has to scrutinise, and in the same town as the European press corps, represemtatives of interest groups, and the embassies of member states. The current dispersal is unacceptable, both in terms of cost and in terms of sheer political lunacy. It is as if the House of Commons held its committee meetings in London, the full House were to meet in York, and the secretariat were based in Leicester.

Similarly, it is the governments who are responsible for another problem, which the 1996 treaty revision gives them a chance to remedy. The treaties negotiated and ratified by the national governments now include so many different procedures — and each one complex — for involving Parliament in the adoption of European legislation, that it is impossible for a Member to explain to a constituent the exact nature of Parliament's powers in anything less than an hour. There is a formidable array of procedures: the co-decision procedure, the co-operation procedure, the consultation procedure, the assent procedure, the budgetary procedure, the conciliation procedure, and so on. The 1996 intergovernmental conference should seek to simplify and standardise this by applying a streamlined co-decision procedure to all areas where Council adopts legislation by a qualified majority.

The Press too, having frequently pointed to Parliament's increased importance in the course of the election campaign, must follow this up by increased coverage when Parliament gets down to work. In the United Kingdom, this will mean for many newspapers a change in attitude and a change from the tradition whereby Westminster lobby correspondents are considered a class apart, with political stories from any other source being secondary. Yes, it costs money too to have a European Parliament correspondent, but every serious newspaper must devote more attention to a forum where our future is being shaped.

However, the Parliament can do much to put its own house in order. A good start was made last year with a complete overhaul of Parliament's rules of procedure, allowing it to concentrate its work on more important matters, to devote less time to general debates on issues where it has no powers and more time to matters where it does have power, to limit the possibilities for fillibustering by small groups, and far better management procedures. A challenge for the new Parliament will be to handle a situation in which the Centre-Right of the Parliament is far more divided and fragmented than before, with an extreme Right contingent introducing an element of instability and even conflict. Even more than in the past, it will be up to the Group of the Party of European Socialists to lead the Parliament, despite the absence of an overall majority for any party group.

The political groups will also have to exert more discipline on their members. Absenteeism is, to a certain degree, inevitable in a Parliament with more than 80 different political parties from 12 countries, and soon more. There is always some national party holding its annual conference, some country or region in the middle of its election campaign, or an airport where the weather prevents easy travel to Brussels or (especially) Strasbourg.

But the level of absenteeism goes beyond this, with a number of members chosen because they can feature prominently in their party's campaign at election time, but who do not subsequently get involved in the nitty-gritty of Parliament's work, possibly because they hold extra responsibilities as members of their national parliaments, as mayors, or as regional councillors. This is not so much a British problem, but it does affect the perception of Parliament across Europe.

All in all, the prospects for the new Parliament to use its new powers effectively are good. Its chances of gaining recognition for this are also good, but the big question is how the national governments will face up to their responsibilities in the 1996 constitutional revision.

The cost of Parliament

Do taxpayers get value for money?

By Robert Morgan

Despite the popular view that the European Parliament is nothing more than an expensive talking shop and a gravy train for its members, it costs each United Kingdom voter much less than the running of the House of Commons.

The total cost of the European Parliament in 1994 will be about £500 million which works out at £900,000 per MEP, or £1.80 per voter. Westminster, on the other hand, costs £261,000 per MP, or £4.25 per voter.

A large part of the outlay stems from interpretation and translation costs and from the Parliament having three locations: Strasbourg for most plenary sessions; Brussels for committee work and some plenary sessions; and Luxembourg, the administrative headquarters.

MEPs are paid and taxed nationally in line with members of their national legislatures and British members are among the lowest paid. The Italians top the list with an annual salary of about £73,000. This contrasts markedly with the Spaniards who get about £21,500. British MEPS are paid nearly £31,000, the same as their Westminster counterparts.

National governments foot the salary bill, but allowances are paid by the European Union.

MEPs are also entitled to £154 a day to cover hotel bills and meals; a flat rate allowance of £2,310 a year for travel; a general expenses allowance of £26,149 for running their offices; an allowance of £71,951 to pay secretaries and assistants; a computer allowance of £770; a car mileage allowance of 58.5p per kilometer up to 400 kilometers and 29p thereafter; first class air fare for travel on European Parliament business.

Although the expense allowances seem generous, most MEPs maintain an office in their constituency as well as staff in Brussels and Strasbourg.

ANNUAL SALARIES OF MEPs

Italy	£73,051	France	£54,700	Germany	£48,953
Belgium	£43,612	Netherlands	£42,559	Denmark	£32,460
Ireland	£31,203	United Kingdom	£30,854	Portugal	£27,258
Luxembourg	£25,225	Greece	£22,730	Spain	£21,436

Members elected to the European Parliament

The following members were elected to the European Parliament in the fourth direct elections held on June 9 and June 12 1994.

Abbreviations used to designate the political groups of the newly-elected Parliament are: PES — Party of European Socialists; EPP — European People's Party (including Christian Democrats and Conservatives); LDR — Liberal and Democratic Reformist; Verts — Greens; EUL — European United Left (including former Communists); FE — Forza Europa (made up entirely of Forza Italia MEPs); EDA — European Democratic Alliance (Gaullist and Fianna Fail); ERA — European Radical Alliance (left of centre and regionalists); EDN — Europe des Nations (De Villiers's list and some other right-wing anti-EU members); Ind — Non-attached (including National Front in France and some right-wing Italians).

Abbreviations of member state political parties of MEPs are set out at the end of this list on Page 43.

* denotes those who were members of the outgoing 1989-94 Parliament.
† denotes those elected in more than one seat.

Silvio Berlusconi, who was elected in five seats in Italy, announced that he would resign and the next in order of preference on his list will become MEPs. Other MEPs elected under the list system may also decline to take their seats or resign and be replaced by candidates lower down their party lists. Those candidates are shown in the results for individual countries. Several Luxembourg MEPs became government ministers and therefore resigned from the EP.

Name	Member state	Political group	Party
A			
Aboville, Gérard d'	France	EPP	UDF/RPR
*Adam, Gordon	UK (Northumbria)	PES	Lab
Aelvoet, Magda	Belgium	Verts	Greens
Aglietta, Adelaide	Italy	Verts	Verdi
Ahern, Nuala	Ireland	Verts	Green
*Ainardi, Sylviane	France	EUL	PCF
*Alavanos, Alexandros	Greece	EUL	SYN
*Alber, Siegbert	Germany	EPP	CDU
Aldo, Blaise	France	EPP	UDF/RPR
Amadeo, Amedeo	Italy	Ind	AN
*Anastassopoulos, Georgios	Greece	EPP	ND
Ancona, Hedy D'	Netherlands	PES	ESD
*Andre-Leonard, Anne	Belgium	LDR	LDP
*Andrews, Niall	Ireland	EDA	FF
Angelilli, Roberta	Italy	Ind	AN
Añoveros Trias De Bes, Julio	Spain	EPP	PP
*Antony, Bernard	France	Ind	FN
Aparicio Sanchez, Pedro	Spain	PES	PSOE
Apolinário, José	Portugal	PES	PS
Aramburu Del Rio, María Jesús	Spain	EUL	IU-IC
*Areitio Toledo, Javier	Spain	EPP	PP
Argyros, Stylianos	Greece	EEP	ND
*Arias Cañete, Miguel	Spain	EPP	PP
Arroni, Aldo	Italy	FE	FI
Augias, Corrado	Italy	PES	PDS
*Avgerinos, Paraskevas	Greece	PES	PASOK
Azzolini, Claudio	Italy	FE	FI

Name	Member state	Political group	Party

B

Name	Member state	Political group	Party
Baggioni, Jean	France	EPP	UDF/RPR
Baldarelli, Francesco	Italy	PES	PDS
Baldi, Stefania	Italy	FE	FI
Baldini, Valerio	Italy	FE	FI
*Balfe, Richard	UK (London South Inner)	PES	Lab
*Banotti, Mary	Ireland	EPP	FG
Bardong, Otto	Germany	EPP	CDU
*Baron Crespo, Enrique	Spain	PES	PSOE
Barros Moura, José	Portugal	PES	PS
Barthet-Mayer, Christine	France	PES	ER
*Barton, Roger	UK (Sheffield)	PES	Lab
Barzanti, Roberto	Italy	PES	PDS
Baudis, Dominique	France	EPP	UDF/RPR
Bazin, Jean-Pierre	France	EPP	UDF/RPR
Bébéar, Jean-Pierre	France	EPP	UDF/RPR
Bellere Spalato	Italy	Ind	AN
Bennasar Tous, Francisca	Spain	EPP	PP
Berend, Rolf	Germany	EPP	CDU
Beres, Pervenche	France	PES	ES
Bernardini, François	France	PES	ES
*Bernard-Reymond, Pierre	France	EPP	UDF/RPR
*Bertens, Jan Willem	Netherlands	LDR	D'66
Berthu, Georges	France	EDN	l'autre Europe
Bertinotti, Fausto	Italy	EUL	RC
Bianco, Gerardo	Italy	EPP	PPI
Billingham, Angela	UK (Northamptonshire and Blaby)	PES	Lab
Bladel, Leonie van	Netherlands	PES	ESD
*Blak, Freddy	Denmark	PES	SPD
Blokland, Hans	Netherlands	PES	SP
*Blot, Yvan	France	Ind	FN
*Böge, Reimer	Germany	EPP	CDU
*Bonde, Jens-Peter	Denmark	EDN	June Mov
Boniperti, Giampiero	Italy	FE	FI
Bontempi, Rinaldo	Italy PES	PDS	
Boogerd-Quaak, Johanna	Netherlands	LDR	D'66
†Bossi, Umberto	Italy	Ind	Lega Nord
Botz, Gerhard	Germany	PES	SPD
*Bourlanges, Jean-Louis	France	EPP	UDF/RPR
*Bowe, David	UK (Cleveland & Richmond)	PES	Lab
Bredin, Frédérique	France	PES	ES
*Brémond d'Ars, Georges de	France	EPP	UDF/RPR
*Breyer, Hiltrud	Germany	Verts	Grüne
Brinkhorst, Laurens-Jan	Netherlands	LDR	D'66
*Brok, Elmar	Germany	EPP	CDU
Burtone, Giovanni	Italy	EPP	PPI

C

Name	Member state	Political group	Party
*Cabezon Alonso, Jesús	Spain	PES	PSOE
Cabrol, Christian	France	EPP	UDF/RPR
Caccavale, Ernesto	Italy	FE	FI
Caligaris, Luigi	Italy	FE	FI
Campos, António	Portugal	PES	PS
Campoy Zueco, Luis	Spain	EPP	PP
*Capucho, Antonio	Portugal	LDR	PSD

Name	Member state	Political group	Party
Carnero Gonzalez, Carlos	Spain	EUL	IU-IC
*Carniti, Pierre	Italy	PES	PDS
Carrère d'Encausse, Hélène	France	EPP	UDF/RPR
*Casini, Carlo	Italy	EPP	PPI
Casini, Pierferdinando	Italy	FE	FI
*Cassidy, Bryan	UK (Dorset & Devon East)	EPP	C
Castagnede, Bernard	France	PES	ER
Castagnetti, Pierluigi	Italy	EPP	PPI
*Castellina, Luciana	Italy	EUL	RC
Castricum, Frits	Netherlands	PES	ESD
*Caudron, Gérard	France	PES	ES
Cellai, Marco	Italy	Ind	AN
*Chanterie, Raphael	Belgium	EPP	CVP
*Chesa, Raymond	France	EPP	UDF/RPR
Chichester, Giles	UK (Devon and Plymouth East)	EPP	C
*Christodoulou, Efthimios	Greece	EPP	ND
*Clercq, Willy de	Belgium	LDR	PVV
*Coates, Kenneth	UK (Nottinghamshire North and Chesterfield)	PES	Lab
Coene Philippe de	Belgium	PES	SP
Cohn-Bendit, Daniel	Germany	Verts	Grüne
*Colajanni, Luigi	Italy	PES	PDS
*Colino Salamanca, Juan Luis	Spain	PES	PSOE
Colli, Ombretta	Italy	FE	FI
Collins, Gerard	Ireland	EDA	FF
*Collins, Kenneth	UK (Strathclyde East)	PES	Lab
Colombo Svevo, Maria Paloa	Italy	EPP	PPI
*Colom i Naval, Joan	Spain	PES	PSOE
*Cornelissen, Petrus	Netherlands	EPP	CDA
Corrie, John	UK (Worcestershire and Warwickshire South	EPP	C
Costa Neves, Carlos	Portugal	PES	PSD
*Cot, Jean-Pierre	France	PES	PS
*Cox, Pat	Ireland	LDR	Ind
*Crampton, Peter	UK (Humberside)	PES	Lab
*Crawley, Christine	UK (Birmingham East)	PES	Lab
Crowley, Brian	Ireland	EDA	FF
Cunha, Arlindo	Portugal	PES	PSD
Cunningham, Tony	UK (Cumbria and Lancashire North)	PES	Lab
*Cushnahan, John	Ireland	EPP	FG

D

D'Andrea, Vittorio	Italy	EPP	PPI
Danesin, Alessandro	Italy	FE	FI
Dankert, Pieter	Netherlands	PES	ESD
Darras, Danièle	France	PES	ES
Dary, Michel	France	PES	ER
Daskalaki, Katerina	Greece	EDA	POLA
*David, Wayne	UK (South Wales Central)	PES	Lab
Decourrière, Francis	France	EPP	UDF/RPR
De Frutos Gama, Manuela	Spain	PES	PSOE
*De Giovanni, Biagio	Italy	PES	PDS
De La Merced Monge, Mercedes	Spain	EPP	PP
Dell'Alba, Gianfranco	Italy	Ind	PR

Name	Member state	Political group	Party
De Luca, Stefano	Italy	FE	FI
Delvaux-Stehres, Mady	Luxembourg	PES	LSAP
De Melo, Eurico	Portugal	PES	PSD
*Deprez, Gerard	Belgium	EPP	PSC
De Sá, Luís	Portugal	EUL	UDC
*Desama, Claude	Belgium	PES	SP
Des Places, Edouard	France	EDN	l'autre Europe
Diez De Rivera Icaza, Carmen	Spain	PES	PSOE
*Dijk, Nel van	Netherlands	Verts	Green Left
*Dillen, Karel	Belgium	Ind	Far Right
Dimitrakopoulos, Georgios	Greece	EPP	ND
Di Prima, Pietro	Italy	FE	FI
Donnay, Jacques	France	EPP	UDF/RPR
*Donnelly, Alan	UK (Tyne and Wear)	PES	Lab
Donnelly, Brendan	UK (Sussex South and Crawley)	EPP	C
*Dührkop Dührkop, Barbara	Spain	PES	PSOE
*Dury, Raymonde	Belgium	PES	PS
Dybkjaer, Lone	Denmark	LDR	RLP

E

Name	Member state	Political group	Party
Ebner, Michael	Italy	EPP	SV
Eisma, Doeke	Netherlands	LDR	D'66
*Elles, James	UK (Buckinghamshire & Oxfordshire East)	EPP	C
*Elliott, Michael	UK (London West)	PES	Lab
*Elmalan, Mireille	France	EUL	PCF
*Ephremidis, Vassilis	Greece	EUL	KKE
*Escudero Lopez, José Antonio	Spain	EPP	PP
Esteban Martin, Laura Elena	Spain	EPP	PP
Estevan Bolea, Maria Teresa	Spain	EPP	PP
Evans, Robert	UK (London North West)	PES	Lab
*Ewing, Winifred	UK (Highlands & Islands)	ERA	SNP

F

Name	Member state	Political group	Party
Fabra Valles, Juan Manuel	Spain	EPP	PP
Fabre-Aubrespy, Hervé	France	EDN	l'autre Europe
*Falconer, Alexander	UK (Scotland Mid & Fife)	PES	Lab
*Fantuzzi, Giulio	Italy	PES	PDS
Farassino, Gipo	Italy	Ind	Lega Nord
Fassa, Raimondo	Italy	Ind	Lega Nord
Ferber, Markus	Germany	EPP	CSU
Feret, Daniel	Belgium	Ind	NF
*Fernandez Albor, Gerardo	Spain	EPP	PP
Fernandez Martin, Fernando	Spain	EPP	PP
Ferraz Mendonça, Nélio	Portugal	PES	PSD
*Ferrer i Casals, Concepcio	Spain	EPP	CDC-CiU
*Ferri, Enrico	Italy	PES	PSDI
Filippi, Livio	Italy	EPP	Patto Segni
*†Fini, Gianfranco	Italy	Ind	AN
*Fitzsimons, James	Ireland	EDA	FF
*Florenz, Karl-Heinz	Germany	EPP	CDU
Florio, Luigi	Italy	FE	FI
*Fontaine, Nicole	France	EPP	UDF/RPR
Fontana, Alessandro	Italy	FE	FI
*Ford, Glyn	UK (Greater Manchester East)	PES	Lab

Name	Member state	Political group	Party
Formentini, Marco	Italy	Ind	Lega Nord
Fouque, Antoinette	France	PES	ER
Fraga Estevez, Carmen	Spain	EPP	PP
*Friedrich, Ingo	Germany	EPP	CSU
Frutos Gama, Manuela	Spain	PES	PSOE
*Funck, Honor	Germany	EPP	CDU

G

Name	Member state	Political group	Party
Galeote Quecede, José Gerardo	Spain	EPP	PP
Gallagher, Pat	Ireland	EDA	FF
*Galland Yves	France	EPP	UDF/RPR
Gallou, Jean-Yves Le	France	Ind	FN
*Garcia Arias, Ludivina	Spain	PES	PSOE
Garcia Margallo, José Manuel	Spain	EPP	PP
Garosci, Riccardo	Italy	FE	FI
Garriga Polledo, Salvador	Spain	EPP	PP
*Gasoliba i Bohm, Carles Alfred	Spain	LDR	CDC-CiU
Gaulle, Charles de	France	EDN	l'autre Europe
Gebhardt, Evelyne	Germany	PES	SPD
Ghilardotti, Fiorella	Italy	EUL	PDS
Gillis, Alan	Ireland	EPP	FG
*Gil-Robles Gil-Delgardo, Jose Maria	Spain	EPP	PP
Girão Pereira, José	Portugal	EPP	CDSP
Glante, Norbert	Germany	PES	SPD
Glase, Anne-Karin	Germany	EPP	CDU
Goepel, Lutz	Germany	EPP	CDU
Gol, Jean	Belgium	LDR	PVV
Goldsmith, Sir James	France	EDN	l'autre Europe
*Gollnisch, Bruno	France	Ind	FN
Gomolka, Alfred	Germany	EPP	CDU
*Gonzalez Alvarez, Laura	Spain	EUL	IU-IC
Gonzalez Triviño, Antonio	Spain	PES	PSOE
*Görlach, Willi	Germany	PES	SPD
*Graefe zu Baringdorf, Friedrich Wilhelm	Germany	Verts	Grüne
Graziani, Antonio	Italy	EPP	PPI
*Green, Pauline	UK (London North)	PES	Lab
*Gröner, Lieselotte	Germany	PES	SPD
Grosch, Mathieu	Belgium	EPP	CD
Grossetête, Françoise	France	EPP	UDF/RPR
Guigou, Elisabeth	France	PES	ES
Guinebertière, Armelle	France	EPP	UDF/RPR
*Günther, Maren	Germany	EPP	CSU
*Gutierrez Diaz, Antoni	Spain	EUL	IU
Gyldenkilde, Lilli	Denmark	Verts	SF

H

Name	Member state	Political group	Party
Haarder, Bertel	Denmark	LDR	V
Hallam, David	UK (Hertforshire and Shropshire	PES	Lab
*Hänsch, Klaus	Germany	PES	SDP
Hansen, Eva Kjer	Denmark	LDR	V
*Happart, Jose	Belgium	PES	PS
Hardstaff, Veronia	UK (Lincolnshire and Humberside South)	PES	Lab

Name	Member state	Political group	Party
*Harrison, Lyndon	UK (Cheshire West & Wirral)	PES	Lab
Hatzidakis, Constantinos	Greece	EPP	ND
Haug, Jutta	Germany	PES	SPD
Heinisch, Renate	Germany	EPP	CDU
Hendrick, Mark	UK (Lancashire Central)	PES	Lab
*Herman, Fernand	Belgium	EPP	CVP
Hermange, Marie-Thérèse	France	EPP	UDF/RPR
*Hersant, Robert	France	EPP	UDF/RPR
*Herzog, Philippe	France	EUL	PCF
*Hindley, Michael	UK (Lancashire South)	PES	Lab
*Hoff, Magdalene	Germany	PES	SDP
*Hoppenstedt, Karsten	Germany	EPP	CDU
*Hory, Jean-Francois	France	PES	ER
Howitt, Richard	UK (Essex South)	PES	Lab
*Hughes, Stephen	UK (Durham)	PES	Lab
*Hume, John	UK (Northern Ireland)	PES	SDLP
Hyland, Liam,	Ireland	EDA	FF

I

Name	Member state	Political group	Party
Imaz San Miguel, Josu Jon	Spain	EPP	NC
*Imbeni, Renzo	Italy	EUL	PDS
Izquierdo Collado, Juan de Bois	Spain	PES	PSOE
*Izquierdo Rojo, María	Spain	PES	PSOE

J

Name	Member state	Political group	Party
*Jackson, Caroline	UK (Wiltshire North & Bath)	EPP	C
Jacob, Christian	France	EPP	UDF/RPR
*Janssen van Raay, Jim	Netherlands	EPP	CDA
*Jarzembowski, Georg	Germany	EPP	CDU
Jean Pierre, Thierry	France	EDN	l'autre Europe
*Jensen, Kirsten	Denmark	PES	S
Jensen, Lis	Denmark	EDN	Anti-EU
Jöns, Karin	Germany	PES	SPD
Jove Peres, Salvador	Spain	EUL	IU-IC
Juncker, Jean-Claude	Luxembourg	PES	CSV
*Junker, Karin	Germany	PES	SPD

K

Name	Member state	Political group	Party
Kaklamanis, Nikitas	Greece	EDA	POLA
Katiforis, Georgios	Greece	PES	PASOK
*Kellett-Bowman, Edward	UK (Itchen, Test & Avon)	EPP	C
*Keppelhoff-Wiechert, Hedwig	Germany	EPP	CDU
Kerr, Hugh	UK (Essex West and Hertfordshire East)	PES	Lab
Kestelyn-Sierens, Mimi	Belgium	LDR	PVV
*Killilea, Mark	Ireland	EDA	FF
Kindermann, Heinz	Germany	PES	SPD
Kinnock, Glenys	UK (South Wales East)	PES	Lab
Kittelmann, Peter	Germany	EPP	CDU
Klass, Christa	Germany	EPP	CDU
Klironomos, Constantinos	Greece	PES	PASOK
Koch, Dieter-Lebrecht	Germany	EPP	CDU
*Kofoed, Niels Anker	Denmark	LDR	V
Kokkola, Angela	Greece	PES	PASOK
Konrad, Christoph	Germany	EPP	CDU

Name	Member state	Political group	Party
Kouchner, Bernard	France	PES	ES
Krarup, Ole	Denmark	EDN	Anti-EU
Krehl, Constanze	Germany	PES	SDP
Kreissl-Dörfler, Wolfgang	Germany	Verts	Grüne
Kristoffersen, Frode	Denmark	EPP	KF
Kuckelkorn, Wilfried	Germany	PES	SPD
*Kuhn, Annemarie	Germany	PES	SPD
Kuhne, Helmut	Germany	PES	SPD

L

Name	Member state	Political group	Party
Lage, Carlos	Portugal	PES	PS
Laignel, André	France	PES	ES
Lalumière, Catherine	France	PES	ER
Lambraki, Irini	Greece	PES	PASOK
*Lambrias, Panagiotis	Greece	EPP	ND
*La Malfa, Giorgio	Italy	LDR	PRI
Lang, Carl	France	Ind	FN
Lang, Jack	France	PES	ES
Lange, Bernd	Germany	PES	SPD
Langen, Werner	Germany	EPP	CDU
*Langenhagen, Brigitte	Germany	EPP	CDU
*Langer, Alexander	Italy	Verts	Verdi
*Lannoye, Paul	Belgium	Verts	Greens
*Larive, Jessica	Netherlands	LDR	VVD
*Le Chevallier, Jean-Marie	France	Ind	FN
Lehne, Klaus-Heiner	Germany	EPP	CDU
*Lenz, Marlene	Germany	EPP	CDU
Leopardi, Giacomo	Italy	FE	FI
*Le Pen, Jean-Marie	France	Ind	FN
Le Rachinel, Fernand	France	Ind	FN
Liese, Hans-Peter	Germany	EPP	CDU
Ligabue, Giancarlo	Italy	FE	FI
Lindeperg, Michèle	France	PES	ES
*Linkohr, Rolf	Germany	PES	SPD
*Lomas, Alfred	UK (London North East)	PES	Lab
*Lucas Pires, Francisco	Portugal	EPP	PSD
*Lüttge, Gunter	Germany	PES	SPD

M

Name	Member state	Political group	Party
Macartney, Allan	UK (Scotland North East)	ERA	SNP
McCarthy, Arlene	UK (Peak District)	PES	Lab
*McCartin, Joe	Ireland	EPP	FG
*McGowan, Michael	UK (Leeds)	PES	Lab
*McIntosh, Anne	UK (Essex and Suffolk South)	EPP	C
McKenna, Patricia	Ireland	Verts	Green
*McMahon, Hugh	UK (Strathclyde West)	PES	Lab
*McMillan-Scott, Edward	UK (Yorkshire North)	EPP	C
McNally, Eryl	UK (Bedfordshire and Milton Kynes)	PES	Lab
Maij-Weggen, Hanja	Netherlands	EPP	CDA
*Malangre, Kurt	Germany	EPP	CDU
Malerba, Franco	Italy	FE	FI
*Malone, Bernie	Ireland	PES	Lab
Mamère, Noël	France	PES	ER

Name	Member state	Political group	Party
Manisco, Lucio	Italy	EUL	RC
Mann, Erika	Germany	PES	SPD
Mann, Thomas	Germany	EPP	CDU
Manzella, Andrea	Italy	PES	PDS
Marin, Marilena	Italy	Ind	Lega Nord
*Marinho, Luis	Portugal	PES	PS
Marinucci, Elena	Italy	PES	PSI-AD
Marra, Alfonso	Italy	FE	FI
Marset Campos, Pedro	Spain	EUL	IU-IC
Martens, Wilfried	Belgium	EPP	CD
*Martin, David	UK (Lothians)	PES	Lab
Martin, Philippe	France	EDN	l'autre Europe
*Martinez, Jean-Claude	France	Ind	FN
Mather, Graham	UK (Hampshire North and Oxford)	EPP	C
Matutes Juan, Abel	Spain	EPP	PP
Mayer, Franz Xaver	Germany	EPP	CSU
*Medina Ortega, Manuel	Spain	PES	PSOE
*Megahy, Thomas	UK (Yorkshire South West)	PES	Lab
*Megret, Bruno	France	Ind	FN
*Mendez de Vigo, Iñigo	Spain	EPP	PP
Mendiluce Pereiro, Jose María	Spain	PES	PSOE
*Menrad, Winfried	Germany	EPP	CDU
*Metten, Alman	Netherlands	PES	SD
Mezzaroma, Roberto	Italy	FE	FI
Miller, Bill	UK (Glasgow)	PES	Lab
*Miranda da Silva, Joaquim	Portugal	EUL	PCP
*Miranda de Lage, Ana Clara	Spain	PES	PSOE
Mombaur, Peter-Michael	Germany	EPP	CDU
Moniz, Fernando	Portugal	PES	PS
Monteiro, Manuel	Portugal	EDA	CDSP
Montesano, Enrico	Italy	PES	PDS
*Moorhouse, James	UK (London South & Surrey East)	EPP	C
*Moran Lopez Fernando	Spain	PES	PSOE
Moreau, Gisèle	France	EUL	PC
Moretti, Luigi	Italy	Ind	Lega Nord
Morgan, Eluned	UK (Wales Mid and West)	PES	Lab
*Morris, David	UK (South Wales West)	PES	Lab
Moscovici, Pierre	France	PES	ES
Mosiek-Urbahn, Marlies	Germany	EPP	CDU
Mouskouri, Nana	Greece	EPP	ND
Mulder, Jan	Netherlands	LDR	VVD
Müller, Edith	Germany	Verts	Grüne
Murphy, Simon	UK (Midlands West)	PES	Lab
*Muscardini, Cristiana	Italy	Ind	AN
Musumeci, Nello	Italy	Ind	AN

N

Name	Member state	Political group	Party
Nassauer, Hartmut	Germany	EPP	CDU
Needle, Clive	UK (Norfolk)	PES	Lab
Nencini, Riccardo	Italy	PES	PSI-AD
*Newens, Stanley	UK (London Central)	PES	Lab
*Newman, Edward	UK (Greater Manchester Central)	PES	Lab

Name	Member state	Political group	Party
Neyts-Uyttebroeck, Annemie	Belgium	LDR	PVV
*Nicholson, James	UK (Northern Ireland)	EPP	UUP

O

*†Occhetto, Achille	Italy	PES	PDS
*Oddy, Christine	UK (Coventry & Warwickshire North)	PES	Lab
*Oomen-Ruijten, Maria	Netherlands	EPP	CDA
*Oostlander, Arie	Netherlands	EPP	CDA
Orlando, Leoluca	Italy	Verts	La Rete

P

*Pack, Doris	Germany	EPP	CDU
Pailler, Aline	France	EUL	PC
*Paisley, The Rev Ian	UK (Northern Ireland)	Ind	DUP
Palacio Vallersundi, Ana Isabel	Spain	EPP	PP
Panagopoulos, Stylianos	Greece	PES	PASOK
*†Pannella, Marco	Italy	EDA	PR
Papakyriazis, Nikolaos	Greece	PES	PASOK
*Papayannakis, Mihail	Greece	EUL	SYN
*Papoutsis, Christos	Greece	PES	PASOK
Parigi, Gastone	Italy	Ind	AN
Parodi, Eolo	Italy	FE	FI
*Pasty, Jean-Claude	France	EPP	UDF/RPR
*Peijs, Karla	Netherlands	EPP	CDA
*Pérez Royo, Fernando	Spain	PES	PSOE
Perry, Roy	UK (Wight and Hampshire South)	EPP	C
*Péry, Nicole	France	PES	ES
*Peter, Helwin	Germany	PES	SPD
Pettinari, Luciano	Italy	EUL	RC
Pex, Peter	Netherlands	EPP	CDA
*Piecyk, Willi	Germany	PES	SPD
*Pimenta, Carlos	Portugal	LDR	PSD
*Piquet, Rene-Emile	France	EUL	PC
Plooij-van Gorsel, Elly	Netherlands	LDR	VVD
*Plumb, Lord	UK (Cotswolds)	EPP	C
Podesta, Guido	Italy	FE	FI
*Poettering, Hans-Gert	Germany	EPP	CDU
Poggiolini, Danilo	Italy	EPP	Patto Segni
Poisson, Anne-Christine	France	EDN	l'autre Europe
*Pollack, Anita	UK (London South West)	PES	Lab
*Pompidou, Alain	France	EPP	UDF/RPR
*Pons Grau, Josep Enrique	Spain	PES	PSOE
Poos, Jacques	Luxembourg	PES	LSAP
*Porto, Manuel	Portugal	PES	SD
Posselt, Bernd	Germany	EPP	CSU
Pradier, Pierre	France	PES	ER
*Pronk, Bartho	Netherlands	EPP	CDA
Provan, James	UK (South Downs West)	EPP	C
*Puerta Gutierrez, Alonso José	Spain	EUL	IU-IC
*Putten, Maartje van	Netherlands	PES	ESD

Name	Member state	Political group	Party

Q

Name	Member state	Political group	Party
*Quisthoudt-Rowohl, Godelieve	Germany	EPP	CDU

R

Name	Member state	Political group	Party
*Raffarin, Jean-Pierre	France	EPP	UDF/RPR
*Randzio-Plath, Christa	Germany	PES	SPD
Rapkay, Bernhard	Germany	PES	SPD
*Rauti, Pino	Italy	Ind	AN
*Read, Ismelda	UK (Nottingham & Leicestershire North West)	PES	Lab
Redondo Jimenez, Encarnación	Spain	EPP	PP
Rehder, Klaus	Germany	PES	SPD
*Ribeiro, Sérgio	Portugal	EUL	UDC
Riis-Jorgensen, Karin	Denmark	LDR	V
*Rinsche, Günter	Germany	EPP	CDU
*†Ripa di Meana, Carlo	Italy	Verts	Verdi
*Robles Piquer, Carlos	Spain	EPP	PP
Rocard, Michel	France	PES	ES
Rosado Fernandes, Raúl	Portugal	EDA	CDSP
Rose, Marie-France de	France	EDN	l'autre Europe
*Roth, Claudia	Germany	Verts	Grüne
*Roth-Behrendt, Dagmar	Germany	PES	SPD
*Rothe, Mechthild	Germany	PES	SPD
*Rothley, Willi	Germany	PES	SDP
Roubatis, Ioannis	Greece	PES	PASOK
*Rovsing, Christian	Denmark	EPP	KF
Ruffolo, Giorgio	Italy	PES	PDS

S

Name	Member state	Political group	Party
*Sainjon, Andre	France	PES	ER
Saint-Pierre, Dominique	France	PES	ER
*Sakellariou, Jannis	Germany	PES	SPD
Salafranca Sanchezneyra, José Ignacio	Spain	EPP	PP
*Salisch, Heinke	Germany	PES	SPD
*Samland, Detlev	Germany	PES	SPD
Sanchez Garcia, Isidoro	Spain	EPP	Nat Co
*Sandbaek, Ulla	Denmark	EDN	June Mov
Santer, Jacques	Luxembourg	PES	CSV
Santini, Giacomo	Italy	FE	FI
*Sanz Fernandez, Francisco Javier	Spain	PES	PSOE
*Sarlis, Pavlos	Greece	EPP	ND
Sauquillo Perez del Arco, Francisca	Spain	PES	PSOE
Scapagnini, Umberto	Italy	FE	FI
Schäfer, Axel	Germany	PES	SPD
Schaffner, Anne-Marie	France	EPP	UDF/RPR
Schiedermeier, Edgar	Germany	EPP	CSU
*Schleicher, Ursula	Germany	EPP	CSU
Schlüter, Poul	Denmark	EPP	KF
*Schmid, Gerhard	Germany	PES	SPD
*Schmidbauer, Barbara	Germany	PES	SPD
Schnellhardt, Horst	Germany	EPP	CDU
Schröder, Jürgen	Germany	EPP	CDU
Schroedter, Elisabeth	Germany	Verts	Grüne
Schulz, Martin	Germany	PES	SPD

Name	Member state	Political group	Party
Schwaiger, Konrad	Germany	EPP	CDU
*Seal, Barry	UK (Yorkshire West)	PES	Lab
Secchi, Carlo	Italy	EPP	PPI
*†Segni Mario	Italy	EPP	Pat Segni
Seillier, Françoise	France	EDN	l'autre Europe
Sierra Gonzalez, Angela de Carmen	Spain	EUL	(IU-IC)
*Simpson, Brian	UK (Cheshire East)	PES	Lab
Sindal, Niels	Denmark	PES	SDP
*Siso Cruellas, Joaquin	Spain	EPP	PP
Skinner, Peter	UK (Kent West)	PES	Lab
*Smith, Alex	UK (Scotland South)	PES	Lab
Soares, João	Portugal	PES	PS
Soltwedel, Irene	Germany	Verts	Grüne
*Sonneveld, Jan	Netherlands	EPP	CDA
Sornosa Martinez, María	Spain	EUL	IU-IC
Souchet, Dominique	France	EDN	l'autre Europe
*Soulier, André	France	EPP	UDF/RPR
Spaak, Antionette	Belgium	LDR	PVV
*Speciale, Roberto	Italy	PES	PDS
*Spencer, Tom	UK (Surrey)	EPP	C
Spiers, Shaun	UK (South Downs West)	EPP	C
Stasi, Bernard	France	EPP	UDF/RPR
*Stevens, John	UK (Thames Valley)	EPP	C
*Stewart, Kenneth	UK (Merseyside West)	PES	Lab
*Stewart-Clark, Sir Jack	UK (Sussex East & Kent South)	EPP	C
Stirbois, Marie-France	France	Ind	FN
Stockmann, Ulrich	Germany	PES	SPD
Striby, Frédéric	France	EDN	l'autre Europe
Sturdy, Robert	UK (Cambridgeshire)	EPP	C

T

Name	Member state	Political group	Party
Tajani, Antonio	Italy	FE	FI
Tannert, Christof	Germany	PES	SPD
Tapie, Bernard	France	PES	RE
Tappin, Michael	UK (Staffordshire West and Congleton)	PES	Lab
Tatarella, Salvatore	Italy	Ind	AN
Taubira-Delannon, Christiane	France	PES	RE
Telkämper, Wilfried	Germany	Verts	Grüne
Terron i Cusi, Ana	Spain	PES	PSOE
Teverson, Roger	UK (Cornwall and Plymouth West)	LDR	LD
*Theato, Diemut	Germany	EPP	CDU
Theonas, Ioannis	Greece	EUL	KKE
Thomas, David	UK (Suffolk and Norfolk South West)	PES	Lab
Thyssen, Marianne	Belgium	EPP	CVP
Tillich, Stanislaw	Germany	EPP	CDU
*Tindemans, Leo	Belgium	EPP	CVP
*Titley, Gary	UK (Greater Manchester West)	PES	Lab
Todini, Luisa	Italy	FE	FI
*Tomlinson, John	UK (Birmingham West)	PES	Lab
*Tongue, Carole	UK (London East)	PES	Lab
*Torres Couto, José	Portugal	PES	PS

Name	Member state	Political group	Party
Torres Marques, Helena	Portugal	PES	Soc
Trakatellis, Antonios	Greece	EPP	ND
*Trautmann, Catherine	France	PES	ES
Trizza, Antonello	Italy	Ind	AN
Truscott, Peter	UK (Hertfordshire)	PES	Lab
Tsatsos, Dimitrios	Greece	PES	PASOK

U

Ullmann, Wolfgang	Germany	Verts	Grüne

V

Valdivielso De Cue, Jaime	Spain	EPP	PP
Vallve i Ribera, Joan	Spain	LDR	CDC-CIU
*Valverde Lopez, Jose Luis	Spain	EPP	PP
*Vandemeulebroucke, Jaak	Belgium	ERA	VU
Vanhecke, Frank	Belgium	Ind	Far Right
Van Lancker, Anne	Belgium	PES	SP
Varela Suances-Carpegna, Daniel Luis	Spain	EPP	PP
Vaz Da Silva, Helena	Portugal	LDR	PSD
*Vecchi, Luciana	Italy	PES	PDS
Velzen, Wim G van	Netherlands	EPP	CDA
*Velzen, Wim J van	Netherlands	PES	ESD
*Verde i Aldea, Josep	Spain	PES	PSOE
Verrier, Odile	France	PES	RE
*Verwaerde, Yves	France	EPP	UDF/RPR
Viceconte, Walter	Italy	FE	FI
Villalobos Talero, Celia	Spain	EPP	PP
Villiers, de Philippe	France	EDN	l'autre Europe
Vinci, Luigi	Italy	EUL	RC
Vitorino, António	Portugal	PES	PS
von Blottnitz, Undine	Germany	Verts	Grüne
von Habsburg, Otto	Germany	EPP	CSU
*Vries, Gijs de	Netherlands	LDR	VVD

W

*Waal, Leen van der	Netherlands	PES	SP
Waddington, Sue	UK (Leicester)	PES	Lab
Walter, Ralf	Germany	PES	SPD
Watson, Graham	UK (Somerset and North Devon)	LDR	LD
Watts, Mark	UK (Kent East)	PES	Lab
Weber, Jup	Luxembourg	Verts	GLEI-GAP
Weiler, Barbara	Germany	PES	SPD
Wemheuer Rosemarie	Germany	PES	SPD
*West, Norman	UK (Yorkshire South)	PES	Lab
*White, Ian	UK (Bristol)	PES	Lab
Whitehead, Phillip	UK (Staffordshire East and Derby)	PES	Lab
Wiebenga, Jan Kees	Netherlands	LDR	VVD
Wiersma, Jan Marinus	Netherlands	PES	ESD
*Wijsenbeek, Florus	Netherlands	LDR	VVD
Willockx, Freddy	Belgium	PES	SP
*Wilson, Joe	UK (Wales North)	PES	Lab
*Wogau, Karl von	Germany	EPP	CDU

Name	Member state	Political group	Party
Wolf, Frieder Otto	Germany	Verts	Grüne
*Wurth-Polfer, Lydie	Luxembourg	LDR	DP
*Wurtz, Francis	France	EUL	PCF
*Wynn, Terry	UK (Merseyside East & Wigan)	PES	Lab

Z

Name	Member state	Political group	Party
Zimmermann, Wilmya	Germany	PES	SPD

Member state political parties

BELGIUM

CVP ....Christelijke Volkspartij
PSC ....Parti social-Chretien
PRL ....Parti reformateur liberal
PVV ....Partij voor vrijheid envooruitgang
(Liberals)
SP ....Socialistische Partij
PS ....Parti Socialiste
VU ....Volksunie-Europese

DENMARK

June Mov ....June Movement (Anti-EU)
KF ....Det Konservative Folkeparti
RLP ....Radical Liberal Party
SDP ....Social Democratic Party
S ....Socialdemokratiet
SF ....Socialistisk Folkeparti
V ....Venstre Danmarks Liberale Parti

FRANCE

ER ....Energie Radicale (Tapie list)
ES ....Europe Solidaire (Socialists)
FN ....Front National
L'autre Europe Majorité pour l'autre Europe
(de Villiers list)
PCF ....Parti Communiste Francais
RPR ....Rassemblement pour la Republique
UDF ....Union pour la Democratie
Francaise
Verts ....Greens

GERMANY

CDU ....Christlich Demokratische Union
CSU ....Christlich Soziale Union
GRÜNE ....Greens
SPD ....Sozilademokratische Partie
Deutschland

GREECE

DI-ANA ....Dimogratiki Ananeossi
KKE ....Communist Party of Greece
ND ....Nea Dimokratia (New Democracy)
POLA ....Political Spring
PASOK ....Panelliniko Socialistiko Kinima
SYN ....Communist Alliance

IRELAND

FF ....Fianna Fail
FG ....Fine Gael Party
Ind ....Independent
Lab ....Italy
Green ....Greens

ITALY

AN ....Alleanza Nazionale (former MSI
Nationalist Party)
FI ....Forza Italia (Silvio Berlusconi's List)
La Rete MD ....La Rete Movimento Democratico
Lega Nord ....Northern Lega (Regional party)
Pat Segni ....Patto Segni (Christian Democrats)

PDS ....Party of Democratic Left (Former
Communists)
PPI ....Popular Party of Italy (Christian
Democrats)
PR ....Pannella Riformatori (Radical
Party
PRI ....Republican Party
PSI-AD ....Socialist Party
PSDI ....Socialist Democratic Party
RC ....Rifondazione Comunista
(Refounded Communists)
SV ....Südtiroler Volkspartei (South Tyrol
People's Party — regional party)
Verdi ....Federazione dei Verdi (Greens)

LUXEMBOURG

CSV ....Christian Social People's Party
LSAP ....Luxembourg Socialist Workers'
Party
GLEI-GAP ......Greens
DP ....Democratic party

NETHERLANDS

CDA ....Christen Democratisch Appel
D'66 ....Democraten 66
ESD ....European Social Democrats
Green Left ....Greens
LDP ....Liberal Democratic Party
SP ....Socialist Party
VVD ....Volkspartij voor Vrijheid en
Democratie (Freedom and
Democracy — Liberals)

PORTUGAL

CDSP ....Partido do Centro Democratico
Social (Central Democratic
and Social Party)
PS ....Partido Socialista (Socialist Party)
PSD ....Partido Socila Democrata (Social
Democratic Party)
UDC ....Coligacao Democratica Unitaria
(United Democratic Coalition —
Communist Party and Greens)

SPAIN

CDC-CIU ....Catalan Party
IU-IC ....Izquierda Unida (United Left)
PP ....Partido Popular (Popular Party)
PSOE ....Partido Socialista Obrero Espanol
(Socialists)
Nat Co ....National Coalition

UNITED KINGDOM

C ....Conservative Party
DUP ....Democratic Unionist Party
(Northen Ireland)
Lab ....Labour Party
UUP ....Ulster Unionist Party (Northern
Ireland)
SDLP ....Social Democratic and Labour
Party (Northern Ireland)
SNP ....Scottish National Party

Six extra constituencies posed formidable problems in drawing electoral map

As a result of decisions reached at the Edinburgh summit in December 1992, the number of seats in the United Kingdom was increased by six to 87. The Government proposed and Parliament agreed that England should have five extra seats and Wales one more. The extra seats led to widespread changes in boundaries with all the Welsh constituencies changing and all but 17 in England changing. Scotland's eight seats remained as they were in 1989. Northern Ireland elected three MEPs by proportional representation.

In the constituencies unaffected by boundary changes, the 1989 Euro-election results have been appended to the results. Where there have been boundary changes, notional results in percentages of what would have happened in 1989 under the present boundaries are shown in italics. These notional results were supplied by the Press Association and compiled by Dr Colin Rallings and Dr Michael Thrasher, directors of the Local Government Chronicle Elections Centre at the University of Plymouth.

The 1992 figures shown after each constituency are the aggregate votes from the Westminster constituencies that comprise the Euro-constituency.

The creation of five new seats in England and one in Wales posed formidable problems for the special committees set up under the European Parliamentary Elections Act of 1993 to draw up the new boundaries.

The two committees were required to ensure that the number of voters in each constituency was as near as possible equal. In drawing up their recommendations, which were published in January 1994, the committee calculated that the electorate in each English constituency should be 512,851 and that for Wales should be 444,535.

All the Euro-constituencies embrace complete Westminster constituencies and in drawing the boundaries the committees had regard to community interests and cultural ties as well as geographical features. The constituencies do not cross the Pennines nor the Thames and Humber estuaries. Cornwall, the English committee felt, did not warrant being a separate constituency because its population is too small.

In Wales, the committee faced problems posed by the sparsity of voters in the middle and north of the principality. After wide-ranging consultations, it opted for a North Wales constituency and a Mid and West Wales constituency. Those in the South, the committee said, were compact, had good communications and a community of interest.

UNITED KINGDOM
England, Scotland and Wales   84 seats

Polling day: June 9

Electorate: 42,293,640   (1989 electorate: 42,590,060)

Votes cast: 15,267,550   **Turnout** (36.1%) (1989: 15,353,154 Turnout: 35.9%)

Seats: 84

	Votes	1994 % of poll	Seats	Votes	1989 % of poll	Seats
Labour	6,753,863	44.24	62	6,153,640	40.1	45
Conservative	4,248,531	27.83	18	5,331,077	34.7	32
LD	2,552,730	16.72	2	986,292	6.2	-
Scot Nat	487,239	3.19	2	406,686	2.7	1
Green	494,561	3.24	-	2,292,705	14.9	-
Plaid Cymru	162,478	1.06	-	115,062	0.8	-
SDP	-	-	-	75,886	0.5	-
Others	568,151	3.72	-	41,295	0.3	-
Totals	15,267,550	100	84	15,353,154	100	78

Voting system: Simple majority — first-past-the-post

There was a marked swing away from the ruling Conservative Party, mainly to the benefit of Labour, although the Liberal Democrats picked up two seats to give them MEPs for the first time.

The Scottish National Party took more than 32 per cent of the vote in Scotland and added one seat to the one it already held. Plaid Cymru took 17 per cent of the vote in Wales.

Those elected were:

Labour (62 seats)
*Gordon Adam
*Richard Balfe
*Roger Barton
Angela Billingham
*Dave Bowe
*Ken Coates
*Ken Collins
*Peter Crampton
*Christine Crawley
Tony Cunningham
*Wayne David
*Alan Donnelly
*Michael Elliott
Robert Evans
*Alex Falconer
*Glyn Ford
*Pauline Green
David Hallam
Veronica Hardstaff
*Lyndon Harrison
Mark Hendrick
*Michael Hindley
Richard Howitt
*Stephen Hughes
Hugh Kerr
Glenys Kinnock
*Alf Lomas
Arlene McCarthy
*Michael McGowan
*Hugh McMahon
Eryl McNally
*David Martin
*Tom Megahy

Bill Miller
Eluned Morgan
*David Morris
Simon Murphy
Clive Needle
*Stan Newens
*Eddie Newman
*Christine Oddy
*Anita Pollack
*Mel Read
*Barry Seal
*Brian Simpson
Peter Skinner
*Alex Smith
Shaun Spiers
*Ken Stewart
Michael Tappin
David Thomas
*Gary Titley
*John Tomlinson
*Carole Tongue
Peter Truscott
Sue Waddington
Mark Watts
*Norman West
*Ian White
Phillip Whitehead
*Joe Wilson
*Terence Wynn

Conservative (18 seats)
*Bryan Cassidy
Giles Chichester
John Corrie

Brendan Donelly
*James Elles
*Caroline Jackson
*Edward Kellett-Bowman
*Anne McIntosh
*Edward McMillan-Scott
Graham Mather
*James Moorhouse
Roy Perry
*Lord Plumb of Coleshill
James Provan
*Tom Spencer
*John Stevens
*Sir Jack Stewart-Clark
Robert Sturdy

Liberal Democrat (2 seats)
Robin Teverson
Graham Watson

Scottish National Party (2 seats)
*Winnie Ewing
Allan Macartney

Northern Ireland (3 seats)

Democratic Unionist Party
*The Rev Ian Paisley

Social Democratic and Labour Party
*John Hume

Ulster Unionist
*James Nicholson

45

NORTHERN IRELAND

Voting system: All 17 Westminster constituencies make up one three-member constituency in the European Parliament. Voting is by single transferable vote.

Electorate: 1,150,304   (1989: 1,120,508)
Total poll: 559,867 **Turnout:** 48.67% (1989: 540,254 Turnout: 48.8%)
Seats: 3

| | | 1994 | | | 1989 | |
Name and party	Votes	% of poll	Seats	Votes	% of poll	Seats
Elected						
*Rev Ian Paisley (DUP)	163,246	29.16	1	160,110	29.6%	1
*John Hume (SDLP)	161,992	28.93	1	136,335	25.2%	1
*James Nicholson (UU)	133,459	23.84	1	118,785	22.0%	1
Not elected						
Mrs Mary Clark-Glass (All)	23,157	4.14%				
Tom Hartley (SF)	21,273					
Ms Dodie McGuinness (SF)	17,195	(9.86%)				
Francie Molloy (SF)	16,747					
Rev Hugh Ross (Ulster I)	7,858					
Miss Myrtle Boal (C)	5,583					
John Lowry (WP)	2,543	(4.07%)				
Niall Cusack (Ind Lab)	2,464					
Jim Anderson (NLP)	1,418					
Mrs June Campion (Peace)	1,088					
Robert Mooney (Con NI)	400					
David Kerr (I Ulster)	571					
Ms Suzanna Thompson (NLP)	454					
Michael Kennedy (NLP)	419					

The same three MEPs were returned in Northern Ireland, but John Hume recieved a marked increase in the number of his first preference votes. This was seen as an endorsement of his peace efforts. As in the Republic, Sinn Fein candidates failed to gain much support.

UK constituency results in England, Scotland and Wales

Results from the 84 constituencies in England, Scotland and Wales. * Denotes member of the outgoing Parliament.

The following main party abbreviations have been used: C - Conservative; Lab - Labour; Lab Co-op - Labour Co-operative; LD - Liberal Democrat; PC - Plaid Cymru; SNP - Scottish National Party; Grn - Green; NLP - Natural Law Party; Lib - Liberal Party; UU - Ulster Unionist; DUP - Democratic Unionist Party; SDLP - Social Democratic and Labour Party; SF - Sinn Fein; All - Alliance; WP - Workers' Party; Anti-Fed - United Kingdom Independence Anti-Federal; Anti-Fed C - Official Anti-Federalist Conservative; C Non-Fed - Conservative Non-Federal Party; Comm - Communist Party; Meb Ker - Mebyon Kernow (Cornish nationalist); NF - National Front; Literal - Literal Democrat.

ENGLAND

BEDFORDSHIRE & MILTON KEYNES

Electorate: 525,524
Bedfordshire Mid; Bedfordshire North; Bedfordshire South West; Luton North; Luton South; Milton Keynes North East; Milton Keynes South West

		%
E McNally (Lab)	94,837	46.6
Mrs E Currie (C)	61,628	30.3
Ms M Howes (LD)	27,994	13.8
A Sked (UK Ind)	7,485	3.7
A Francis (Grn)	6,804	3.3
A Howes (N Brit)	3,878	1.9
L Sheaff (NLP)	939	0.5

Lab maj: 33,209

Total vote: 203,565 (38.7%)
Lab gain
1992 Electorate and turnout: 514,358 (80.98%). C 217,427 (50.20%); Lab 126,592 (30.39%); LD 65,671 (15.77%); Others 6,860 (1.65%). Seats: C 7. *1989: Turnout 32.4%. C 40.7 Lab 34.8 Grn 18.5 LD 5.15 SDP 0.98.*

BIRMINGHAM EAST

Electorate: 520,782 (535,951)
Edgbaston; Erdington; Hall Green; Hodge Hill; Northfield; Selly Oak; Small Heath; Sparkbrook; Yardley

		%
*Mrs C Crawley (Lab)	90,291	58.2
A Turner (C)	35,171	22.7
Ms C Cane (LD)	19,455	12.6
P Simpson (Grn)	6,268	4.0
R Cook (Soc)	1,969	1.8
M Brierley (NLP)	1,885	1.2

Lab maj: 55,120

Total vote: 155,039 (29.8%)
No change
1989: Total vote 179,722 (33.8%). Lab 96,588 (53.7%); C 49,640 (27.6%); Grn 22,589 (12.5%); SDP 5,424 (3.0%); LD 4,010 (2.2%); NF 1,471 (0.8%).
1992 Electorate and turnout: 527,503 (72.65%). Lab 182,188 (47.54%); C 147,944 (38.60%); LD 49,451 (12.90%) Others 3,659 (0.95%). Seats: Lab 7; C 2.

BIRMINGHAM WEST

Electorate: 509,948 (521,662)
Aldridge-Brownhills; Birmingham Ladywood; Birmingham Perry Barr; Sutton Coldfield; Walsall North; Walsall South; West Bromwich East; West Bromwich West

		%
*J Tomlinson (Lab Co-op)	77,957	53.7
D Harman (C)	38,607	26.6
N McGeorge (LD)	14,603	10.1
Dr B Juby (Anti-F)	5,237	3.6
M Abbott (Grn)	4,367	3.0
A Carmichael (NF)	3,727	2.6
H Meads (NLP)	789	0.5

Lab Co-op maj: 39,350

Total vote: 145,287 (26.5%)
No change
1989: Total vote: 171,287 (33.2%). Lab 86,545 (50.5%); C 55,685 (32.5%); Grn 21,384 (12.4%); LD 7,673 (4.4%).
1992 Electorate and turnout: 513,786 (74.80%). Lab 168,975 (43.97%); C 166,992 (43.45%); LD 46,113 (12.00%); Others 2,255 (0.59%). Seats: Lab 6; C 2.

BRISTOL

Electorate: 503,218
Bristol East; Bristol North West; Bristol South; Bristol West; Kingswood; Northavon; Woodspring

		%
*I White (Lab)	90,790	44.1
Earl of Stockton (C)	60,835	30.0
J Barnard (LD)	40,394	19.6
J Boxall (Grn)	7,163	3.5
T Whittingham (UKI)	5,798	2.8
T Dyball (NLP)	876	0.4

Lab maj: 29,955

Total vote: 205,856 (40.9%)
No change
1992 Electorate and turnout: 502,948 (81.07%). C 178,411 (43.75%); Lab 132,889 (32.59%); LD 90,431 (22.18%); Others 6,028 (1.48%). Seats: C 4; Lab 3.
1989: Turnout 40.7%. Lab 39.8% C 35.6% Grn 17.8% LD 6.4% Others 0.42%.

47

BUCKINGHAMSHIRE & OXFORDSHIRE EAST

Electorate: 487,692
Aylesbury; Banbury; Beaconsfield; Buckingham; Chesham & Amersham; Henley; Wycombe

		%
*J Elles (C)	77,037	42.3
D Enright (Lab)	46,372	25.5
Ms S Bowles (LD)	42,836	23.5
L Roach (Grn)	8,433	4.6
Ms A Micklen (Ind Li)	5,111	2.8
Dr G Clements (NLP)	2,156	1.2

C maj: 30,665

Total vote: 181,945 (37.3%)
No change
1992 Electorate and turnout: 478,540 (81.04%). C 229,217 (59.11%); LD 87,668 (22.61%); Lab 64,666 (16.68%); Others 6,239 (1.61%). Seats: C 7.
1989: Turnout 36.0%. C 50.5% Grn 20.3% Lab 20.2% LD 6.9% Others 2.09%.

CAMBRIDGESHIRE

Electorate: 495,383
Cambridge; Cambridgeshire North East; Cambridgeshire South East; Cambridgeshire South West; Huntingdon; Peterborough

		%
R Sturdy (C)	66,921	37.6
Ms M Johnson (Lab)	62,979	35.4
A Duff (LD)	36,114	20.3
Ms M Wright (Grn)	5,756	3.2
P Wiggin (Lib)	4,051	2.2
F Chalmers (NLP)	2,077	1.2

C maj: 3,942

Total vote: 177,898 (36.0%)
No change
1992 Electorate and turnout: 492,526 (78.20%). C 209,831 (54.48%); Lab 89,734 (23.30%); 75,972 (19.72%); Others 9,622 (2.50%). Ca 5; Lab 1.
1989: Turnout 32.5%. C 45.2% Lab 25.9% Grn 20.9% LD 8.0%.

CHESHIRE EAST

Electorate:502,726
Altrincham & Sale; Halton; Macclesfield; Manchester Wythenshawe; Tatton; Warrington North; Warrington South

		%
*B Simpson (Lab)	87,586	53.7
P Slater (C)	48,307	49.6
P Harris (LD)	20,552	12.6
D Wild (Grn)	3,671	2.3
P Dixon (Loony CP)	1,600	1.0
P Leadbetter (NLP)	1,488	0.1

Lab maj: 39,279

Total vote: 163,204 (32.5%)
No change
1992 Electorate and turnout: 498,226 (79.10%). C 172,612 (43.80%); Lab 160,187 (40.64%); LD 58,478 (14.84%) Others 2,842 (0.72%). Seats: Lab 4; C 3.
1989: Turnout 35.6%. Lab 45.1% C 37.1% Grn 11.3%; LD 6.5%.

CHESHIRE WEST & WIRRAL

Electorate: 538,571
Birkenhead; Chester City; Crewe & Nantwich; Eddisbury; Ellesmere Port & Neston; Wallasey; Wirral South; Wirral West

		%
*L Harrison (Lab)	106,160	53.6
D Senior (C)	58,984	29.8
I Mottershaw (LD)	20,746	10.5
D Carson (Home Rl)	6,167	3.1
M Money (Grn)	5,096	2.6
A Wilmot (NLP)	929	0.5

Lab maj: 47,176

Total vote: 198,082 (36.8%)
No change
1992 Electorate and turnout: Total vote: 536,951 (81.56%). C 192,848 (44.03%); 185,909 (42.45%); LD 53,264 (12.16%) Other 5,923 (1.35%). Seats: C 4; Lab 4.
1989: Turnout 39.9%. Lab 45.5% C 37.9% Grn 12.2 LD 4.4%.

CLEVELAND & RICHMOND

Electorate:499,580
Hartlepool; Langbaurgh; Middlesbrough; Redcar; Richmond (Yorks); Stockton North; Stockton South

		%
*D Bowe (Lab)	103,355	58.7
R Goodwill (C)	45,787	26.0
B Moore (LD)	21,574	12.2
G Parr (Grn)	4,375	2.5
R Scott (NLP)	1,068	0.6

Lab maj: 57,568

Total vote: 176,159 (34.9%)
No change
1992 Electorate and turnout: 497,161 (78.19%). Lab 169,287 (43.55%); 160,282 (41.23%); LD 58,027 (14.93%); Others 1,120 (0.29%). Seats: Lab 4; C 3.
1989: Turnout 34.9%. Lab 51.3% C 32.9% Grn 8.5% LD 3.7% SDP 3.53%.

CORNWALL & PLYMOUTH WEST

Electorate: 484,697
Cornwall North; Cornwall South East; Falmouth & Camborne; Plymouth Devonport; Plymouth Drake; St Ives; Truro

		%
R Teverson (LD)	91,113	41.8
*C Beazley (C)	61,615	28.3
Mrs D Kirk (Lab)	42,907	19.7
Mrs P Garnier (UKI)	6,466	3.0
P Holmes (Off Li)	6,414	2.9
Ms K Westbrook (Grn)	4,372	2.0
Dr L Jenkin (Meb K)	3,315	1.5
F Lyons (NLP)	921	0.4
M Fitzgerald (Sub)	606	0.3

LD maj: 29,498

Total vote: 217,729 (44.9%)
LD gain
1992 Electorate and turnout: 484,292 (80.37%). C 162,294 (41.70%); LD 136,761 (35.14%); Lab 81,608 (20.97%); Others 8,552 (2.20%). Seats: C 4: LD 2; Lab 1.
1989: Turnout 40.6%. C 38.0% LD 31.5% Lab 17.5% Grn 10.9% Others 2.12%.

COTSWOLDS

Electorate: 497,588
Cheltenham; Cirencester & Tewkesbury; Gloucester; Gloucestershire West; Stroud; Witney

		%
*Lord Plumb (C)	67,484	34.5
Ms T Kingham (Lab)	63,216	32.4
J Thomson (LD)	44,269	22.7
M Rendell (BnB)	11,044	5.7
D McCanlis (Grn)	8,254	4.2
H Brighouse (NLP)	1,151	0.6

C maj: 4,268

Total vote: 195,418 (39.3%)
No change
1992 Electorate and turnout: 489,766 (82.16%). C 196,500 (48.83%); LD 109,039 (27.10%); Lab 91,989 (22.84%); Others 4,953 (1.23%). Seats: C 5 LD 1.
1989: Turnout 36.1%. C 42.6% Lab 26.2% Grn 22.5% LD 8.7%

COVENTRY & WARWICKSHIRE NORTH

Electorate: 523,448
Coventry North East; Coventry North West; Coventry South East; Coventry South West; Meriden; Nuneaton; Solihull; Warwickshire North

		%
*Ms C Oddy (Lab)	89,500	52.6
Ms J Crabb (C)	45,599	26.8
G Sewards (LD)	17,453	10.3
R Meacham (Free Tr)	9,432	5.5
P Baptie (Grn)	4,360	2.6
R Wheway (Lib)	2,885	1.7
R France (NLP)	1,098	0.6

Lab maj: 43,901

Total vote: 170,327 (32.4%)
No change
1992 Electorate and turnout: 524,403 (79.57%). Lab 184,471 (44.21%); 162,999 (39.07%) LD 52,926 (12.68%); Others 16,850 (4.04%). Seats: Lab 5; C 3.
1989: Turnout 37.0%. Lab 42.6% C 34.5% Grn 19.3% LD 3.6%.

CUMBRIA & LANCASHIRE NORTH

Electorate: 498,557
Barrow & Furness; Carlisle; Copeland; Lancaster; Morecambe & Lunesdale; Penrith & the Border; Westmorland & Lonsdale; Workington

		%
T Cunningham (Lab)	97,599	48.0
*Lord Inglewood (C)	74,611	36.7
R Putnam (LD)	24,233	11.9
D Frost (Grn)	5,344	2.6
I Docker (NLP)	1,500	0.7

Lab maj: 22,988

Total vote: 203,287 (40.8%)
Lab gain
1992 Electorate and turnout: 496,186 (80.09%). C 185,717 (46.74%); Lab 142,530 (35.87%); LD 65,194 (16.41%). Others 3,939 (0.99%). Seats: C 4; Lab 4.
1989: Turnout 35.7%. Lab 40.5% C 40.5% Grn 10.5% LD 6.4% SDP 2.14%.

DEVON & PLYMOUTH EAST

Electorate: 524,320
Devon West & Torridge; Exeter; Plymouth Sutton; South Hams; Teignbridge; Tiverton; Torbay

		%
G Chichester (C)	74,953	31.7
A Sanders (LD)	74,253	31.4
Ms L Wade (Lab)	47,596	20.1
D Morrish (Lib)	14,621	6.2
P Edwards (Grn)	11,172	4.7
R Huggett (Lit)	10,203	4.3
J Everard (Ind)	2,629	1.1
A Pringle (NLP)	908	0.4

C maj: 700

Total vote: 236,335 (45.1%)
No change
1992 Electorate and turnout: 521,234 (81.67%). C 208,465 (48.97%); LD 137,173 (32.22%); Lab 71,287 (16.75%): Others 8,773 (2.06%). Seats: C 7.
1989: Turnout 40.0%. C 45.2% Lab 19.0% Grn 21.1% LD 10.8% SDP 2.72% Others 1.10%.

DORSET & DEVON EAST

Electorate: 531,842
Bournemouth East; Bournemouth West; Dorset North; Dorset South; Dorset West; Honiton; Poole

		%
*B Cassidy (C)	81,551	37.2
P Goldenberg (LD)	79,287	36.2
A Gardner (Lab)	39,856	15.9
M Floyd (UKI)	10,548	4.8
Mrs K Bradbury (Grn)	8,642	3.9
I Mortimer (C N-Fed)	3,229	1.5
M Griffiths (NLP)	1,048	0.5

C maj: 2,264

Total vote: 219,161 (41.2%)
No change
1992 Electorate and turnout: 528,033 (78.36%). C 218,937 (52.91%); LD 130,472 (31.53%); Lab 55,758 (13.48%); Others 8,620 (2.08%0). Seats: C 7.
1989: Turnout 35.7%. C 49.0% Grn 22.0% Lab 18.5% LD 10.6%.

DURHAM

Electorate: 532,051 (535,728
Bishop Auckland; Blaydon; Darlington; Durham City of; Durham North; Durham North West; Easington; Sedgefield

		%
*S Hughes (Lab)	136,671	72.1
P Bradbourn (C)	25,033	13.2
Dr N Martin (LD)	20,935	11.0
S Hope (Grn)	5,670	3.0
C Adamson (NLP)	1,198	0.6

Lab maj: 111,638

Total vote: 189,507 (37.6%)
No change
1989: Total vote 189,187 (35.6%). Lab 124,448 (65.7%); C 37,600 (19.8%); Grn 18,770 (9.9%); LD 8,369 (4.4%).
1992 Electorate and turnout: 533,793 (76.70%). Lab 231,465 (56.53%); C 115,305 (28.16%); LD 61,485 (15.02%); Other 1,167 (0.29%). Seats: Lab 8.

ESSEX NORTH & SUFFOLK SOUTH

Electorate: 497,098
Braintree; Colchester North; Colchester South & Maldon; Harwich; Saffron Walden; Suffolk South

		%
*Miss A McIntosh (C)	68,311	33.2
C Pearson (Lab)	64,678	31.5
S Mole (LD)	52,536	25.6
S De Chair (Ind A)	12,409	6.4
J Abbott (Grn)	6,641	3.2
N Pullen (NLP)	884	0.4

C maj: 3,633

Total vote: 205,459 (41.3%)
No change
1992 Electorate and turnout: 491,740 (80.67%). C 209,590 (52.84%); Lab 85,016 (21.43%); LD 98,613 (24.86%) Other 3,452 (0.87%0). Seats C 6.
1989: Turnout 34.4%. C 42.8% Lab 26.4% Grn 22.4% LD 8.4%.

ESSEX SOUTH

Electorate: 487,221
Basildon; Billericay; Castle Point; Rochford; Southend East; Southend West; Thurrock

		%
R Howitt (Lab)	71,883	44.6
L Stanbrook (C)	50,516	31.3
G Williams (LD)	26,132	16.2
B Lynch Lib	6,780	4.2
G Rumens (Grn)	4,691	2.9
M Heath (NLP)	1,177	0.7

Lab maj: 21,367

Total vote: 161,179 (33.1%)
Labour gain
1992 Electorate and turnout: 481,148 (79.59%). C 205,690 (53.71%); Lab 102,305 (26.72%); 70,682 (18.46%); Other 4,259 (1.11%). Seats: C 6; Lab 1.
1989: Turnout 32.8%. C 42.4% Lab 34.6% Grn 17.2% LD 5.8%

ESSEX WEST & HERTFORDSHIRE EAST

Electorate: 504,095
Brentwood & Ongar; Broxbourne; Chelmsford; Epping Forest; Harlow; Hertford & Stortford; Stevenage

		%
H Kerr (Lab)	66,379	36.2
*Ms P Rawlings (C)	63,312	34.5
Ms G James (LD)	39,695	19.5
B Smalley (Brit)	10,277	5.6
Ms F Mawson (Grn)	5,632	3.1
P Carter (Sprtmn)	1,127	0.6
L Davis (NLP)	1,026	0.6

C maj: 3,067

Total vote: 183,448 (36.4%)
Lab gain
1992 Electorate and turnout: 504,474 (82.38%). C 228,665 (55.03%); Lab 95,990 (23.10%); LD 87,841 (21.14%); Other 3,067 (0.74%) Seats C 7.
1989: Turnout 33.0%. C 45.6% Lab 28.5% Grn 18.1% LD 7.7%.

GREATER MANCHESTER CENTRAL

Electorate: 481,779
Cheadle; Hazel Grove; Manchester Blackley; Manchester Central; Manchester Gorton; Manchester Withington; Stockport; Stretford

		%
*E Newman (Lab)	74,935	53.4
Mrs S Mason (C)	32,490	23.2
J Begg (LD)	22,988	16.4
B Candeland (Grn)	4,952	3.5
P Burke (Lib)	3,862	2.7
P Stanley (NLP)	1,017	0.7

Lab maj: 42,445

Total vote: 140,244 (29.1%)
No change
1992 Electorate and turnout: 480,923 (72.69%). Lab 150,228 (42.97%); C 125,380 (35.86%); LD 69,796 (19.97%); Other 4,185 (1.20%). Seats: Lab 8.
1989: Turnout 34.3%. Lab 47.4% C 30.2% Grn 11.6% LD 9.3% SDP 0.87% Others 0.63%.

GREATER MANCHESTER EAST

Electorate: 501,125
Ashton-under-Lyne; Denton & Reddish; Heywood & Middleton; Littleborough & Saddleworth; Oldham Central & Royton; Oldham West; Rochdale; Stalybridge & Hyde

		%
*G Ford (Lab)	82,289	60.4
J Pinniger (C)	26,303	19.3
A Riley (LD)	20,545	15.1
T Clarke (Grn)	5,823	4.3
W Stevens (NLP)	1,182	0.9

Lab maj: 55,986

Total vote: 136,143 (27.2%)
No change
1992 Electorate and turnout: 503,023 (75.93%). Lab 178,570 (46.75%); C 122,429 (32.05%); LD 73,663 (19.29%); Others 7,296 (1.91%). Seats: Lab 6; C 1; LD 1.
1989: Turnout 35.9%. Lab 56.2% C 25.8% Grn 10.7% LD 7.3%.

GREATER MANCHESTER WEST

Electorate: 512,618
Bolton North East; Bolton South East; Bolton West; Bury South; Davyhulme; Eccles; Salford East; Worsley

		%
*G Titley (Lab)	94,129	61.8
D Newns (C)	35,494	23.3
F Harasiwka (LD)	13,650	9.0
R Jackson (Grn)	3,950	2.6
G Harrison (McC)	3,693	2.4
T Brotheridge (NLP)	1,360	0.9

Lab maj: 56,635

Total vote: 152,232 (29.7%)
No change
1992 Electorate and turnout: 512,845 (78.00%). Lab 194,715 (48.67%); C 154,029 (38.50%); LD 44,534 (11.13%); Others 6,755 (1.68%). Seats: Lab 4; C 4.
1989: Turnout 38.0%. Lab 54.0% C 28.6% Grn 11.4% LD 3.8% SDP 2.23%

HAMPSHIRE NORTH & OXFORD

Electorate: 525,982
Aldershot; Basingstoke; Hampshire North West;
Newbury; Oxford East; Oxford West & Abingdon;
Wantage

		%
G Mather (C)	72,209	35.8
Ms J Hawkins (LD)	63,015	31.3
J Tanner (Lab)	48,525	24.1
D Wilkinson (UKI)	8,377	4.2
Dr M Woodin (Grn)	7,310	3.6
H Godfrey (NLP)	1,027	0.5
R Boston (Bos)	1,018	0.5

C maj: 9,194

Total vote: 201,481 (38.3%)
No change
1992 Electorate and turnout: 521,790 (80.01%). C
217,842 (52.18%); LD 114,976 (27.54%); Lab
78,579 (18.82%); Others 6,092 (1.46%). Seats: C 6;
Lab 1.
*1989: Turnout 33.7%. C 44.4% Lab 23.9% Grn 22.1% LD
9.6%.*

HEREFORDSHIRE & SHROPSHIRE

Electorate: 536,470
Hereford; Leominster; Ludlow; Shrewsbury &
Atcham; Shropshire North; The Wrekin; Wyre
Forest

		%
D Hallam (Lab)	76,120	36.7
*Sir C Prout (C)	74,270	35.8
J Gallagher (LD)	44,130	21.2
Ms F Norman (Grn)	11,578	5.6
T Mercer (NLP)	1,480	0.7

Lab maj 1,850

Total vote: 207,578 (38.7%)
No change
1992 Electorate and turnout: 527,221 (80.32%). C
203,553 (48.07%); Lab 107,802 (25.46%); LD
106,922 (25.25%); Others 5,182 (1.22%). Seats: C
6; Lab 1.
*1989: Turnout 32.6%. C 42.6% Lab 30.3% Grn 19.9% LD
7.2%.*

HERTFORDSHIRE

Electorate: 522,338
Hertfordshire North; Hertfordshire South West;
Hertfordshire West; Hertsmere; St Albans;
Watford; Welwyn Hatfield.

		%
Dr P Truscott (Lab)	81,821	39.1
P Jenkinson (C)	71,517	34.1
D Griffiths (LD)	38,995	18.6
Ms L Howitt (Grn)	7,741	3.7
M Biggs (N Brit)	6,555	3.1
J McAuley (NF)	1,755	0.8
D Lucas (NLP)	734	0.4
J Laine (21 C)	369	0.2

Lab maj: 10,304

Total vote: 209,487 (40.1%)
Lab gain
1992 Electorate and turnout: 518,051 (83.12%). C
224,205 (52.07%); Lab 113,239 (26.30%); LD
88,743 (20.61%); Others 4,408 (1.02%). Seats: C 7.
*1989: Turnout 35.0%. C 43.4% Lab 27.4% Grn 19.8% LD
6.8% SDP 2.52%.*

HUMBERSIDE

Electorate: 519,013
Beverley; Boothferry; Bridlington; Glanford &
Scunthorpe; Hull East; Hull North; Hull West

		%
*P Crampton (Lab)	87,296	51.9
D Stewart (C)	46,678	27.8
Ms D Wallis (LD)	28,818	17.2
Ms S Mummery (Grn)	4,170	2.5
Ms A Miszewska (NLP)	1,100	0.7

Lab maj: 40,618

Total vote: 168,062 (32.4%)
No change
1992 Electorate and turnout: 516,763 (74.67%). C
158,761 (41.14%); Lab 153,811 (39.86%); LD
71,227 (18.46%); Others 2,079 (0.54%). Seats: Lab
4; C 3.
*1989: Turnout 32.0%. Lab 44.4% C 36.1% Grn 14.7%
LD3.2%% SDP 1.59%.*

ITCHEN, TEST & AVON

Electorate: 550,406
Christchurch; Eastleigh; New Forest; Romsey &
Waterside; Salisbury; Southampton Itchen;
Southampton Test

		%
*E Kellett-Bowman (C)	81,456	35.4
T Barron (LD)	74,553	32.4
E Read (Lab)	52,416	22.8
N Sarage (UK Ind)	12,423	5.4
Ms F Hulbert (Grn)	7,998	3.5
A Miller-Smith (NLP)	1,368	0.6

C maj: 6,903

Total vote: 230,214 (41.8%)
No change
1992 Electorate and turnout: 542,167 (80.39%). C
230,887 (52.97%); LD 111,685 (25.62%); Lab
90,246 (20.71%); Others 3.033 (0.70%). Seats: C 6;
Lab 1.
*1989: Turnout 34.9%. C 45.9% Lab 25.1% Grn 20.2 LD
8.8%.*

KENT EAST

Electorate: 499,662
Ashford; Canterbury; Dover; Faversham;
Folkestone & Hythe; Thanet North; Thanet South

		%
M Watts (Lab)	69,641	34.4
*C Jackson (C)	69,006	34.2
J Macdonald (LD)	44,549	22.1
C Bullen (UK Ind)	9,414	4.7
S Dawe (Grn)	7,196	3.8
C Beckley (NLP)	1,746	0.9

Lab maj: 635

Total vote: 201,552 (40.3%)
Lab gain
1992 Electorate and turnout: 497,162 (79.19%). C
202,565 (51.45%); Lab 94,011 (23.88%); 91,840
(23.33%); Others 5,305 (1.35%). Seats: C 7.
*1989: Turnout 33.8%. C 43.4% Lab 29.8% Grn 19.0% LD
7.8%.*

KENT WEST

Electorate: 505,658
Dartford; Gillingham; Gravesham; Kent Mid; Maidstone; Medway; Tonbridge and Malling

		%
P Skinner (Lab)	77,346	41.0
*B Patterson (C)	60,569	32.1
J Daly (LD)	33,869	17.9
C Mackinlay (UK Ind)	9,750	5.2
Ms P Kemp (Grn)	5,651	3.0
J Bowler (NLP)	1,598	0.9

Lab maj: 16,777

Total vote: 188,783 (37.3%)
Lab gain
1992 Electorate and turnout: 501,278 (81.39%). C 218,427 (53.54%); Lab 111,444 (27.32%); LD 72,898 (17.87%); Other 5,225 (1.28%). Seats: C 7.
1989: Turnout 33.2%. C 42.7% 32.7% Grn 17.1% 7.5%.

LANCASHIRE CENTRAL

Electorate: 505,224
Blackpool North; Blackpool South; Burnley; Fylde; Pendle; Preston; Ribble Valley; Wyre

		%
M Hendrick	73,420	43.7
*M Welsh (C)	61,229	36.5
Ms J Ross-Mills (LD)	20,578	12.3
D Hill (Home Rl)	6,751	4.0
C Maile (Grn)	4,169	2.5
Ms J Ayliffe (NLP)	1,127	1.0

Lab Co-op maj: 12,191

Total vote: 167,874 (33.2%)
Lab change
1992 Electorate and turnout: 508,408 (78.48%). C 180,532 (45.25%); Lab 143,154 (35.88%); LD 73,452 (18.41%); Others 1,843 (0.46%) Seats: C 5; Lab 3.
1989: Turnout 34.4%. Lab 40.8% C 40.2% Grn 13.7% LD 5.2%.

LANCASHIRE SOUTH

Electorate: 514,840
Blackburn; Bury North; Chorley; Hyndburn; Lancashire West; Rossendale & Darwen; South Ribble

		%
*MHindley (Lab)	92,598	54.3
R Topham (C)	51,194	30.0
J Ault (LD)	17,008	10.0
J Gaffney (Grn)	4,774	2.8
Mrs E Rokas (Ind)	3,439	2.4
J Renwick (NLP)	1,605	1.0

Lab maj: 41,404

Total vote: 170,618 (33.1%)
No change
1992 Electorate and turnout: 512,394 (82.13%). C 188,456 (44.78%); Lab 183,649 (43.64%); LD 44,718 (10.63%); Others 3,994 (0.95%). Seats: Lab 4; C 3.
1989: Turnout 37.8%. Lab 48.0% C 36.9% Grn 11.8% LD 3.2%.

LEEDS

Electorate: 521,989 (508,109)
Elmet; Leeds Central; Leeds East; Leeds North East; Leeds North West; Leeds South & Morley; Leeds West; Pudsey

		%
*M McGowan (Lab)	89,160	56.9
N Carmichael (C)	36,078	23.0
Ms J Harvey (LD)	17,557	11.2
M Meadowcroft (Lib)	6,617	4.2
Ms C Nash (Grn)	6,283	4.0
Ms S J Hayward (NLP)	1,018	0.7

Lab maj: 53,082

Total vote: 156,731 (30.0%)
No change
1989: Total vote 186,530 (35.9%). Lab 97,385 (52.2%); C 54,867 (29.4%); Grn 22,558 (12.1%); LD 11,720 (6.3%).
1992 Electorate and turnout: 529,127 (73.79%). Lab 171,919 (44.03%); C 146,847 (37.61%); LD 64,717 (16.58%); Others 6,966 (1.78%). Seats: Lab 4; C 4.

LEICESTER

Electorate: 515,343
Harborough; Leicester East; Leicester South; Leicester West; Loughborough; Rutland & Melton; Stamford & Spalding

		%
Ms S Waddington (Lab)	87,048	44.9
A Marshall (C)	66,764	34.4
M Jones (LD)	28,890	14.9
G Forse (Grn)	8,941	4.6
Ms P Saunders (NLP)	2,283	1.2

Lab maj: 20,284

Total vote: 193,926 (37.6%)
Lab gain
1992 Electorate and turnout: 508,157 (78.70%). C 192,809 (48.21%) Lab 131,459 (32.87%); LD 71,027 (17.76%); Others 4,633 (1.16%). Seats: C 4; Lab 3.
1989: Turnout 35.3%. C 38.7% Lab 35.9% Grn 16.7% LD 4.9% Others 3.86%.

LINCOLNSHIRE & HUMBERSIDE SOUTH

Electorate: 539,981
Brigg & Cleethorpes; Gainsborough & Horncastle; Grantham; Great Grimsby; Holland with Boston; Lincoln; Lindsey East

		%
Mrs V Hardstaff (Lab)	83,172	42.4
*B Newton Dunn (C)	69,427	35.4
K Melton (LD)	27,241	13.9
Ms R Robinson (Grn)	8,563	4.4
E Wheeler (Lib)	3,434	1.8
I Selby (Network)	2,973	1.5
H Kelly (NL)	1,129	0.7

C maj: 13,745

Total vote: 196,239 (36.3%)
Lab gain
1992 Electorate and turnout: 532,136 (78.44%). C 208,569 (49.97%); Lab 129,164 (30.95%); LD 75,750 (18.15%); Others 3,911 (0.94%). Seats: C 6 Lab 1.
1989: Turnout 32.7%. C 44.7% Lab 35.8% Grn 12.9% LD 6.6%.

LONDON CENTRAL

Electorate: 494,610 (493,067)
Chelsea; City Of London & Westminster South; Fulham; Hampstead & Highgate; Holborn & St Pancras; Islington North; Islington South & Finsbury; Kensington; Westminster North

		%
*S Newens (Lab Co-op)	75,711	47.0
A Elliott (C)	50,652	31.4
Ms S Ludford (LD)	20,176	12.5
Ms N Kortvelyessy (Grn)	7,043	4.4
H Le Fanu (UKI)	4,157	2.6
M Slapper (Soc P)	1,593	1.0
Ms S Hamza (NLP)	1,215	0.8
G Weiss (Rainbow)	547	0.3

Lab Co-op maj: 25,059

Total vote: 161,094 (32.6%)
No change
1989: *Total vote 186,340 (38.3%). Lab Co-op 78,561 (42.1%); C 67,019 (35.9%); Grn 28,087 (15.0%); LD 7,864 (4.2%); SDP 2,957 (1.5%); Others (0.8%).*
1992 Electorate and turnout: 485,602 (69.69%). C 145,279 (42.93%); C 140,961 (41.65%); LD 44,311 (13.09%); Others 7,883 (2.33%). Seats: C 5; Lab 4.

LONDON EAST

Electorate: 511,523 (535,582)
Barking; Dagenham; Hornchurch; Ilford North; Ilford South; Newham North East; Romford; Upminster; Wanstead & Woodford

		%
*Ms C Tongue (Lab)	98,759	57.8
Ms V Taylor (C)	41,370	24.2
K Montgomery (LD)	15,566	9.1
G Batten (UKI)	5,974	3.5
J Baguley (Grn)	4,337	2.5
O Tillett (Third W)	3,484	2.0
N Kahn (NLP)	1,272	0.7

Lab maj: 57,389

Total vote: 170,762 (33.4%)
No change
1989: *Total vote 187,667 (35.3%). Lab 92,803 (49.4%); C 65,418 (34.8%); Grn 21,388 (11.4%); LD 7,341 (3.9%); ICP 717 (0.3%).*
1992 Electorate and turnout: 518,547 (74.76%). C 186,557 (48.12%); Lab 149,605 (38.59%); LD 49,438 (12.75%) Others 2,083 (0.54%). Seats: C 5; Lab 4.

LONDON NORTH

Electorate: 541,269 (577,420)
Chipping Barnet; Edmonton; Enfield North; Enfield Southgate; Finchley; Hendon North; Hendon South; Hornsey & Wood Green; Tottenham

		%
*Mrs P Green (Lab Co-op)	102,059	55.5
M Keegan (C)	53,711	29.2
I Mann (LD)	15,739	8.6
Ms H Jago (Grn)	5,666	3.1
I Booth (UKI)	5,099	2.8
G Sabrizi (Judo)	880	0.5
J Hinde (NLP)	856	0.5

Lab Co-op maj: 48,348

Total vote: 184,010 (34.0%)
No change
1989: *Total vote 207,825 (36.2%). Lab Co-op 85,536 (41.1%); C 79,699 (38.3%); Grn 30,807 (14.8%); LD 8,917 (4.2%); Ind 2,016 (0.9%); Comm 850 (0.4%).*
1992 Electorate and turnout: 546,568 (74.93%). C 201,261 (49.14%); 153,312 (37.43%) LD 49,067 (11.98%); Others 5,930 (1.45%). Seats: C 7; Lab 2.

LONDON NORTH EAST

Electorate: 486,016 (513,302)
Bethnal Green & Stepney; Bow & Poplar; Chingford; Hackney North & Stoke Newington; Hackney South & Shoreditch; Leyton; Newham North West; Newham South; Walthamstow

		%
*A Lomas (Lab)	80,256	63.0
S Gordon (C)	23,171	17.9
K Appiah (LD)	10,242	7.9
Ms J Lambert (Grn)	8,386	6.4
E Murat (Lib)	2,573	2.0
P Compobassi (UKI)	2,015	1.6
R Archer (NLP)	1,111	8.9
M Fischer (Com GB)	869	0.7
A Hyland (ICP4)	679	0.5

Lab maj: 57,085

Total vote: 129,302 (26.7%)
No change
1989: *Total vote 141,056 (27.6%). Lab 76,085 (53.9%); C 28,318 (20.0%); Grn 25,949 (18.4%); LD 9,575 (6.7%); Comm 1,129 (0.8%).*
1992 Electorate and turnout: 484,376 (66.05%). Lab 156,296 (48.86%); C 99,890 (31.22%); LD 53,776 (16.81%); Others 9,945 (3.11%). Seats: Lab 8; C 1.

LONDON NORTH WEST

Electorate: 481,272 (510,858)
Brent East; Brent North; Brent South; Harrow East; Harrow West; Hayes & Harlington; Ruislip-Northwood; Uxbridge

		%
R Evans (Lab)	80,192	47.4
* Lord Bethell (C)	62,750	37.1
Ms H Leighter (LD)	18,998	11.2
D Johnson (Grn)	4,743	2.8
Ms A Murphy (Com GB)	858	0.5
Ms T Sullivan (NLP)	807	0.5
C Palmer (21 C)	740	0.4

Lab maj: 17,442

Total vote: 169,088 (35.1%)
Lab gain
1989: *Total vote 181,228 (35.7%). C 74,900 (41.3%); Lab 67,500 (37.2%); Grn 28,275 (15.6%); LD 10,553 (5.8%).*
1992 Electorate and turnout: 482,963 (75.29%). C 183,883 (50.57%); Lab 127,410 (35.04%); 46,577 (12.81%); Other 5,739 (1.58%). Seats: C 6; Lab 2.

LONDON SOUTH & SURREY EAST

Electorate: 486,358
Carshalton & Wallington; Croydon Central; Croydon North East; Croydon North West; Croydon South; Epsom & Ewell; Surrey East; Sutton & Cheam

		%
*J Moorhouse (C)	64,813	38.8
Ms G Rolles (Lab)	56,074	33.5
M Reinisch (LD)	32,059	19.2
J Cornford (Grn)	7,048	4.2
J Major (Loony X)	3,339	2.0
A Reeve (Captl)	2,982	1.8
P Levy (NLP)	887	0.5

C maj: 8,739

Total vote: 167,201 (34.4%)
No change
1992 Electorate and turnout: 494,356 (77.38%). C 212,203 (55.47%); LD 85,029 (22.23%); Lab 82,442 (21.55%); Others 2,849 (0.74%). Seats: C 7 Lab 1.
1989: *Turnout 35.4%. C 45.6% Lab 27.5% Grn 18.4% LD 8.5%.*

53

LONDON SOUTH EAST

Electorate: 493,178
Beckenham; Bexleyheath; Chislehurst; Eltham; Erith & Crayford; Old Bexley & Sidcup; Orpington; Ravensbourne; Woolwich

		%
S Spiers (Lab Co-op)	71,505	41.0
*P Price (C)	63,483	36.4
J Fryer (LD)	25,271	14.5
I Mouland (Grn)	6,399	3.7
R Almond (Lib)	3,881	2.2
K Lowne (NF)	2,926	1.7
J Small (NLP)	1,025	0.6

Lab maj: 8,022

Total vote: 174,490 (35.4%)
Lab gain
1992 Electorate and turnout: 502,110 (79.45%). C 205,404 (51.49%); Lab 106,733 (26.77%); LD 66,005 (16.55%); Others 20,728 (5.20%). Seats: C 8 Lab 1.
1989: Turnout 38.3%. C 40.3% Lab 33.2% Grn 17.7% LD 4.0% SDP 4.54% Others 0.21%.

LONDON SOUTH INNER

Electorate: 510,609
Dulwich; Greenwich; Lewisham Deptford; Lewisham East; Lewisham West; Norwood; Peckham; Southwark & Bermondsey; Vauxhall

		%
*R Balfe (Lab Co-op)	85,079	61.0
A Boff (C)	25,859	18.6
A Graves (LD)	20,708	14.9
S Collins (Grn)	6,570	4.7
M Leighton (NLP)	1,179	0.9

Lab Co-op maj: 59,220

Total vote: 139,395 (27.3%)
No change
1992 Electorate and turnout: 510,424 (66.49%). Lab 165,596 (48.80%); C 103,199 (30.41%); LD 52,986 (15.61%); Others 17,589 (5.18%). Seats: Lab 8 LD 1.
1989: Turnout 33.7%. Lab 52.1% C 24.2% Grn 15.6% LD 7.2% Other 0.96%.

LONDON SOUTH WEST

Electorate: 479,246
Battersea; Kingston-upon-Thames; Mitcham & Morden; Putney; Streatham; Surbiton; Tooting; Wimbledon

		%
*Ms A Pollack (Lab)	81,850	49.7
Prof P Treleaven (C)	50,875	30.9
G Blanchard (LD)	18,697	11.4
T Walsh (Grn)	5,460	3.3
A Scholefield (UKI)	4,912	3.0
C Hopewell (Captl)	1,840	1.1
M Simson (NLP)	625	0.4
J Quanjer (Spirit)	377	0.2

Lab maj: 30,975

Total vote: 164,636 (34.4%)
No change
1992 Electorate and turnout: 474,401 (77.52%). C 178,508 (48.54%); Lab 130,495 (35.49%); LD 51,101 (13.90%); Others 7,628 (2.07%). Seats: C 6; Lab 2.
1989: Turnout 39.6%. Lab 41.6% C 35.8% Grn 17.9% LD 4.7%.

LONDON WEST

Electorate: 505,791 (519,646)
Brentford & Isleworth; Ealing Acton; Ealing North; Ealing Southall; Feltham & Heston; Hammersmith; Richmond & Barnes; Twickenham

		%
*M Elliott (Lab)	94,562	51.9
R Guy (C)	52,287	28.7
B Mallinson (LD)	21,561	11.8
J Bradley (Grn)	6,134	3.4
G Roberts (UKI)	4,583	2.5
W Binding (NF)	1,963	1.1
R Johnson (NLP)	1,105	0.6

Lab maj: 42,275

Total vote: 182,195 (36.0%)
No change
1989: *Total vote 215,982 (41.8%). Lab 92,959 (43.0%); C 78,151 (36.1%); Grn 32,686 (15.1%); LD 9,309 (4.3%); SDP 2,877 (1.3%).*
1992 Electorate and turnout: 503,272 (77.59%). C 176,777 (45.27%); Lab 133,186 (34.11%); LD 70,405 (18.03%); Others 10,123 (2.59%). Seats: C 5 Lab 3.

MERSEYSIDE EAST & WIGAN

Electorate: 518,196 (523,254)
Knowsley North; Knowsley South; Leigh; Liverpool Garston; Makerfield; St Helens North; St Helens South; Wigan

		%
*T Wynn (Lab)	91,986	72.0
C Manson (C)	17,899	14.0
Ms F Clucas (LD)	8,874	6.9
J Melia (Lib)	4,765	3.7
L Brown (Grn)	3,280	2.6
G Hutchard (NLP)	1,009	0.8

Lab maj: 74,087

Total vote: 127,813 (24.7%)
No change
1989: *Total vote 163,385 (31.4%). Lab 107,288 (65.6%); C 30,421 (18.6%); Grn 20,018 (12.2%); LD 5,658 (3.6%).*
1992 Electorate and turnout: 521,555 (74.76%). Lab 244,950 (62.82%); C 95,017 (24.37%) LD 43,379 (11.12%); Others 6,578 ((1.69%). Seats: Lab 8.

MERSEYSIDE WEST

Electorate: 515,909 (506,387)
Bootle; Crosby; Liverpool Broadgreen; Liverpool Mossley Hill; Liverpool Riverside; Liverpool Walton; Liverpool West Derby; Southport

		%
*K Stewart (Lab)	78,819	58.4
C Varley (C)	27,008	20.0
D Bamber (LD)	19,097	14.1
S Radford (Off Li)	4,714	3.5
Ms L Lever (Grn)	4,573	3.4
J Collins (NLP)	852	0.6

Lab maj: 51,811

Total vote: 135,063 (26.2%)
No change
1989: *Total vote 178,743 (35.1%). Lab 93,717 (52.4%); C 43,900 (24.5%); Grn 23,052 (12.9%); LD 16,327 (9.1%); PRP 1,747 (0.9%).*
1992 Electorate and turnout: 520,192 (71.29%). Lab 177,605 (47.89%); 91,661 (24.72%); LD 86,733 (23.39%); Others 14,867 (4.01%). Seats: Lab 5; C 2; LD 1,

MIDLANDS WEST

Electorate: 533,742 (535,395)
Dudley East; Dudley West; Halesowen & Stourbridge; Warley East; Warley West; Wolverhampton North East; Wolverhampton South East; Wolverhampton South West

		%
S Murphy (Lab)	99,242	59.5
M Simpson (C)	44,419	26.6
G Baldauf-Good (LD)	12,195	7.3
M Hyde (Lib)	5,050	3.0
C Mattingly (Grn)	4,390	2.6
J Oldbury (NLP)	1,641	1.0

Lab maj: 54,823

Total vote: 166,937 (31.3%)
No change
1989: *Total vote 197,455 (37.2%). Lab 105,529 (53.4%); C 63,165 (31.9%); Grn 21,787 (11.0%); LD 6,974 (3.5%).*
1992 Electorate and turnout: 534,653 (71.29%): Lab 191,077 (46.23%); C 174,769 (42.28%); LD 42,176 (10.20%); Others 5,318 (1.29%). Seats: Lab 5; C 3.

NORFOLK

Electorate: 513,553
Great Yarmouth; Norfolk Mid; Norfolk North; Norfolk North West; Norfolk South; Norwich North; Norwich South

		%
C Needle (Lab)	102,711	45.2
*P Howell (C)	76,424	33.7
P Burall (LD)	39,107	17.2
A Holmes (Grn)	7,938	3.5
B Parsons (NLP)	1,075	0.5

Lab maj: 26,287

Total vote: 227,255 (44.2%)
Lab gain
1992 Electorate and turnout: 508,375 (81.18%). C 199.773 (48.41%); 131,248 (31.80%); 77,092 (18.68%); Others 4,593 (1.11%). Seats: C 6; Lab 1.
1989: Turnout 37.0%. C 41.5% Lab 33.3% Grn 18.8% LD 4.1% SDP 2.26%.

NORTHAMPTONSHIRE & BLABY

Electorate: 524,916
Blaby; Corby; Daventry; Kettering; Northampton North; Northampton South; Wellingborough

		%
Mrs A Billingham (Lab)	95,317	46.1
*A Simpson (C)	69,232	33.5
K Scudder (LD)	27,616	13.4
Ms A Bryant (Grn)	9,121	4.4
I Whitaker (Ind)	4,397	2.1
B Spivack (NL)	972	0.5

Lab maj: 26,085

Total vote: 206,655 (39.4%)
Labour gain
1992 Electorate and turnout: 516,291 (81.70%). C 222,599 (52.77%); 132,785 (31.48%); LD 64,216 (15.22%); Others 2,219 (0.53%). Seats: C 7.
1989: Turnout 34.9%. C 40.8% Lab 34.1% Grn 20.3% LD 4.8%.

NORTHUMBRIA

Electorate: 516,680 (521,980)
Berwick-upon-Tweed; Blyth Valley; Hexham; Newcastle-upon-Tyne Central; Newcastle-upon-Tyne North; Tynemouth; Wallsend; Wansbeck

		%
*Dr G Adam (Lab)	103,087	59.3
J Flack (C)	36,929	21.2
L Opik (LD)	20,197	11.6
D Lott (UKI)	7,210	4.1
J Hartshorne (Grn)	5,714	3.3
L Walch (NLP)	740	0.4

Lab maj: 66,158

Total vote: 173,875 (33.7%)
No change
1989: *Total vote 197,201 (38.3%). Lab 110,688 (56.1%); C 50,648 (25.6%); Grn 24,882 (12.6%); LD 10,983 (5.5%).*
1992 Electorate and turnout: 516,157 (77.93%). Lab 182,867 (45.46%); C 132,480 (32.93%); LD 84,398 (20.98%); Others 2,504 (0.62%). Seats: Lab 5; C 2 LD 1.

NOTTINGHAM & LEICESTERSHIRE NW

Electorate: 507,915
Bosworth; Gedling; Leicestershire North West; Nottingham East; Nottingham North; Nottingham South; Rushcliffe

		%
*Ms M Read (Lab)	95,344	49.8
M Brandon-Bravo (C)	55,676	20,9
A Wood (LD)	23,836	12.5
Ms S Blount (Grn)	7,035	3.7
J Downes (UKI)	5,849	3.1
P Walton (Ind Out)	2,710	1.4
Mrs J Christou (NLP)	927	0.5

Lab maj: 39,668

Total vote: 191,277 (37.7%)
No change
1992 Electorate and turnout: 508,083 (79.46%).C 187,881 (46.54%) Lab 159,009 (39.39%); LD 52,099 (12.90%); Others: 4,734 (1.17%). Seats: C 4; Lab 3.;
1989: Turnout 34.9%. Lab 41.8% C 38.4% Grn 16.2% LD 3.5%.

NOTTINGHAMSHIRE NORTH & CHESTERFIELD

Electorate: 490,330
Bassetlaw; Bolsover; Chesterfield; Derbyshire North East; Mansfield; Newark; Sherwood

		%
*K Coates (Lab)	114,353	63.1
D Hazell (C)	38,093	21.0
Ms S Pearce (LD)	21,936	12.1
G Jones (Grn)	5,159	2.9
Ms S Lincoln (NLP)	1,632	1.0

Lab maj: 76,260

Total vote: 181,173 (37.0%)
No change
1992 Electorate and turnout: 487,677 (81.31%). Lab 198,345 (50.02%); C 138,030 (34.81%); LD 59,750 (15.06%); Others 435 (0.11%). Seats: Lab 6; C 1.
1989: Turnout 37.3%. Lab 54.5% C 28.6% Grn 12.6% LD 4.3%.

PEAK DISTRICT

Electorate: 511,357
Amber Valley; Ashfield; Broxtowe; Derbyshire West; Erewash; High Peak; Staffordshire Moorlands

		%
Ms A McCarthy (Lab)	105,853	53.1
R Fletcher (C)	56,546	28.3
Ms S Barber (LD)	29,979	15.0
M Shipley (Grn)	5,598	2.8
D Collins (NLP)	1,533	0.8

Lab maj: 49,307

Total vote: 199,509 (39.0%)
No change
1992 Electorate and turnout: 511,010 (83.23%). C 197,109 (46.34%); Lab 162,210 (38.14%) LD 61,883 (14.55%); Others 4,114 (0.97%). Seats C 6; Lab 1.
1989: Turnout 36.0%. Lab 44.7% Lab 39.4% Grn 11.1% LD 3.2%.

SHEFFIELD

Electorate: 476,530
Barnsley West & Penistone; Sheffield Attercliffe; Sheffield Brightside; Sheffield Central; Sheffield Hallam; Sheffield Heeley; Sheffield Hillsborough

		%
*R Barton (Lab)	76,397	58.3
Ms S Anginotti (LD)	26,109	19.3
Ms K Twitchen (C)	22,374	17.1
B New (Grn)	4,742	3.6
M England (Com)	834	0.6
R Hurford (NLP)	577	0.4

Lab maj: 50,288

Total vote: 131,033 (27.5%)
No change
1992 Electorate and turnout: 480,300 (70.24%). Lab 175,561 (52.04%); C 88,488 (26.23%); LD 69,721 (20.67%) Others 3,598 (1.07%). Seats: Lab 6; C 1.
1989: Turnout 33.7%. Lab 58.0% C 20.0% Grn 16.3% LD 5.3%.

SOMERSET & DEVON NORTH

Electorate: 517,349
Bridgwater; Devon North; Somerton & Frome; Taunton; Wells; Weston-Super-Mare; Yeovil

		%
G Watson (LD)	106,187	43.6
*Mrs M Daly (C)	83,678	34.3
J Pilgrim (Lab)	34,540	14.2
D Taylor (Grn)	10,870	4.5
M Lucas (NLP)	1,200	0.5
G Livings (N Brit)	7,165	2.9

LD maj: 22,509

Total vote: 243,640 (47.0%)
LD gain
1992 Electorate and turnout: 511,684 (81.89%). C 191,625 (45.73%); LD 171,868 (41.02%); Lab 48,884 (11.67%) Others 6,616 (1.58%). Seats: C 5; LD 2.
1989: Turnout 39.0%. C 44.1% Grn 24.0% Lab 17.6% LD 13.7%.

SOUTH DOWNS WEST

Electorate: 486,793
Arundel; Chichester; Hampshire East; Havant; Horsham; Surrey South West

		%
J Provan (C)	83,813	43.6
Dr J Walsh (LD)	62,746	32.7
Ms L Armstrong (Lab)	32,344	16.8
E Paine (Grn)	7,703	4.0
B Weights (Lib)	3,630	1.9
P Kember (NLP)	1,794	0.9

C maj: 21,067

Total vote: 192,030 (39.4%)
No change
1992 Electorate and turnout: 484,167 (79.69%). C 230,303 (59.69%); LD 102,757 (26.63%); Lab 43,906 (11.38%); Others 8,884 (2.30%). Seats: C 6.
1989: Turnout 36.4%. C 48.5% Grn 25.1% Lab 15.4% LD 11.1%.

STAFFORDSHIRE EAST & DERBY

Electorate: 519,553
Burton; Cannock & Burntwood; Derby North; Derby South; Derbyshire South; Staffordshire Mid; Staffordshire South East

		%
P Whitehead (Lab)	102,393	62.4
Ms J Evans (C)	30,197	18.4
Ms D Brass (LD)	17,469	10.6
I Crompton (UKI)	6,993	4.3
R Clarke (Grn)	4,272	2.6
R Jones (NF)	2,098	1.3
Ms D Grice (NLP)	793	0.5

Lab maj: 72,196

Total vote: 164,215 (31.6%)
No change
1992 Electorate and turnout: 513,351 (82.44%). C 199,706 (47.19%); Lab 179,613 (42.44%); LD 41,288 (9.76%); Others 2,580 (0.61%). Seats: C 5; Lab 2.
1989: Turnout 34.2%. Lab 48.0% C 37.4% Grn 11.5% LD 3.1%.

STAFFORDSHIRE WEST & CONGLETON

Electorate: 502,395
Congleton; Newcastle-Under-Lyme; Stafford; Staffordshire South; Stoke Central; Stoke North; Stoke South

		%
M Tappin (Lab)	84,337	53.1
A Brown (C)	44,060	27.8
J Stevens (LD)	24,430	15.4
D Hoppe (Grn)	4,533	2.9
D Lines (NLP)	1,403	0.9

Lab maj: 40,277

Total vote: 158,763 (31.6%)
No change
1992 Electorate and turnout: 504,477 (78.06%). C 163,753 (41.58%); Lab 157,929 (40.10%); LD 70,166 (17.82%); Others 1,941 (0.49%). Seats: Lab 4; C 3.
1989: Turnout 32.3%. Lab 45.1% C 35.3% Grn 13.8% LD 5.8%.

SUFFOLK & NORFOLK SOUTH WEST

Electorate: 477,668
Bury St Edmunds; Ipswich; Norfolk South West;
Suffolk Central; Suffolk Coastal; Waveney

		%
D Thomas (Lab)	74,304	40.5
*A Turner (C)	61,769	33.7
R Atkins (LD)	37,975	20.7
T Slade (Grn)	7,760	4.2
E Kaplan (NLP)	1,530	0.8

Lab maj: 12,535

Total vote: 183,338 (38.4%)
Lab gain
1992 Electorate and turnout: 471,129 (80.30%). C
191,377 (50.58%); Lab 110,748 (29.27%) LD
72,416 (19.14%); Others 3,789 (1.00%). Seats: C 5;
Lab 1.
*1989: Turnout 34.0%. C 43.1% Lab 31.6 Grn 19.0% LD
6.3%.*

SURREY

Electorate: 514,130
Chertsey & Walton; Esher; Guildford; Mole Valley;
Reigate; Surrey North West; Woking

		%
*T Spencer (C)	83,405	43.7
Mrs S Thomas (LD)	56,387	29.2
Ms F Wolf (Lab)	30,894	16.0
Mrs S Porter (UKI)	7,717	4.0
H Charlton (Grn)	7,198	3.7
J Walker (I Brit)	4,627	2.4
Mrs J Thomas (NLP)	2,638	1.4

C maj: 27,018

Total vote: 192,866 (37.5%)
No change
1992 Electorate and turnout: 509,862 (79.58%). C
243,080 (59.91%); LD 104,645 (25.79%); Lab
54,666 (13.47%); Others 3,376 (0.83%). Seats C 7.
*1989: Turnout 34.7%. C 49.5% Grn 21.8% Lab 17.5% LD
9.6%.*

SUSSEX EAST & KENT SOUTH

Electorate: 513,550
Bexhill & Battle; Eastbourne; Hastings & Rye;
Lewes; Sevenoaks; Tunbridge Wells; Wealden

		%
*Sir J Stewart-Clark (C)	83,141	38.6
D Bellotti (LD)	76,929	35.8
N Palmer (Lab)	35,273	16.4
A Burgess (UKI)	9,058	4.2
Ms R Addison (Grn)	7,439	3.5
Ms M Williamson (Lib)	2,558	1.2
P Cragg (NLP)	765	0.4

C maj: 6,212

Total vote: 215,163 (41.9%)
No change
1992 Electorate and turnout: 510,232 (79.59%). C
226,457 (55.76%); LD 128,593 (31.67%); Lab
45,282 (11.15%); Others 5,768 (1.42%). Seats C 7.
1989: Turnout 33.0%. C 52.9% Grn 20.4% Lab 14.5% 11.5%.

SUSSEX SOUTH & CRAWLEY

Electorate: 492,413
Brighton Kemptown; Brighton Pavilion; Crawley;
Hove; Shoreham; Sussex Mid; Worthing

		%
B Donelly (C)	62,860	33.9
Ms J Edmond Smith (Lab)	61,114	33.0
J Williams (LD)	41,410	22.3
Ms P Beever (Grn)	9,348	5.0
D Horner (Sceptic)	7,106	3.8
N Furness (Anti-F C)	2,618	1.4
A Hankey (NLP)	901	0.5

C maj: 1,746

Total vote: 185,367 (37.6%)
No change
1992 Electorate and turnout: 490,608 (78.48%). C
202,880 (52.69%); 89,477 (23.24%); LD 83,379
(21.65%); Others 9,303 (2.42%). Seats C 7.
*1989: Turnout 38.2%. C 42.4% Lab 25.4% Grn 23.3% LD
8.9%.*

THAMES VALLEY

Electorate: 543,685 (548,243)
Berkshire East; Reading East; Reading West;
Slough; Spelthorne; Windsor & Maidenhead;
Wokingham

		%
*J Stevens (C)	70,485	37.3
J Howarth (Lab)	69,727	36.9
N Bathurst (LD)	33,187	17.5
P Unsworth (Grn)	6,120	3.2
J Clark (Lib)	5,381	2.8
P Owen (Loony C)	2,859	1.5
M Grenville (NLP)	1,453	0.8

C maj: 758

Total vote: 189,212 (34.8%)
No change
*1989: Total vote 171,117 (31.5%). C 73,070 (42.7%); Lab
46,579 (27.2%); Grn 36,865 (21.5%); LD 14,603 (8.5%).*
1992 Electorate and turnout: 536,926 (79.75%). C
238,086 (55.60%); Lab 95,685 (22.35%); LD
87,496 (20.43%) Others 6,932 (1.62%). Seats: C 7.

TYNE & WEAR

Electorate: 516,436 (536,205)
Gateshead East; Houghton & Washington;
Jarrow; Newcastle-upon-Tyne East; South
Shields; Sunderland North; Sunderland South;
Tyne Bridge

		%
*A Donnelly (Lab)	107,604	74.4
I Liddell-Grainger (C)	19,224	13.3
P Maughan (LD)	8,706	6.0
G Edwards (Grn)	4,375	3.0
Ms W Lundgren (Lib)	4,174	2.9
A Fisken (NLP)	650	0.5

Lab maj: 88,380

Total vote: 144,723 (28.0%)
No change
*1989: Total vote 182,711 (34.4%). Lab 126,682 (69.3%); C
30,902 (16.9%); Grn 18,107 (9.9%); LD 6,101 (3.3%); SPGB
919 (0.5%).*
1992 Electorate and turnout: 521,408 (70.24%).
Lab 225,215 (61.49%); C 93,901 (25.64%); LD
44,938 (12.27%); Others 2,181 (0.60%). Seats: Lab
8.

WIGHT & HAMPSHIRE SOUTH

Electorate: 488,398
Fareham; Gosport; Isle of Wight; Portsmouth North; Portsmouth South; Winchester

		%
R Perry (C)	63,306	34.9
M Hancock (LD)	58,205	32.1
Ms S-L Fry (Lab)	40,442	22.3
J De La Valette Browne (Ind)	12,140	6.7
P Fuller (Grn)	6,697	3.7
W Treend (NLP)	722	0.4

C maj: 5,101

Total vote: 181,512 (37.2%)
No change
1992 Electorate and turnout: 487,055 (78.15%). C 197,890 (51.99%); LD 125,102 (32.87%); Lab 51,958 (13.65%) Others 5,663 (1.49%). Seats C 6.
1989: Turnout 32.3%. C 45.6% Lab 24.9% Grn 17.6% LD 11.9%.

WILTSHIRE NORTH & BATH

Electorate: 496,591
Bath; Devizes; Swindon; Wansdyke; Westbury; Wiltshire North

		%
*Dr C Jackson (C)	71,872	34.9
Ms J Matthew (LD)	63,085	30.6
Ms J Norris (Lab)	50,489	24.5
P Cullen Lib	6,760	3.3
M Davidson (Grn)	5,974	2.9
T Hedges (UKI)	5,842	2.8
D Cooke (NLP)	1,148	0.6
Dr J Day (People)	725	0.4

C maj: 8,787

Total vote: 205,895 (41.5%)
No change
1992 Electorate and turnout: 493,864 (82.40%). C 199,780 (49.09%); LD 118,257 (29.06%); Lab 80,720 (19.84%); Others 8,198 (2.01%). Seats C 5: LD 1.
1989: Turnout 36.6%. C 41.8% Lab 26.3% Grn 20.4% LD 8.8%.

WORCESTERSHIRE & WARWICKSHIRE SOUTH

Electorate: 551,162
Bromsgrove; Rugby & Kenilworth; Stratford-on-Avon; Warwick & Leamington; Worcester; Worcestershire Mid; Worcestershire South

		%
J Corrie (C)	73,573	35.2
Ms G Gschaider (Lab)	72,369	34.6
P Larner (LD)	44,168	21.1
Ms J Alty (Grn)	9,273	4.4
C Hards (Nat Ind)	8,447	4.0
J Brewster (NLP)	1,510	0.7

C maj: 1,204

Total vote: 209,340 (38.0%)
No change
1992 Electorate and turnout: 541,863 (81.69%). C 230,802 (52.14%); Lab 122,511 (27.68%); LD 82,975 (18.75%); Others 6,333 (1.43%). Seats: C 7.
1989: Turnout 36.2%. C 42.3% Lab 30.4% LD 21.8% LD 5.5%.

YORKSHIRE NORTH

Electorate: 475,686
Harrogate; Ryedale; Scarborough; Selby; Skipton & Ripon; York

		%
*E McMillan-Scott (C)	70,036	38.0
B Regan (Lab)	62,964	34.2
M Pitts (LD)	43,171	23.5
Dr D Richardson (Grn)	7,036	3.8
S Withers (NLP)	891	0.5

C maj: 7,072

Total vote: 184,098 (38.7%)
No change
1992 Electorate and turnout: 471,710 (79.95%). C 193,432 (51.29%); Lab 96,704 (25.64%); LD 84,678 (22.45%); Others 2,304 (0.61%). Seats: C 5; Lab 1.
1989: Turnout 32.7%. C 46.5% Lab 30.5% Grn 14.1% LD 8.9%.

YORKSHIRE SOUTH

Electorate: 523,401 (526,040)
Barnsley Central; Barnsley East; Don Valley; Doncaster Central; Doncaster North; Rotherham; Rother Valley; Wentworth

		%
*N West (Lab)	109,004	72.7
J Howard (C)	20,695	13.8
Ms C Roderick (LD)	11,798	7.9
P Davies (UKI)	3,948	2.6
J Waters (Grn)	3,775	2.5
N Broome (NLP)	681	0.5

Lab maj: 88,309

Total vote: 149,901 (28.6%)
No change
1989: Total vote 174,438 (33.6%). Lab 121,060 (69.4%); C 29,276 (16.7%); Grn 19,063 (10.9%); LD 5,039 (2.8%).
1992 Electorate and turnout: 523,527 (73.73%). Lab 243,231 (63.02%); C 97,782 (25.33%); LD 43,971 (11.39%); Others 987 (0.26%). Seats: Lab 8.

YORKSHIRE SOUTH WEST

Electorate: 547,469
Batley & Spen; Colne Valley; Dewsbury; Hemsworth; Huddersfield; Normanton; Pontefract & Castleford; Wakefield

		%
*T Megahy (Lab)	94,025	59.1
Mrs C Adamson (C)	34,463	21.7
D Ridgway (LD)	21,595	13.6
A Cooper (Grn)	7,163	4.5
G Mead (NLP)	1,674	1.0

Lab maj: 59,562

Total vote: 158,920 (29.0%)
No change
1992 Electorate and turnout: 544,586 (77.27%). Lab 209,616 (49.82%); C 149,247 (35.47%); LD 58,586 (13.92%); Others 3,336 (0.79%). Seats: Lab 6; C 2.
1989: Turnout 34.6%. Lab 57.1% C 25.5% Grn 12.0% LD 5.4%.

YORKSHIRE WEST

Electorate: 490,078
Bradford North; Bradford South; Bradford West; Calder Valley; Halifax; Keighley; Shipley

		%
*Dr B Seal (Lab)	90,652	53.4
R Booth (C)	42,455	25.0
C Bidwell (LD)	20,452	12.1
R Pearson (N Brit)	8,027	4.7
C Harris (Grn)	7,154	4.2
D Whitley (NLP)	894	0.5

Lab maj: 48,197

Total vote: 169,634 (34.6%)
No change
1992 Electorate and turnout: 489,641 (77.80%). Lab 161,109 (42.29%); C 159,419 (41.85%); LD 55,813 (14.65%); Others 4,609 (1.21%). Seats: Lab 4; C 3.
1989: Turnout 37.8%. Lab 49.9% C 32.2% Grn 13.2% LD 4.7%.

SCOTLAND

GLASGOW

Electorate: 463,364 (491,905)
Glasgow Cathcart; Glasgow Central; Glasgow Garscadden; Glasgow Govan; Glasgow Hillhead; Glasgow Maryhill; Glasgow Pollok; Glasgow Provan; Glasgow Shettleston; Glasgow Springburn

		%
B Miller (Lab)	83,953	52.6
T Chalmers (SNP)	40,795	25.6
T Sheridan (Mil Lab)	12,113	7.6
R Wilkinson (C)	10,888	6.8
J Money (LD)	7,291	4.6
P O'Brien (Grn)	2,252	1.1
J Fleming (Soc)	1,195	0.7
M Wilkinson (NLP)	868	0.5
C Marsden (ICP)	381	0.2

Lab maj: 43,158

Total vote: 159,666 (34.5%)
No change
1989: Total vote 194,638 (39.9%); Lab 107,818 (55.3%); SNP 48,586 (24.9%); C 20,761 (10.6%); Grn 12,229 (6.2%); LD 3,887 (2.0%); Comm 1,164 (0.6%); ICP 193 (0.1%).
1992 Electorate and turnout: 466,007 (68.99%). Lab 176,266 (54.82%); SNP 66,435 (20.66%); C 44,269 (13.77%); LD 25,727 (8.00%). Seats: Lab 10.

HIGHLANDS & ISLANDS

Electorate 328,104 (317,129)
Argyll & Bute; Caithness & Sutherland; Inverness, Nairn & Lochaber; Moray; Orkney & Shetland; Ross, Cromarty & Skye; Western Isles

		%
*Dr W Ewing (SNP)	74,872	58.4
M Macmillan (Lab)	19,956	15.6
M Tennant (C)	15,767	12.3
H Morrison (LD)	12,919	10.1
Dr E Scott (Grn)	3,140	2.5
M Carr (UKI)	1,096	0.9
Ms M Gilmour (NLP)	522	0.4

SNP maj: 54,916

Total vote: 128,272 (39.1%)
No change
1989: Total vote 128,590 (40.9%). SNP 66,297 (51.5%); C 21,602 (16.8%); Lab 17,848 (13.8%); Grn 12,199 (9.4%); LD 10,644 (8.2%).
1992 Electorate and turnout: 321,302 (72.57%). LD 65,856 (28.25%); SNP 61,479 (26.37%); C 59,096 (25.35%); Lab 44,709 (19.18%); Others 2,014 (0.86%). Seats: LD 5; SNP 1; Lab 1.

LOTHIANS

Electorate: 520,943 (527,785)
Edinburgh Central; Edinburgh East; Edinburgh Leith; Edinburgh Pentlands; Edinburgh South; Edinburgh West; Linlithgow; Livingston; Midlothian

		%
*D Martin (Lab)	90,531	44.9
K Brown (SNP)	53,324	26.5
Dr P McNally (C)	33,526	16.6
Ms H Campbell (LD)	17,883	8.9
R Harper (Grn)	5,149	2.6
J McGregor (Soc)	637	0.3
M Siebert (NLP)	500	0.2

Lab maj: 37,207

Total vote: 201,550 (38.7%)
No change
1989: Total vote 219,994 (42.0%). Lab 90,840 (41.2%); C 52,014 (23.6%); SNP 44,935 (20.4%); Grn 22,983 (10.4%); LD 9,222 (4.1%).
1992 Electorate and turnout: 517,083 (75.75%). Lab 147,940 (37.77%); C 106,993 (27.31%); SNP 74,266 (18.96%); LD 55,178 (14.09%); Others 7,330 (1.87%). Seats: Lab 7; C 2.

SCOTLAND MID & FIFE

Electorate: 546,060 (539,276)
Clackmannan; Dunfermline East; Dunfermline West; Falkirk East; Falkirk West; Fife Central; Fife North East; Kirkcaldy; Perth & Kinross; Stirling

		%
*A Falconer (Lab)	95,667	45.1
D Douglas (SNP)	64,254	38.8
P Page (C)	28,192	13.5
Ms H Lyall (LD)	17,192	8.2
M Johnston (Grn)	3,015	1.4
T Pringle (NLP)	532	0.2

Lab maj: 31,413

Total vote: 208,852 (38.3%)
No change
1989: Total vote 221,862 (41.5%). Lab 102,246 (46.0%); SNP 50,089 (22.5%); C 46,505 (20.9%); Grn 14,165 (6.3%); LD 8,857 (3.9%).
1992 Electorate and turnout: 537,471 (77.09%). Lab 162,460 (39.21%); C 108,933 (26.29%); SNP 90,906 (21.94%); LD 51,242 (12.37%); Others 789 (0.19%). Seats: Lab 7; C 2; LD 1.

SCOTLAND NORTH EAST

Electorate: 575,748 (559,275)
Aberdeen North; Aberdeen South; Angus East; Banff & Buchan; Dundee East; Dundee West; Gordon; Kincardine & Deeside; Tayside North

		%
Dr A Macartney (SNP)	92,892	42.8
* H McCubbin (Lab)	61,665	28.4
Dr R Harris (C)	40,372	18.6
S Horner (LD)	18,008	8.2
K Farnsworth (Grn)	2,559	1.2
Ms M Ward (Com GB)	689	0.3
L Mair (Neeps)	584	0.3
D Paterson (NLP)	371	0.2

SNP maj: 31,227
Total vote: 217,150(37.7%)
SNP gain
1989: Total vote 213,206 (38.4%). Lab 65,348 (30.6%); SNP 62,735 (29.4%); C 56,835 (26.6%); Grn 15,584 (7.3%); LD 12,704 (5.9%).
1992 Electorate and turnout: 568,742 (72.84%). C 138,928 (33.53%); SNP 111,542 (26.92%); Lab 96,763 (23.36%); LD 65,259 (15.75%); Other 1,793 (0.43%). Seats: C 3; Lab 3: SNP 2 LD 1.

SCOTLAND SOUTH

Electorate: 500,643 (497,108)
Ayr; Carrick, Cumnock & Doon Valley; Clydesdale; Cunninghame South; Dumfries; East Lothian; Galloway & Upper Nithsdale; Roxburgh & Berwickshire; Tweeddale, Ettrick & Lauderdale

		%
*A Smith (Lab)	90,750	45.1
A Hutton (C)	45,595	22.7
Mrs C Creech (SNP)	45,032	22.4
D Millar (LD)	13,363	6.7
J Hein (Lib)	3,249	1.6
Ms L Hendry (Grn)	2,429	1.2
G Gay (NLP)	539	0.3

Lab maj: 45,155

Total vote: 200,957 (40.1%)
No change
1989: Total vote 204,220 (41.5%). Lab 81,366 (39.8%); C 65,673 (32.1%); SNP 35,155 (17.2%); Grn 11,658 (5.7%); LD 10,368 (5.0%).
1992 Electorate and turnout: 496,995 (79.51%). Lab 140,588 (35.58%); C 124,631 (31.54%); SNP 72,591 (18.37%); LD 56,177 (14.22%); Others 1,198 (0.30%). Seats: Lab 4; C 3; LD 2.

STRATHCLYDE EAST

Electorate: 492,618 (500,935)
Cumbernauld & Kilsyth; East Kilbride; Glasgow Rutherglen; Hamilton; Kilmarnock & Loudon; Monklands East; Monklands West; Motherwell North; Motherwell South

		%
*K Collins (Lab)	106,476	58.0
I Hamilton (SNP)	54,136	29.5
B Cooklin (C)	13,915	7.6
B Stewart (LD)	6,383	3.9
A Whitelaw (Grn)	1,874	1.0
D Gilmour (NLP)	787	0.4

Lab maj: 52,340

Total vote: 183,571 (37.3%)
No change
1989: Total vote 194,281 (39.3%). Lab 109,170 (56.1%); SNP 48,853 (25.1%); C 22,233 (11.4%); Grn 9,749 (5.0%); LD 4,276 (2.2%).
1992 Electorate and turnout: 491,803 (77.41%). Lab 209,204 (54.95%); SNP 83,223 (21.86%); C 61,316 (16.11%); LD 26,757 (7.03%); Others 208 (0.05%). Seats: Lab 9.

STRATHCLYDE WEST

Electorate: 489,129 (499,616)
Clydebank & Milngavie; Cunninghame North; Dumbarton; Eastwood; Greenock & Port Glasgow; Paisley North; Paisley South; Renfrew West & Inverclyde; Strathkelvin & Bearsden

		%
*H McMahon (Lab)	86,957	44.4
C Campbell (SNP)	61,934	31.6
J Godfrey (C)	28,414	14.5
D Herbison (LD)	14,772	7.5
Ms K Allan (Grn)	2,886	1.5
Ms S Gilmour (NLP)	918	0.5

Lab maj: 25,023

Total vote: 195,881 (40.1%)
No change

1989: Total vote 210,094 (42.6%). Lab 89,627 (42.6%); SNP 50,036 (23.8%); C 45,872 (21.8%); Grn 16,461 (7.8%); LD 8,098 (3.8%).

1992 Electorate and turnout: 488,630 (77.92%). Lab 164,978 (43.33%); C 107,729 (28.29%); SNP 69,122 (18.15%); LD 37,660 (9.89%); Others 1,275 (0.33%). Seats: Lab 8; C 1.

60

WALES

SOUTH WALES CENTRAL

Electorate: 477,182
Cardiff Central; Cardiff North; Cardiff South & Penarth; Cardiff West; Cynon Valley; Pontypridd; Rhondda; Vale of Glamorgan

		%
*W David (Lab)	115,396	61.4
Ms L Verity (C)	29,340	15.6
G Llywelyn (PC)	18,857	10.0
J Dixon (LD)	18,471	9.8
C von Ruhland (Grn)	4,002	2.1
R Griffiths (Com Y)	1,073	0.6
G Duguay (NLP)	889	0.5

Lab maj: 86,082

Total vote: 188,002 (39.4%)
No change
1992 Electorate and turnout: 472,826 (78.52%). Lab 201,701 (54.33); C 109,692 (29.54%); LD 38,689 (10.42%); PC 18,838 (5.07%); Others 2,362 (0.64%). Seats: Lab 6; C 2.
1989: Turnout 36.6%. Lab 56.0% C 22.0% Grn 13.4% PC 5.3% LD 2.0%.

SOUTH WALES EAST

Electorate: 454,794
Blaenau Gwent; Caerphilly; Islwyn; Merthyr Tydfil & Rhymney; Monmouth; Newport East; Newport West; Torfaen

		%
Mrs G Kinnock (Lab)	144,907	74.0
Mrs R Blomfield-Smith (C)	24,660	12.6
C Woolgrove (LD)	9,963	5.1
C Mann (PC)	9,550	4.9
R Coghill (Grn)	4,509	2.3
Ms S Williams (W Soc)	1,270	0.7
Dr R Brussatis (NLP)	1,027	0.5

Lab maj: 120,247

Total vote: 195,886 (43.1%)
No change
1992 Electorate and turnout: 456,401 (79.93%). Lab 227,060 (62.24%); C 87,559 (24.00%); LD 35,397 (9.70%); PC 11,883 (3.26%); Others 2,904 (0.80%). Seats: Lab 7; C 1.
1989: Turnout 38.1%. Lab 62.6% C 15.8% Grn 12.7% PC 6.5% LD 2.3%.

SOUTH WALES WEST

Electorate: 395,131
Aberavon; Bridgend; Gower; Neath; Ogmore; Swansea East; Swansea West

		%
*D Morris (Lab)	104,263	66.1
R Buckland (C)	19,293	12.2
J Bushell (LD)	15,499	9.8
Ms C Adams (PC)	12,364	7.8
Ms J Evans (Grn)	4,114	2.6
Ms H Evans (NLP)	1,112	0.7
Capt Beany (Beanus)	1,106	0.7

Lab maj: 84,970

Total vote: 157,751 (39.9%)
No change
1992 Electorate and turnout: 394,980 (78.51%). Lab 190,011 (61.27%); C 73,565 (23.72%); LD 28,684 (9.25%); PC 15,946 (5.14%); Others 1,907 (0.61%). Seats: Lab 7.
1989: Turnout 40.1% Lab 59.7% C 18.8% Grn 13.0% PC 5.6% LD 2.8%.

WALES MID & WEST

Electorate: 401,529
Brecon & Radnor; Carmarthen; Ceredigion & Pembroke North; Llanelli; Meirionnydd Nant Conwy; Montgomeryshire; Pembroke

		%
Ms E Morgan (Lab)	78,092	40.5
M Phillips (PC)	48,858	25.4
P Bone (C)	31,606	16.4
Ms J Hughes (LD)	23,719	12.3
D Rowlands (UK Ind)	5,536	2.9
Dr C Busby (Grn)	3,938	2.0
T Griffith-Jones (NLP)	988	0.5

Lab maj: 29,234

Total vote: 192,737 (48.0%)
No change
1992 Electorate and turnout: 398,620 (81.07%). Lab 105,298 (32.58%); C 93,324 (28.88%); LD 65,445 (20.25%); PC 57,089 (17.67%). Seats: Lab 3; PC 2; C 1; LD 1.
1989: Turnout 39.9%. Lab 33.9% C 26.6% PC 21.3 Grn 11.9% LD 6.3%.

WALES NORTH

Electorate: 475,829
Alyn & Deeside; Caernarfon; Clwyd North West; Clwyd South West; Conwy; Delyn; Wrexham; Ynys Mon

		%
*J Wilson (Lab)	88,091	40.8
D Wigley (PC)	72,849	33.8
G Mon Hughes (C)	33,450	15.5
Ms R Parry (LD)	14,828	6.9
P Adams (Grn)	2,850	1.3
D Hughes (NLP)	2,065	1.0
M Cooksey (Ind)	1,623	0.8

Lab maj: 15,242

Total vote: 215,756 (45.3%)
No change
1992 Electorate and turnout: 472,202 (80.35%). Lab 141,593 (37.32%); C 135,537 (35.72%); LD 49,242 (12.98%); PC 50,634 (13.35%); Others 2,403 (0.63%). Seats: Lab 4; C 2; PC 2.
1989: Turnout 45.9%. Lab 35.6% C 31.7% PC 23.1% Grn 6.2% LD 3.3%.

Results of voting in the Republic of Ireland and continental Europe

At the Edinburgh summit in December 1992, the heads of government of the Twelve agreed to increase the number of seats in the European Parliament from 518 to 567.

Germany's allocation was increased from 81 to 99 to take account of the reunification of the eastern and western parts of the country. At the same time the United Kingdom, France and Italy were each given six more seats, bringing their representation up to 87 MEPs. Spain was given four extra seats, bringing it up to 64. The Netherlands got an extra six, bringing it up to 31, Portugal, Greece and Belgium were increased by one each to 25, while Denmark, Ireland and Luxembourg were unchanged at 16, 15 and six respectively.

BELGIUM

Polling day June 12

Electorate: 7,211,311 (1989 electorate: 7,096,273)

Votes cast: 6,512,722

Valid votes: 5,937012 Turnout 90.7% (1989: 5,899,285 Turnout: 90.7%)

Seats: 25 of which 14 are for Flanders and 10 are for Wallonia with one allocated to the German speaking region.

Party	Votes	1994 % of poll	Seats	Votes	1989 % of poll	Seats
Socialist (SP-Flanders)	646,376	10.8	3	733,247	12.4	3
Socialist (PS-Wallonia)	671,555	11.3	3	854,148	14.5	5
Christian People's (CVP-Flanders)	1,013,268	17.0	4	1,247,090	21.1	5
Social Christian (Wallonia)	415,071	6.9	2	476,802	8.1 2	2
Christian Social Party (German region)	11,999	0.2	1			-
Liberal Democratic Party (Flanders)	678,424	11.4	3		10.6	2
Liberal Democratic Party (Wallonia)	535,870	9.0	3		8.7	2
People's Union (Flanders)	262,045	4.4	1		5.4	1
Vlaams Blok (Far Right)	463,924	7.8	2		4.1	1
National Front (Far Right)	174,233	2.9	1			
Agalev, Flanders (Green)	396,200	6.7	1		7.6	1
Ecologists (Wallonia)	288,066	4.8	1		6.3	2
Others	379,981	6.9	-		1.2	-
Totals	5,937,012	100	25	5,899,285	100	24

Voting system: Proportional Representation with a regional list. One Flemish constituency of 14 seats, one Walloon constituency of 10 seats and one seat for the German-speaking region. Voting is compulsory.

The share of the vote for the Christian Democrats and the Socialists was down on 1989, with both losing seats, although the Christian Democrats retrieved their loss through the extra allocation for the German-speaking region. The Liberals and extreme right in both Flanders and Wallonia made gains in votes and seats.

Those elected were:

Christian Democrats (7 seats)
*Raf Chanterie
*Gérard Deprez
Mathieu Grosch
*Fernand Herman
Wilfried Martens
*Marianne Thyssen
*Leo Tindemans

Socialists (6 seats)
*Claude Desama
*Raymonde Dury
José Happart
Louis Tobback
Anne Van Lancker
Freddy Willocks

Liberals (6 seats)
*Anne Andre-Leonard
*Willy de Clercq
Jean Gol
Mimi Kestelyn-Sierens
Annemie Neyts-Uyttebroeck
Antoinette Spaak
Far Right (3 seats)
*Karel Dillen
Daniel Feret
Frank Vanhecke
Greens (2 seats)
Magda Aelvoet
*Paul Lannoye
People's Union (1 seat)
*Jaak Vandemeulebroucke

DENMARK

Polling day: June 9
Electorate: 3,900,000 (1989 electorate: 3,923,549)
Votes cast: 2,078,082 Turnout 52.5% (1989: Votes cast: 1,789,395 Turnout: 46.2%)
Seats: 16

Party	Votes	**1994** % of poll	Seats	Votes	**1989** % of poll	Seats
Liberal Party	329,202	19.0	4	297,565	16.6	3
Conservative People's	368,490	17.7	3	238,760	13.4	2
Social Democratic Party	329,113	15.8	3	417,076	23.3	4
June Movement (Anti-Europe)	315,938	15.2	2			
People's Movement against EU	214,880	10.3	2	338,953	18.9	4
Socialist People's Party	178,513	8.6	1	162,902	9.1	1
Radical Liberal Party	176,498	8.5	1			
Progress (Far Right)	59,532	2.9	-	93,985	5.3	-
Christian People's Party	23,169	1.1	-			
Centre Democracy	18,340	0.9	-	142,190	7.9	2
Others				97,964	5.5	-
Totals	2,078,082	100.0	16	1,789,395	100.0	16

Voting system: Proportional representation/National list with all Denmark a 16 seat constituency.
The Liberal party and the Conservatives made gains, but the Soical Democrats lost ground and the Centre Democrats lost their two seats. The Anti-Europe groupings continued to attract support with one in four of the people voting supporting them.

Those elected were:
Liberal Party
Eva Kjer Hansen
Bertel Haarder
*Niels Anker Kofoed
Karin Riis-Jorgensen
Conservative People's Party
Poul Schluter
*Christian Rovsing
Frode Kristoffersen
Social Democratic Party
*Kirsten Jensen
*Freddy Blak
Niels Sindal
June Movement
*Jens-Peter Bonde
*Ulla Sandbaek
People's Movement against EU
Ole Krarup
Lis Jensen
Radical Liberal Party
Lone Dyubkjaer
Socialist People's party
Lilli Gyldenkilde

FRANCE

Polling day: June 12
Electorate: 39,044,441 (1989 electorate: 38,348,191)
Votes cast: 20,590,577
Valid votes: 19,486,482. Turnout 52.73%. (1989 votes: 18,145,588 Turnout: 48.7%)
Seats: 87

Party	Votes	1994 % of poll	Seats	Votes	1989 % of poll	Seats
UDF/RPR (Centre Right)	4,985,057	25.58	28	5,241,354	28.9	26†
				1,528,931	8.4	7†
Socialist Party (Europe Solidaire)	2,824,173	14.49	15	4,284,734	23.61	22
L'Autre Europe (de Villiers list)	2,404,105	12.34	13			
Energie Radicale (Tapie list)	2,344,457	12.03	13			
National Front (FN)	2,050,086	10.52	11	2,128,589	11.73	10
Communist Party (PCF)	1,342,222	6.89	7	1,399,939	7.71	7
Union of Ecologists	575,247	2.95	-	1,922,353	10.59	9
Other Green party	391,905	2.01	-	-	-	-
Regional Lists	76,503	0.39	-			
Others	2,493,211	12.8	-	1,639,688	9.06	-
Totals	19,486,482	100.0	87	18,145,588	100.0	81

Voting system: PR national list. Minimum of 5 per cent needed to obtain seat.
Both main parties, the Centre Right Alliance and the Socialists, lost to the Alternative Europe (de Villiers) list opposed to further integration and the separate list headed by Bernard Tapie. The Communists and the National Front maintained their respective positions, but support for the Greens fell away.

Those elected were:
†Two lists in 1989.

UDF/RPR (28 seats)
Dominique Baudis
Hélène Carrère d'Ecausse
*Yves Galland
Christian Jacob
*Jean-Pierre Raffarin
Armelle Guinebèrtiere
*Nicole Fontaine
*Alain Pompidou
*Yves Verwaerde
Marie-Thérèse Hermange
Jean-Louis Bourlanges
Jacques Donnay
François Grosetête
Blaise Aldo
*Robert Hersant
Anne-Marie Schaffner
Francis Decourrière
Christian Cabrol
Bernard Stasi
*Jean-Claude Pasty
*André Soulier
Jean-Pierre Bazin
*Pierre Bernard-Reymond
*Raymond Chesa
*Georges de Brémond d'Ars
Jean Baggioni
Jean-Pierre Bébéar
Gérard d'Aboville
Socialist Party (Europe Solidaire) (15 seats)
Michel Rocard

*Catherine Trautman
Bernard Kouchner
Danièle Darras
André Laignel
*Nicole Péry
Jack Lang
Frédérique Bredin
Pierre Moscovici
Elisabeth Guigou
*Jean-Pierre Cot
Pervenche Beres
François Bernardini
Michèle Lindeperg
*Gérard Caudron
L'Autre Europe (de Villiers list) (13 seats)
Phillipe de Villiers
Sir James Goldsmith
*Charles de Gaulle
Thierry Jean-Pierre
Phillipe Martin
Françoise Seillier
Georges Berthu
Hervé Fabre-Aubrespy
Dominique Souchet
Anne-Christine Poisson
Frédéric Striby
Edouard Des Places
Marie-France de Rose
Energie Radicale (Tapie List) (13 seats)
Bernard Tapie

*Jean-François Hory
Catherine La Lumière
Christiane Taubira-Delanon
Noël Mamère
Michel Dary
*André Sainjon
Bernard Castagnede
Odile Verrier
Pierre Pradier
Christine Barthet Mayer
Dominique Saint-Pierre
Antionette Fouque
National Front (11 seats)
*Jean-Marie Le Pen
*Bruno Mégret
*Bruno Gollnisch
*Jean-Claude Martinez
Carl Lang
Marie-France Stirbois
*Bernard Antony
*Yvan Blot
*Jean-Marie le Chevallier
Fernand Le Rachinel
Jean-Yves Le Gallou
Communist party (7 seats)
*Francis Wurtz
*Sylviane Ainardi
*Philippe Herzog
Gisèle Moreau
*René Piquet
*Mireille Elmalan
Aline Pailler

64

GERMANY

Polling day: June 12

Electorate: 60,420,775 (1989 electorate: 45,723,901)

Votes cast: 35,403,626 Turnout 60.1% (1989: Votes cast: 28,203,266 Turnout: 62.4%)

Seats: 99

Party	Votes	1994 % of poll	Seats	Votes	1989 % of poll	Seats
Social Democrat Party	11,388,028	32.2	40	10,524,859	37.3	31
Christian Democratic Union	11,344,110	30.2	39	8,334,433	29.5	25
Christian Social Union	2,391,755	6.8	8	2,324,655	8.2	7
Greens	3,560,126	10.1	12	2,381,278	8.4	8
Republicans (Far Right)	1,389,060	3.9	-	2,005,555	7.1	6
Free Democrats (Liberals)	1,443,146	4.1	-	1,576,280	5.6	4
Others	3,887,401	11.0	-	1,056,206	3.7	-
Totals	35,403,626	100	99	28,203,266	100	81

Voting system: Proportional representation on the national and Land list system.
Germany's respresentation was increased by 18 seats to take in the former East Germany. The Christian Democrats made a strong showing as support for the Liberal Democrats and the far right Republic Party fell below the 5 per cent needed to ensure representation. There was increased support for the Greens.

Those elected were:

Social Democrat Party (40 seats)
**Gerhard Botz
Evelyne Gebhardt
Norbert Glante
*Willi Görlach
*Lissy Gröner
*Klaus Hänsch
Jutta Haug
*Magdalene Hoff
Karin Jöns
*Karin Junker
Heinz Kindermann
**Constanze Krehl
Wilfried Kuckelkorn
*Annemarie Kuhn
Helmut Kuhne
Bernd Lange
*Rolf Linkohr
*Günter Lüttge
Erika Mann
*Helwin Peter
*Willi Piecyk
*Christa Randzio-Plath
Bernhard Rapkay
Klaus Rehder
*Dagmar Roth-Behrendt
*Mechthild Rothe
*Willi Rothley
*Jannis Sakellariou
*Heinke Salisch
*Detlev Samland
Axel Schäfer
Gerhard Schmid
*Barbara Schmidbauer
Martin Schulz

**Ulrich Stockmann
Christof Tannert
Ralf Walter
Barbara Weiler
Rosemarie Wemheuer
Wilmya Zimmermann
Christian Democratic Union
*Siegbert Alber
Otto Bardong
**Rolf Berend
Reimer Böge
*Elmar Brok
*Karl-Heinz Florenz
*Honor Funk
**Anne-Karin Glase
Lutz Goepel
Alfred Gomolka
Renate Heinisch
*Karsten Hoppenstedt
*Georg Jarzembowski
*Hedwig Keppelhoff-Wiechert
Peter Kittlemann
Christa Klass
**Dieter-Lebrecht Koch
Christoph Konrad
*Brigitte Langenhagen
*Marlene Lenz
Klaus-Heiner Lehne
Hans-Peter Liese
*Kurt Malangre
Thomas Mann
*Winfried Menrad
Peter-Michael Mombaur
Marlies Mosiek-Urbahn
Hartmut Nassauer

*Doris Pack
*Hans-gert Poettering
*Godelieve Quisthoudt-Rowohl
*Günter Rinsche
Horst Schnellhardt
*Jürgen Schröder
Konrad Schwaiger
*Diemut Theato
**Stanislaw Tillich
*Karl von Wogau
Christian Social Union (8 seats)
Markus Ferber
*Ingo Friedrich
*Maren Günther
Franz Xaver Mayer
Berd Posselt
*Edgar Schiedermeier
*Ursula Schleicher
*Otto von Harsburg
Greens (12 seats)
*Hiltrud Breyer
Daniel Cohn-Bendit
*Friedrich Wilhelm Graffe zu Baringdorf
Edith Müller
*Claudia Roth
Elisabeth Schroedter
Irene Soltwedel
*Wilfried Telkämper
Undine von Blottnitz
Wolfgang Ullmann
Frieder Otto Wolf
** Denotes former observer from East Germany

GREECE

Polling date: June 12
Electorate: 9,485,495 (1989 electorate: 8,347,387)
Valid votes: 6,532,591. Turnout: 71.2% (1989: 6,544,669 Turnout: 79.28%)
Seats: 25

Party	Votes	1994 % of poll	Seats	Votes	1989 % of poll	Seats
Socialist (PASOK)	2,458,619	37.64	10	2,352,271	35.94	9
New Democracy (ND)	2,133,372	32.66	9	2,647,215	40.45	10
Political Spring (POLA)	564,778	8.65	2			
Communist Party of Greece (KKE)	410,741	6.29	2	936,175	14.30	4
Left Alliance (SYN)	408,066	6.25	2			
Centre Right Alliance (DI-ANA)	182,522	2.79	-	89,469	1.37	1
Extreme Right Wing (EPEN)				75,877	1.16	-
Others	374,493	5.72	-	443,662	6.78	-
Totals	6,532,691	100	25	6,544,669	100	24

Voting system: National list. Proportional representation.
There was some increased support for the Socialists as New Democracy lost ground to the new Political Spring movement which had ben formed by dissidents from the party and supporters of a more natiomalist stance on Macedonia.

Those elected were:
PASOK (10 seats)
Dimitrios Tsatsos
*Christos Papoutsis
*Paraskevas Avgerinos
Constantinos Klironomos
Ioannis Roubatis
Angela Kokkola
Stylianos Panagopoulos
Georgios Katiforis
Mikolaos Papakryriazis
Irini Lambraki
New Democracy (9 seats)
*Efthimios Christodoulou
Antonios Trakatellis
Nana Mouskouri
Stylianos Argyros
Georgios Dimitrakopoulos
*Pavlos Sarlis
*Panagiotis Lambrias
*Georgios Anastasopoulos
Constantinos Hatzidakis
Political Spring (2 seats)
Katerina Daskalaki
Nikitas Kaklamanis
Communist Party of Greece (2seats)
*Vassilis Ephremidis
Ioannis Theonas
Communist Alliance (2 seats)
*Alexandros Alavanos
*Michail Papayannakis

IRELAND

Polling day: June 9

Electorate: 2,631,575 (1989 electorate: 2,453,451)

Valid votes: 1,137,490. Turnout: 44.0% Spoiled votes: 19,806 (1989: Valid votes: 1,632,728 Spoiled votes: 42,391 Turnout: 68.3%)

Seats: 15

Party	Votes	1994 % of poll	Seats	Votes	1989 % of poll	Seats
Fianna Fail	398,066	35.0	7	514,537	31.5	6
Fine Gael	276,095	24.27	4	353,094	21.6	4
Labour Party	124,972	10.99	1	155,782	9.5	1
Green Party	90,046	7.92	2	61,041	3.8	-
Independents	78,986	6.94	1	193,823	11.9	2
Progressive Democrats	73,696	6.48	-	194,059	11.9	1
Democratic Left	39,706	3.49	-	123,265	7.5	1
Sinn Fein (PSF)	33,823	2.97	-	37,127	2.3	-
Workers' Party	22,100	1.94	-			
Totals	1,137,90	100	15	1,632,728	100	15

Voting system: Proportional representation using regional list. Country divided into four constituencies. The main development was the gain of two seats for the Greens, the first from English-speaking parts of the Union. Sinn Fein failed to make any impact.

Those elected were:
Fianna Fail (7 seats)
*Niall Andrews
Gerard Collins
Brian Crowley
*James Fitzsimons
Pat Gallagher
Liam Hyland
*Mark Killilea
Fina Gael (4 seats)
*Mary Banotti
*John Cushnahan
Alan Gillis
*Joe McCartin
Green party (2 seats)
Patricia McKenna
Nuala Ahern
Labour Party (1 seat)
*Bernie Mallone
Independent
*Pat Cox

67

ITALY

Polling day: June 12
Electorate: 47,489,843 (1989 electorate: 46,805,457)
Voters: 35,505,023
Valid votes: 32,923,377 Turnout: 74.8% (1989: 34,829,128 Turnout: 81.0%)
Invalid votes: 2,548,298
Seats: 87

Party	Votes	1994 % of poll	Seats
Forza Italia	10,076,653	30.6	27
Democratic Left	6,286,030	19.1	16
National Alliance	4,124,739	12.5	11
Popular party	3,289,143	10.0	8
Northern League	2,172,317	6.6	6
Refounded Communists	1,994,880	6.1	5
Patto Segni (Christian Democrats)	1,073,424	3.3	3
Greens	1,047,681	3.2	3
Radical Party	704,153	2.1	2
Socialist Party	600,106	1.8	2
La Rete Democratic Movement	366,393	1.1	1
Republican Party	241,574	0.7	1
Social Democrat Party	223,099	0.7	1
Lega Meridionale (Regional Party)	222,183	0.7	-
South Tyrol People's Party	197,972	0.6	1
Union Valdostana (Regional Party	126,643	0.4	-
Lega Alpina Lumbarda (Regional Party)	108,831	0.3	-
Liberals	52,646	0.2	-
Solidarity	14,910	0.0	-
Totals	32,923,377	100	87

Voting system: Regional list with five regional constituencies.
Because of the realignment of parties in Italy since the 1989 European election, direct comparisons between 1989 and 1994 are not valid. In the 1989 elections, the Christian Democrats secured 26 seats, the Communists 22 and the Socialist party 12. The remaining seats were widely spread. Full details appear on the following page.
    In 1994 Forza Italia secured the highest number of votes with the Communists slipping back. There was a strong showing for the National Alliance, a right grouping. As the proportional representation system used does not have a threshhold for votes, many small parties managed to win seats.
†Indicates that the candidate was elected in more than one constituency and will be replaced in those he rejects by another name on the list. Silvio Berclusconi was elected in five constituencies, resigned and was replaced by the next five names on the list.

Those elected were:
Forza Italia (27 seats)
†Silvio Berlusconi
Giampiero Boniperti
Guido Podesta
Alessandro Fontana
Eolo Parodi
Luigi Florio
Ombretta Colli
Aldo Arroni
Franco Malerba
Luigi Calligaris
Giancarlo Ligabue
Alessandro Danesin
Giacomo Santini
Luisa Todini
Roberto Mezzaroma
Antonio Tajani
Giacomo Leopardi
Pierferdinando Casini
Alfonso Marra

Ernesto Caccavale
Claudio Azzolini
Pietro di Prima
Umberto Scapagnini
Next in order on the party list:
Riccardo Garosci
Valerio Baldini
Stefania Baldi
Walter Viceconte
Stefano de Luca
Democratic Left (16 seats)
†*Achille Occhetto
Fioella Ghilardotti
*Roberto Speciale
*Renzo Imbeni
Giorgio Ruffolo
*Giulio Fantuzzi
*Luciano Vecchi
*Enrico Montesano
*Pierre Carniti

Francesco Baldarelli
Andrea Manzella
Corrado Augias
*Biagio de Giovanni
*Luigi Colajanni
Next on list:
*Rinaldo Bontempi
*Roberto Barzanti
Gaetano Carroccio
National Alliance (11 seats)
†Gianfranco Fini
*Cristiana Muscardini
Gastone Parigi
*Pino Rauti
Roberta Angelilli
Salvatore Tatarella
Antonello Trizza
Next on list:
Amedeo Amadeo
Sergio Berlato

Marco Cellai
Spalato Bellere
Sabstiano Musumeci
Popular Party (8 seats)
Maria Paola Colombo Svevo
Carlo Secchi
Pierluigi Castagnetti
*Carlo Casini
Antonio Graziani
Gerardo Bianco
Vittorio d'Andrea
Giovanni Burtone
Next on list:
*Agostino Mantovani
Nino Cristofori
Domenico Trucchi
*Giuseppe Mottola
Mario Floris
Northern League (6 seats)
†Umberto Bossi
Marco Formentini

Gipo Farassino
Raimondo Fassa
Marilena Marin
Next on list:
*Luigi Moretti
Aldo Mariconda,
Refounded Communists (5 seats)
Fausto Bertinotti
Luigo Vinci
Lucio Manisco
*Luciana Castellina
Luciano Pettinari
Patto Segni (3 seats)
†Mario Segni
Next on list:
Danilo Poggiolini
Livio Filippi
Vincenzo Viola
Greens (3 seats)
†Carlo Ripa di Meana
*Alexander Langer

Adelaide Aglietta
Next on list:
Massimo Scalia
Radical Party (2 seats)
†Marco Pannella
Gianfranco Dell'Alba
Next on list:
Emma Bonino
*Marco Taradash
Socialist Party (2 seats)
Riccardo Nencini
Elena Marinucci
La Rete Democratic Movement (1 seat)
Leoluca Orlando
Republican party (1 seat)
Giorgio La Malfa
Socialist Democratic Party (1 seat)
*Enrico Ferri
South Tyrol People's Party (1 seat)
Michael Ebner

Results from 1989

Party	Votes	% of poll	Seats
Christian Democracy (DC)	11,460,702	32.9	26
Communist (PCI)	9,602,618	27.6	22
Socialists (PSI)	5,154,515	14.8	12
Green Alliance (Verdi/Arco)	2,148,723	6.2	5
Social Movement (MSI)	1,922,761	5.5	4
Centre Parties (PRI/PLI)	1,533,063	4.4	4
Social Democrat (PSDI)	946,856	2.7	2
Lombardy Regional (Lega L)	626,546	1.8	2
Proletarian Democracy (DP)	450,058	1.3	1
Antiproibizionisti	429,554	1.2	1
Sardinian Action (UV-PSDA)	208,775	0.6	1
South Tyrol People's Party	172,488	0.5	1
Others	162,479	0.5	-
Total	34,829,128	100	81

LUXEMBOURG

Polling day: June 12. Voting compulsory. General election held on the same day

Electorate: 229,328 1989: 218,019

Votes cast: 179,688 Turnout: 86.6%. 1989 votes cast: 191,442 (Turnout 87.4%)
Each elector has up to six votes.

Seats: 6

Party	Votes	1994 % of poll	Seats	Votes	1989 % of poll	Seats
Christian Social People's Party	318,345	31.4	2	346,621	34.87	3
Socialist Workers' Party	251,748	24.8	2	252,920	25.45	2
Democratic Party	191,104	18.9	1	198,254	19.95	1
Green Party	110,930	10.9	1			
Others	141,477	14.0	-	196,951	19.73	-
Totals	1,013,600	100	6	993,951	100	6

Voting system: National list, proportional representation.
The Christian Democrats maintained their position as the leading party, but lost a seat to the Greens who won representation for the first time.

Those elected were
Christian Social People's Party (2 seats)
Jean-Claude Juncker
Jacques Santer
Socialist Workers' Party (2 seats)
Jacques Poos
Mady Delvaux-Stehres
Green Party (1 seat)
Jup Weber
Democratic Party (1 seat)
*Lydie Wurth-Polfer

With the appointment of Mr Santer as President of the Commission, and the appointment of Mr Juncker, Mr Poos and Ms Delvaux-Stehres to the government, the following were appointed to the EP in their places.

Christian Social People's Party
Astrid Lulling
Viviane Reding
Socialist Workers' Party
Ben Fayot
Marcel Schlechter

| Astrid Lulling | Viviane Reding | Ben Fayot | Marcel Schlechter |

THE NETHERLANDS

Polling day: June 9
Electorate: 11,620,300 (1989 electorate: 11,121,477)
Valid votes: 4,133,309 Turnout: 35.6% (1989: 5,243,911 Turnout: 47.2%)
Seats 31

Party	Votes	1994 % of poll	Seats	Votes	1989 % of poll	Seats
Christian Democrats	1,271,840	30.8	10	1,813,935	34.6	10
Social Democrats	945,843	22.9	8	1,609,408	30.7	8
Freedom and Democracy	740,451	17.9	6	715,721	13.6	3
Democrats '66	481,826	11.7	4	311,973	5.9	1
Coalition of Protestants	322,793	7.8	2	309,059	5.9	1
Greens	251,560	6.1	1	365,527	7.0	2
Socialist Party	55,306	1.3	-	-	-	-
Centre Democrats	43,330	1.0	-	-	-	-
List 9	8,844	0.2	-	-	-	-
Others	11,546	0.3	-	117,260	2.3	-
Totals	4,133,309	100	31	5,243,883	100	25

Voting system: National lists, proportional representation.
With just under 36 per cent of the electorate voting, this was the lowest turnout recorded for European elections in The Netherlands. The gainers were the two Liberal parties. Although Christian Democrats and the Social Democrats had a lower percentage share of the vote, each party maintained its same number of seats in the Parliament.

Those elected were:
Christian Democrats (10 seats)
Hanja Maij-Weggen
Wim Van Velzen
*Pam Cornelissen
*Jan Sonneveld
*Ria Oomen-Ruijten
*Karla Peijs
*Jim Janssen Van Raaij
*Arie Oostlander
*Bartho Pronk
Peter Pex
Social Democrats (8 seats)
Hedy D'Ancona
Frits Castricum
Piet Dankert
Leonie van Bladel
*Wim van Velzen
*Maartje van Putten
Jan Marinus Wiersma
*Alman Metten
Freedom and Democracy (6 seats)
*Gijs De Vries
Jan Kees Wiebenga
*Jessica Larive
Jan Mulder
*Florus Wijsenbeek
Elly Plooij-van Gorsel
Democrats 66 (4 seats)
*Jan Willem Bertens
Laurens-Jan Brinkhorst
Doeke Eisma
Johanna Boogerd-Quaak
Socialist party (2 seats)
*Leen van der Waal
Hans Blokland
Green (1 seats)
*Nel van Dijk

71

PORTUGAL

Polling day: June 12
Electorate: 8,476,681 1989: 8,052,025 Turnout: 51.27%
Valid votes: 2,927,306 **Turnout:** 35.6%
Seats 25

Party	Votes	1994 % of poll	Seats	Votes	1989 % of poll	Seats
Socialist	1,051,944	34.79	10	1,175,671	28.5	8
Social Democrat	1,039,840	34.36	9	1,349,996	32.7	9
Central Democratic and						
Social Party	377,485	12.48	3	584,602	14.2	3
United Democratic Coalition	339,330	11.22	3	594,771	14.4	4
(Communist/Green) Democratic Renewal	5,797	0.19	-	-	-	-
Others (incl invalid votes)	210,203	6.96	-	423,644	10.3	-
Totals	3,023,843	100	25	4,128,684	100	24

With elections taking place in the middle of a national holiday, turnout was down. The Socialist Party edged ahead of the Social Democratic Party, the Centre Party held its position, but support for the Left and Greens dropped.

Those elected were:
Socialist Party (10 seats)
António Vitorino
João Soares
*Luís Marinho
*José Torres Couto
José Barros Moura
Carlos Lage
António Campos
Helena Torres Marques
*José Alpinário
Fernando Moniz
Socialist Democratic Party (9 seats)
Eurico De Melo
*António Capucho
Arlindo Cunha
*Francisco Lucas Pires
*Carlos Pimenta
*Manuel Porto
Helena Vaz Da Silva
Carlos Costa Neves
Nélio Mendonça
United Democratic Coalition (3 seats)
Luís SÁ
*Joaquim Miranda Da Silva
*Sergio Ribeiro
Central Democratic amd Social Party (3 seats)
Manuel Monteiro
Raúl Fernandes
José Girao Pereira

SPAIN

Polling day June 12
Electorate: 31,145,446 (1989: 29,160,830)
Votes cast: 18,554,316
Valid votes: 18,256,204 Turnout: 59.58% (1989 15,621,087 Turnout: 54.8%)
Seats: 64

Party	Votes	1994 % of poll	Seats	Votes	1989 % of poll	Seats
Popular Party	7,426,189	40.21	28	3,389,341	21.42	15
Socialists	5,665,537	30.67	22	6,258,749	39.56	27
United Left	2,486,550	13.46	9			
Catalan Party	861,897	4.67	3	662,757	4.19	2
Nationalist Coalition (Regional Parties)	517,882	2.80	2	295,741	1.87	1
People's Coalition (Regional Party)	237,521	1.29	-	238,528	1.51	1
Democratic Centre Party	182,512	0.99	-	1,129,599	7.14	5
Basque party	179,361	0.97	-	269,743	1.71	1
Andalucia Regional Party	139,994	0.76	-	297,218	1.88	1
Galicia National Party	138,051	0.76	-	-	-	-
Greens	107,731	0.68	-	-	-	-
Ruiz Mateos (Financier)	82,069	0.44	-	609,171	3.85	2
Communists and Allies	-	-	-	959,270	6.06	4
Izquierda de los Pueblos	-	-	-	289,915	1.83	1
Others	230,910	2.41	-	-	-	-
Totals	18,256,204	100	64		100	60

The Popular Party made gains at the expense of the Socialists, while the United Left grouping of former Communists also saw an increase in support.

Those elected were:
Popular Party (28 seats)
Abel Matutes Juan
Celia Villalobos Talero
Mercedes De La Merced Monge
*José María Gil-Robles Gil-Delgado
*Miguel Arias Cañete
Maria Teresa Estevan Bolea
José Manuel Garcia-Margallo Marfil
Carmen Fraga Estevez
Luis Campoy Zueco
Ana Isabel Palacio Vallelersundi
*Carlos Robles Piquer
Juan Manuel Fabra Valles
*Gerardo Fernandez Albor
Fernando Fernandez Martin
Jaime Valdivieso De Cue
Encarnación Redondo Jimenez
*Iñigo Mendez De Vigo
*Javier Areitio Toledo
Joaquin Siso Cruellas
Laura Elena Esteban Martin
Daniel Luis Varela Suances-Carpegna
José Gerardo Galeote Quecede

José Ignacio Salafranca Sanchez-Neyra
*José Antonio Escudero Lopez
Francisca Bennasar Tous
*José Luis Valverde Lopez
Salvador Garriga Polledo
Julio Añoveros Trias De Bes
Socialists (22 seats)
*Fernando Moran Lopez
Francisca Sauquillo Perez Del Arco
*Enrique Baron Crespo
*Ludivina Garcia Arias
*Josep Verde i Aldea
*Ana Clara Miranda de Lage
Pedro Aparicio Sanchez
Jose María Mendiluce Pereira
*Manuel Medina Ortega
*Maria Izquierdo Rojo
*Jose Enrique Pons Grau
*Joan Colom i Naval
*Juan Luis Colino Salamanca
*Carmen Diez de Rivera Icaza
Juan de Dios Izquierdo Collado

*Jesus Cabezon Alonso
*Bárbara Dührkop Dührkop
Antonio Gonzalez Triviño
*Francisco Javier Sanz Fernandez
Manuela De Frutos Gama
Fernando Perez Royo
Ana Terron i Cusi
United Left (9 seats)
*Alonso José Puerta Gutierrez
*Antonio Gutierrez Diaz
*Laura Gonzalez Alvarez
María Sornosa Martinez
María Jesús Aramburu Del Rio
Salvador Jove Peres
Carlos Carnero Gonzalez
Angela de Carmen Sierra Gonzalez
Pedro Marset Campos
Catalan Party (3 seats)
*Carles Alfred Gasoliba i Böhm
*Concepció Ferrer i Casals
Joan Vallve i Ribera
Nationalist Coalition (2 seats)
Josu Jon Imaz San Miguel
Isidoro Sanchez Garcia

Political Groups

Group membership after the elections in June 1994

	B	Dk	F	G	Gr	Irl	I	L	Nl	P	S	UK	Total
PES	6	3	15	40	10	1	18	2	8	10	22	63	198
EPP	7	3	13	47	9	4	12	2	10	1	30	19	157
LDR	6	5	1	0	0	1	7	1	10	8	2	2	43
EUL	0	0	7	0	4	0	5	0	0	3	9	0	28
FE	0	0	0	0	0	0	27	0	0	0	0	0	27
EDA	0	0	14	0	2	7	0	0	0	3	0	0	26
Greens	2	1	0	12	0	2	4	1	1	0	0	0	23
ERA	1	0	13	0	0	0	2	0	0	0	1	2	19
EDN	0	4	13	0	0	0	0	0	2	0	0	0	19
Ind	3	0	11	0	0	0	12	0	0	0	0	1	27
Total	**25**	**16**	**87**	**99**	**25**	**15**	**87**	**6**	**31**	**25**	**64**	**87**	**567**

Abbreviations of political groups:
PES — Party of European Socialists; EPP — European People's Party (Christian Democrats and Conservatives); LDR — Liberal and Democratic Reformist; Greens: Group of the Greens; EUL — European United Left (including former Communists); FE — Forza Europa (made up entirely of Forza Italia MEPs); EDA — European Democratic Alliance (Gaullist and Fianna Fail); ERA — European Radical Alliance (left of centre and regionalists); EDN — Europe des Nations (De Villiers's list and some other right-wing anti-EU members); Ind — Non-attached (including National Front in France and some right-wing Italians).

Group membership before the 1994 elections

	B	Dk	F	G	Gr	Irl	I	L	Nl	P	S	UK	Total
PES	8	3	21	31	9	1	33	2	8	8	27	46	**197**
EPP	7	4	12	32	10	4	27	3	10	3	17	33	**162**
LDR	4	2	9	5	0	2	4	1	4	9	5	0	**45**
Green	3	1	8	6	0	0	6	0	2	0	1	0	**27**
EDA	0	0	11	0	1	6	0	0	0	0	2	0	**20**
RBW	1	4	1	1	0	1	1	0	0	1	3	1	**14**
LU	0	0	7	0	3	0	0	0	0	3	0	0	**13**
ER	1	0	9	2	0	0	0	0	0	0	0	0	**12**
Ind	0	2	3	4	1	1	10	0	1	0	5	1	**28**
Total	**24**	**16**	**81**	**81**	**24**	**15**	**81**	**6**	**25**	**24**	**60**	**81**	**518**

PES: Party of European Socialists (including 45 British Labour MEPs and one SDLP from Northern Ireland). EPP: European People's Party (Christian Democrat Group) (including 32 British Conservative and one Ulster Unionist). LDR: Liberal Democratic and Reformist Group. Greens: Group of the Greens. EDA: European Democratic Alliance. RBW: Rainbow Group (including one Scottish nationalist). LU: Left Unity. ER: Technical Group of the European Right. Ind: Non-attached, including one Democratic Unionist).

The European Parliament

The biographies of Members of the European Parliament have been compiled from information supplied to *The Times* by the Directorate-General of Information and Public Relations and its offices in the EU member states, the Secretariats and Press Officers of the Political Groups of the Parliament, and by the successful candidates and their party headquarters in the United Kingdom. Occupations are those at the time of election in June 1994. Addresses and telephone numbers were those published during the July 1994 plenary session in Strasbourg and are subject to change, particularly those of newly-elected MEPs.

All MEPs can also be contacted at the EP political group offices, 97-113 rue Belliard, B-1047 Brussels, at the Palais de l'Europe in Strasbourg during plenary sessions, at the offices of the European Parliament in the member states (see page 270 for addresses and telephone numbers), and through their political party headquarters in their member states.

ABOVILLE, Gérard d'   France EPP (UDF/RPR)

Gérard d'Aboville was elected in 1994. He is a sailor and president of the council for pleasure boats. Aged 48.

Address: Kéantre F-56950 Auray

ADAM, Gordon   UK Northumbria PES (Lab)

Gordon Adam was first elected 1979. Re-appointed a vice-chairman of committee on energy, research and technology. Contested Tynemouth, 1966 Westminster election, and Berwick-upon-Tweed in 1973 by-election and February 1974. Member, Whitley Bay Council, 1971-4; North Tyneside Metropolitan Council, 1973-80 (chairman, 1973-4; mayor, 1974-5); Northern Economic Planning Council, 1974-9; Northern Arts General Council, 1975- . Board member, Newcastle Free Festival. A miner. Born March 28 1934.

Address: 10 Coach Road, Wallsend, Tyne and Wear NE28 6JA. Tel: (091) 263 5838. Fax: (091) 263 7079. East House Farm, Killingworth, Newcastle upon Tyne NE12 0BQ. Tel: 091 216 0154.

75

AELVOET, Magda — Belgium Verts (Green)

Magda Aelvoet, a member of the Chamber of Deputies since 1985, was elected in 1994. A former aid agency worker, Born April 4 1944.

Address: Europees Parlement, Belliardstraat 97-113, B-1047 Brussel. Fax 02 284 91 62.

AGLIETTA, Adelaide — Italy Verts (Verdi)

Adelaide Aglietta was first elected in 1989 on the Green Rainbow for Europe group. Member of the Chamber of Deputies. Former President of the parliamentary radical group (1979-82).

Address: Parlamento Europeo, Groupe des Verts, 97-113 rue Belliard, B-1047 Bruxelles. Centro per un Futuro Sostenibile, Viale Giulio Cesare, 49, I-00 192 Roma. Tel: 06 321 54 91. Fax: 06 321 54 93.

AHERN, Nuala — Ireland Verts (Green)

Nuala Ahern was elected in 1994, one of the first two Green MEPs from English-speaking countries of the Union. Member of Wicklow County Council. Active in environmental campaigns. Counselling psychologist. Born February 1949.

Address: 80 Heathervue, Greystones, Co Wicklow.
Tel: 01 287 65 74. Fax: 01 287 65 74.

AINARDI, Sylviane — France EUL (PCF)

Sylviane Ainardi, a teacher, was first elected to the EP in 1989. Midi-Pyrenees regional councillor; municipal councillor at Toulouse; federal first secretary of PCF at Haute-Garonne. Born December 19 1947.

Address: 1 allee Marc Saint Saens, B.P. 1157, F-31036 Toulouse Cedex. Tel: 61 40 39 65. Fax: 61 76 11 60. 8 rue des Chenes, Lherm, F-31600 Muret.

ALAVANOS, Alexandros — Greece, EUL (SYN)

Alexandros Alavanos was first elected to the EP in 1984. Former member of the central council of the Greek Young Communists. Economist. Born May 22 1950.

Address: Coalition de la Gauche et du Progres, Themistokleous 7 kai Gambetta, GR-106 77 Athina. Tel: (1) 361 92 32/361 92 34/362 16 19. Fax: (1) 363 92 52/364 82 63. Telex: (1) 220343.

ALBER, Siegbert — Germany EPP (CDU)

Siegbert Alber became a member of the appointed Parliament in 1977 and was elected in 1979. A vice-president of the EP, 1984-92. Vice-chairman of EPP Group 1982-4; member of bureau. Chaired EP committee of inquiry into treatment of toxic and dangerous substances by EC and its member states. Member, Bundestag, 1969-80; assemblies of Council of Europe and Western European Union, 1970-80. Chairman, Stuttgart CDU, 1971-9. Legal official and public prosecutor. Born July 27 1936.

Address: Gammertinger Strasse 35, D-70567 Stuttgart. Tel: (0711) 728 54 45.

ALDO, Blaise — France EPP (UDF/RPR)

Blaise Aldo was elected in 1994. Vice-president of Guadeloupe regional council and a local councillor. An education official. Aged 43.

Address: Surgy F-97180 Sainte Anne.

AMADEO, Amedeo — Italy Ind (AN)

Amedeo Amadeo was elected in 1994. A former local councillor (Bergamio). Doctor. Born September 8 1946.

Address: Via Paglia, 8, I-Bergamo. Tel: 035 23 91 91.

ANASTASSOPOULOS, Georgios — Greece EPP (ND)

Georgios Anastassopoulos was first elected in 1984. A vice-president of the outgoing Parliament. A journalist who in 1978 was first Greek appointed to bureau of International Federation of Journalists and was on its bureau until 1984; President, Union of Journalists, 1976-84. Worked for Athens newspapers since 1953 and has been general manager, Athens News Agency. Acting secretary of state attached to president's office in 1977 and 1981 caretaker governments. Born September 25 1935.

Address: Levidou 21, GR-146 71 Nea Erythrea. Tel: (1) 620 89 28. Fax: (1) 800 00 41.

ANCONA, Hedy D'   Netherlands PES (ESD)

Hedy d'Ancona was a member of the EP in 1984-9 and was re-elected in 1994. Appointed a vice-president of the PES Group after the 1994 election. Minister of Health and Culture and former Secretary of State for Social Affairs and Employment. Member of the second chamber of the national Parliament.

Address: Amstel 274, 1017 Am Amsterdam. Tel: (020) 63 85 829.

ANDRE-LEONARD, Anne   Belgium LDR (PRL)

Anne Andre-Leonard was an MEP 1985-9 and returned in 1991. Re-elected in 1994. Mayor of Ottignies. President of the European foundation for the protection of the child and SOS "Drug international". Born November 16 1948.

Address: 40 rue de la Chapelle, B-1340 Orttignies (Louvain-la-Neuvre). Tel: (010) 41 80 70. Fax: (010 41 83 74.

ANDREWS, Niall   Ireland EDA (FF)

Niall Andrews was first elected in 1984. Minister of State, Department of Environment, October to December 1982. Member of the Dail (Irish Parliament) from 1977-89. Former television programmes officer with RTE. Former delegate to the Council of Europe. Born August 19 1937.

Address: 48 Westbrook Road, Dundrum, Dublin 14. Tel: 01 98 47 69.

ANGELILLI, Roberta Italy Ind (AN)

Roberta Angelilli was first elected in 1994. Principal secretary of Fronte Della Gioventi. Born February 1 1965.

Address: Via di Priscilla, 22 , I-00199 Roma. Tel: (06) 86 20 62 39.

AÑOVEROS Trias De Bes, Julio   Spain EPP (PP)

Julio Añoveros Trias De Bes was elected in 1994. University lecturer. Lawyer. Born March 27 1942.

Address: Aribau, 237 (escalera B, entr. 3a), E-08021 Barcelona. Tel: 200 19 33. Fax: 209 16 29. Avda de Madrid, 133-135, E-08028 Barcelona. Tel: 339 24 00. Fax: 330 33 24.

ANTONY, Bernard   France Ind (FN)

Bernard Antony was first elected in 1984. Member of the Midi-Pyrénées regional council. Chairman of the Association for Christianity and Solidarity. Member of the bureau of DR group, the technical group of the European right in the outgoing Parliament. Company director and former teacher. Born November 28 1944.

Address: 61 avenue Lucien Coudert, F-81100 Castres. Tel: 63 59 62 77.
125 rue Albert 1er, F-81000 Castres. Tel: 63 59 79 91.

80

APARICIO SANCHEZ, Pedro Spain PES (PSOE)

Pedro Aparicio Sanchez was elected in 1994. Mayor of Malaga. Former member of the Andalucia regional assembly. Surgeon and university lecturer. Born October 4 1942.

Address: Avenida Cervantes, 4, E-29071 Malaga. Tel: 213 53 48. Fax: 213 54 20.

APOLINÁRIO, José Portugal PSE (PS)

José Apolinário became an MEP in January 1993. Former member of the national Parliament and former leader of the Young Socialists. Businessman. Born July 22 1962.

Address: Grupo Socialists, Largo Jean Monnet, No 1-6, P-1200 Lisboa. Tel: (1) 52 23 07. Damaso da Encarnacao No 53-D-1, P-8700 Olhao. Tel: (89) 70 27 81.

ARAMBURU DEL RIO, María Jesús Spain EUL (IU-IC)

María Jesús Aramburu Del Rio was elected to the EP in 1994. Member of the Andalucia regional assembly. Member of the federal council of the Izquierda Unida party. Teacher. Born 1952.

Address: Lumbreras, 16-3 B, E-41002 Sevilla. Tel: 954 38 81 43.

81

ARIETIO Toledo, Javier — Spain EPP (PP)

Javier Arieto Toledo became an MEP in July 1993. Consultant and head of a private company. Civil engineer. Born Apr 11 1954.

Address: La Moraleja, Calle Camino Viejo 77, E-28104 Alcobendas-Madrid.
Tel: (1) 650 29 86. Fax: (1) 650 60 89.

ARGYROS, Stylianos — Greece EEP (ND)

Stylianos Argyros was elected in 1994. President of the Association of Greek Industries. Former adviser to World Bank. Engineer and business manager. Born 1945.

Address: Ypsilandou 23, GR 106 75 Athina.
Tel: (01) 72 21 936. Fax: (01) 72 21 936.

ARIAS CAÑETE, Miguel — Spain EPP (PP)

Miguel Arias Cañete has been an MEP since January 1986. A former senator for Cadiz and a former member of the Andalucian regional assembly. A lawyer and professor of civil law. Born February 24 1950.

Address: Sevilla 41-43, Jerez de la Frontera, E-11402 Cadiz. Tel: (56) 32 18 55. Fax: (56) 34 85 64. Marques de Bonanza, sin E-11407 Jerez de la / frontera, Cadiz. Tel: (56) 18 52 63.

ARRONI, Aldo — Italy FE (FI)

Aldo Arroni was first elected in 1994. Manager with *Corriere della Sera/Arnaldo Mondadori* newspaper and media group. Former director general of Publitel-France (Berlusconi publishing group). Born December 20 1945.

Address: Via Ferruccio, 3 I-20145 Milano.

AUGIAS, Corrado — Italy PES (PDS)

Corrado Augias was elected in 1994. Journalist. Born January 26 1935.

Address: Via Rubens, 44 I-00197 Roma. Tel: (06) 322 44 93.

AVGERINOS, Paraskevas — Greece PES (PASOK)

Paraskevas Avgerinos is a founder-member of PASOK (Pan-Hellenic Socialist Movement) and a member of its central committee. World War Two resistance veteran. A doctor and former minister of health. First elected in 1984 and a former vice-president of the Parliament. Born Aug 19 1927.

Address: Knossou 10, GR-175 64 P. Faliro. Tel: (1) 93 08 288.

AZZOLINI, Claudio — Italy FE (FI)

Claudio Azzolini was first elected in 1994. A journalist and member of the executive committee of the National Council of Journalists and president of several companies. Born June 9 1940.

Address: S.m. a Cappella Necchia, 8/B, I-80121 Napoli. tel: (0801) 764 69 44. Fax: (081) 525 51 20. CISI Napoli S.p.A. Via A. Olivetti, 1 I-80078 Possuolii (NA). Tel: (081) 525 51 11. Fax: (081) 525 51 20.

BAGGIONI, Jean — France EPP (UDF/RPR)

Jean Baggioni was elected in 1994. President of the executive council of Corsica. Mayor of Ville-Di-Pietrabugno. Aged 55.

Address: Villa Stella, Cité Comte Toga, F-20200 Ville di Pietrabugno. Tel: 95 31 05 45. Fax: 95 32 66 11. Cours Grandval 22, B.P. 277, F-20187 Ajaccio Cedex. Tel: 95 51 12 84. Fax: 95 51 02 78.

BALDARELLI, Francesco — Italy PES (PDS)

Francesco Baldarelli was elected in 1994. Former Mayor of Fano. Secretary-general of local party branch (Marche). Born March 20 1955.

Address: Via Ottava Strada 56, I-61031 Bellocchi di Fano. Tel: 0721 85 44 40. Viale Gransci 56, I-61032 Fano. Tel: 0721 8013 68/82 45 27. Fax: 0721 80 13 86.

BALDI, Stefania — Italy FE (FI)

Stefania Baldi was elected in 1994. Local councillor. Vice-president of the local branch of the Red Cross. Architect and teacher. Born April 26 1959.

Address: Via Barbano 1, I-50129 Firenze.

BALDINI, Valerio — Italy FE (FI)

Valerio Baldini was elected in 1994. Manager and director of Rinascente, Edilnord and RAS. Director general of Fininvest financial group. Doctor of law. Born October 25 1939.

Address: Via Pionabarola 9, I-40086 San Lazzaro (BO). Tel: (059) 28 05 57.

BALFE, Richard — UK London South Inner PES (Lab)

Richard Balfe was first elected in 1979. Reappointed to the foreign affairs and security committee. Treasurer, Labour group of MEPs (EPLP) in the outgoing Parliament. Contested Paddington South, 1970 Westminster general election. Chairman, Co-operative Wholesale Society political committee; director, Royal Arsenal Co-operative Society and associated companies, 1978-85, being political secretary, 1973-9. Member, Greater London Council, 1973-7. Born May 14 1944.

Address: South East Co-op, 132/152 Powis Street, London SE18 6NL. Tel: 081 855 2128. Fax: 081 316 1936. 53 Chatsworth Way, London SE27 9HN. Tel: (081) 761 2510.

BANOTTI, Mary   Ireland EPP (FG)

Mary Banotti was first elected in 1984. State registered nurse, social worker and broadcaster; contributor to newspapers and magazines on social welfare issues. Worked as nurse in Kenya; chairs treatment centre for alcoholism in Dublin; co-founder of hostel for battered wives. Assistant Secretary, Dublin Central Fine Gael constituency. Born May 29 1939.

Address: 8 Cambridge Avenue, Ringsend, Dublin 4. Tel: (1) 68 03 41.

BARDONG, Otto   Germany EPP (CDU)

Otto Bardong was an MEP 1985-9 and was re-elected in 1994. Former member of the Reheinland-Pfalz Assembly. Leader of the local party. Chairman of Europa Union, Rheinland-Pfalz. Lecturer. Born October 2 1953.

Photograph unavailable

Address: Höhenstrasse 9, D-28014 Madrid. Tel: (1) 429 33 52.

BARÓN CRESPO, Enrique   Spain PES (PSOE)

Enrique Barón Crespo was President of the Parliament, 1989-92 and vice-president, 1987-9. Chairman of the foreign affairs committee in the outgoing Parliament. Former vice-chairman of Socialist Group. Spanish Minister for Transport, Tourism and Communications, 1982-5; member, Cortes (Spanish Parliament), 1977-87. President, International European Movement, since 1987. Lawyer and economist. Born March 27 1944.

Address: Fernanflor 4-7, E-28014 Madrid. Tel: (1) 429 33 52.

BARROS MOURA, José — Portugal PES (PS)

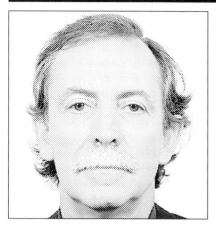

José Barros Moura, a former secretary of state, was and MEP in 1986-91 and was re-elected to the EP in 1994. Lawyer and university lecturer. Born October 8 1944.

Address: Avenida Visconde de Santarém, 14-R/C Esq, P—Lisboa. Tel: 846 28 07. Fax: 846 28 07.

BARTHET-MAYER, Christine — France PES (RE)

Christine Barthet-Mayer was elected in 1994. She is a local councillor. Former member of the Génération Ecologie national council. Born 1948.

Address: Mairie, 1 Place de la Mairie, F-68000 Colmar. 6 rue Clémence Isaure, F-31000 Toulouse. Tel: 61 22 08 09. Fax: 61 22 08 65. 3A rue du Chanoine Boxler, F-68000 Colmar. Tel: 89 41 44 74.

BARTON, Roger — UK Sheffield PES (Lab)

Roger Barton, secretary of Sheffield District Labour Party and Sheffield TUC, 1981-9, was first elected to EP in 1989. Appointed to institutional affairs committee in 1994. Former member, committee on economic and monetary affairs and industrial policy. Former Sheffield city councillor. Founding activist within local authorities' nuclear free zones movement and former chairman UK and international steering committees. Engineering fitter. Born January 6 1945.

Address: The Euro Office, 2nd Floor, Barkers Pool House, Burgess Street, Sheffield S1 2HF. Tel: 0742 753431. Fax: 0742 739666.

BARZANTI, Roberto — Italy PES (PDS)

Roberto Barzanti was first elected in 1984. He has been Mayor and Deputy Mayor of Siena and was a regional assessor for Tuscany. Student of literature and history. Born January 24 1939.

Address: Via di Città 85, 53100 Siena. Tel: (0577) 404 44. Fax: (0577) 28 12 04 (PDS).

BAUDIS, Dominique — France EPP (UDF/RPR)

Dominique Baudis was an MEP 1984-8 and was re-elected in 1994. Former member of the National Assembly. Mayor of Toulouse. Member of the UDF bureau. Former journalist. Born May 14 1947.

Address: Secrétariat particulier du Maire, Maire de Toulouse, F-31000 Toulouse. Tel: 61 22 20 19. Fax: 61 22 23 08. 31 rue des Potiers, F-31000 Toulouse.

BAZIN, Jean-Pierre — France EPP (UDF/RPR)

Jean-Pierre Bazin was elected in 1994. A local councillor and chairman of regional planning committee in the Loire. Historian. Aged 46.

Address: 60 rue de la Ville en Bois, F-44100 Bantes. Tel: 40 41 92 66. Fax 40 41 58 72.

BÉBÉAR, Jean-Pierre 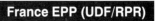 France EPP (UDF/RPR)

Jean-Pierre Bébéar was elected in 1994. Deputy Mayor of Bordeaux. A doctor. Aged 51.

Address: Conseil Régional d'Aquataine, 14 rue François de Sourdis, F-33077 Bordeaux Cedex. Tel: 56 90 53 23. Fax: 56 90 53 55. Clinique Universitaire ORL, Centre Hospitalier Pellegrin, F-33076 Bordeaux Cedex. Tel: 56 79 56 09. Fax: 56 79 56 78. 16 rue Emile Fourcand, F-33000 Bordeaux. Tel: 56 44 74 42.

BELLERE, Spalato Italy Ind (AN)

Spalato Bellere was elected in 1994. Former local and regional councillor. Member of party's executive committee. Doctor. Born May 3 1938.

Address: Via L Sanfelice, 71, I-80100 Napoli. Tel: 081 556 59 69. Via L Pirro 23, I-80100 Napoli.

BENNASAR TOUS, Francisca Spain EPP (PP)

Francisca Bennasar Tous was elected in 1994. A teacher. Born December 11 1943.

Address: Son Toell 1, E-07015 Palma de Mallorca, (Baleares). Tel: (71 40 28 26. Fax: (71 70 01 06.

BEREND, Rolf Germany EPP (CDU)

Rolf Berend was elected in 1994. Former member of the Volkskammer. Former East German observer at the EP. Teacher and musician. Born October 1 1943.

Address: Lindeistrasse 17, D-37339 Gernrode. Tel: (036076) 9522. Fax: (036076) 9522.

BERES, Pervenche France PES (ES)

Pervenche Beres, an official of the National Assembly, was elected in 1994. Born March 10 1957.

Address: 12 rue Oberkampf, F-75011, Paris.

BERNARDINI, François France PES (ES)

François Bernardini was elected in 1994. A regional councillor and deputy mayor of Istres. A civil servant. Born August 24 1953.

Address: Chemin du Rouquier, F-13800 Istres.

90

BERNARD-REYMOND, Pierre — France EPP (UDF/RPR)

Pierre Bernard-Reymond was re-elected in 1989 having been a member, 1984-6. State secretary attached to foreign affairs minister, 1978-81; Hautes Alps deputy (UDF), 1971-7 and 1986-8; vice-chairman, Hautes-Alpes Regional Council, 1982-9; Mayor of Gap (Hautes Alps) since; deputy mayor, 1971-89. Vice-chairman of CDS. Member, EPP Group bureau in the outgoing Parliament. Born January 16 1944.

Address: Mairie de Gap, 3 rue du Colonel Roux, F-05007 Gap. Tel: 92 53 24 01.

BERTENS, Jan Willem — Netherlands LDR (D'66)

Jan Willem Bertens was first elected in 1989, regaining a seat for his party that was previously held in 1979. A former diplomat and former ambassador in Costa Rica. Born January 23 1936.

Address: St. Bernardusstraat 11, 6211 HK Maastricht. Tel: (043) 21 00 41. Fax: (043) 25 89 79.

BERTHU, Georges — France EDN (l'autre Europe)

Georges Berthu, a civil servant, was elected in 1994. He is a member of "Club de l'Horloge", a think-tank. Born 1950.

Address: 18 rue Francois Trinquard, F-77500 Chelles. Tel: 64 26 11 87.

BERTINOTTI, Fausto   Italy EUL (RC)

Fausto Bertinotti was elected in 1994. Member of the Chamber of Deputies. Trade unionist and party secretary. Born March 22 1940.

Address: Direzione Nazionale Rifondazione Communista, Via Barbernini 11, I-00187 Roma.

BIANCO, Gerardo   Italy EPP (PPI)

Gerado Bianco was elected in 1994. Member of the Chamber of Deputies and former President of the Council of Europe Assembly. University professor. Born September 12 1931.

Address: Partito Popolarw Italiano, Piazza del Gesu, I-00586 Roma.

BILLINGHAM, Angela   UK Northamptonshire and Blaby PES (Lab)

Angela Billingham was first elected in 1994. A teacher and former member of the Sports Council. Oxford county councillor and former Mayor of Banbury and leader of Labour group, Cherwell District Council. Born July 1939; ed Aylesbury Grammar School; College of Education (London); Department of Education (Oxford).

Address: Ivy House, The Green, Oxford Road, Banbury, Oxfordshire, OX17 3NG. Tel: 0295 810004. Fax: 0295 810004.

BLADEL, Leonie van — Netherlands PES (ESD)

Leonie van Bladel was elected in 1994. Head of the Africa service of Dutch International Radio. Former president of the party's scientific institute. Born June 22 1939.

Address: Oude Loosdrechtseweg 160, 1215 HL Hilversum. Tel: 035 21 03 03.

BLAK, Freddy — Denmark PES (SDP)

Freddy Blak was first elected in 1989 Re-appointed a vice-chairman of the Committee on Budgetary Control after the 1994 elections. Member of the budgets committee in the outgoing Parliament. A fitter and trade unionist. Born March 8 1945.

Address: Marie Bregendahlsvej 18, DK-4700 Naestved. Tel: (53) 73 47 81. Fax: 55 77 12 39.

BLOKLAND, Hans — Netherlands PES (SP)

Hans Blokland was elected in 1994. A former president of the GPV party. Teacher. Born March 5 1943.

Address: Carolinen 11, 2904 Ve Capelle a/d Ijssel. Tel: (010) 450 53 09. Fax: (010) 450 53 09.

BLOT, Yvan — France Ind (FN)

Yvan Blot, a former member of the French National Assembly as deputy for Calais, was elected to the European Parliament in 1989. Vice-president of Alsace regional council. President of "Club de l'Horloge", a right-wing think-tank. Lecturer at Institute for Political Studies in Paris. Former county councillor for Pas-de-Calais and town councillor in Calais. Born June 29 1948.

Addresses: 35 avenue de la Paix, F-67000 Strasbourg. Tel: 88 25 68 67 post 18 20. Fax: 88 32 94 27. 12 rue des Dardanelles, F-75017 Paris. tel: (1) 45 74 89 07. Fax (1) 47 74 89 07. 86 bld de Cimiez, F-06000 Nice. Tel: 93 81 93 01.

BÖGE, Reimer — Germany EPP (CDU)

Reimer Böge, an agricultural engineer and farmer, was elected in 1989. Member of land bureau of Schleswig-Holstein CDU. Former municipal councillor. President, European Council of Young Farmers and member of bureau of European Farmers' Association, 1977-80. Born December 18 1951.

Address: *CDU-Landesverband/Europaburo, Sophienblatt 44-46, D-24114 Kiel. Tel: (0431) 66 09 25. Fax: (0431) 66 09 27. Dorfstrasse 50, D-24640 Hasenmoor. Tel: (04195) 412. Fax: (04195) 14 07.*

BONDE, Jens-Peter — Denmark EDN (June Mov)

Jens-Peter Bonde, who was first elected in 1979, was largely responsible for starting Danish anti-EC popular movement journal *Det ny Notat (The New Report)*. Member, central committee, Danish Communist Party. Journalist. Born March 27 1948.

Address: JuniBevaegelsen, Amagertorv 33.3, DK-1160 Kobenhavin K. Tel: 33 91 47 48. Fax: 33 91 46 18. Skovbrynet 39 DK-2880 Bagsvaerd. Tel: 44 49 02 51. Fax: 44 49 49 28.

BONIPERTI, Giampiero — Italy FE (FI)

Giampiero Boniperti was elected in 1994. Former Italian international footballer with Juventus and Turin. President of Juventus football club until 1994. Born January 29 1936.

Address: Via Casteggio 10, I-10131 Torino.

BONTEMPI, Rinaldo — Italy PES (PDS)

Rinaldo Bontempi was first elected in 1989. A regional councillor. Former member of the regional secretariat of the Italian Communist Party. Degree in jurisprudence. Born January 2 1944.

Photograph unavailable

Address: Via Maria Vittoria 18, I-10123 Torino. Tel: (011) 839 70 40.

BOOGERD-QUAAK, Johanna — Netherlands LDR (D'66)

Johanna Boogerd-Quaak was elected in 1994. Former member of the Zeeland regional council. Joint owner of an agricultural company. Born March 1 1944.

Address: Koning Willem III weg 4, 4543 RD Zaamslag. Tel: (01153) 16 18. Fax: (01153) 22 79.

BOSSI, Umberto   Italy Ind (Lega Nord)

Umberto Bossi was elected in 1994 in two constituencies. Founder and secretary general of the Lega Nord movement. Ally of Silvio Berlusconi in Italian government. Member of the Chamber of Deputies. Born April 19 1941.

Address: Via Verbano 11, I-21036 Gemonio (Varese). Tel: (02) 66 23 41.

BOTZ, Gerhard   Germany PES (SDP)

Gerhard Botz was elected in 1994. Former East German observer at the Parliament. Former member of the Volkskammer and then the Bundestag. Soil engineer. Born September 15 1955.

Address: Ortstrasse 31, D-98744 Lichtenhain/Bergbahn. Tel: 036705 23 29. Fax: 036705 23 29.

BOURLANGES, Jean-Louis   France EPP (UDF/RPR)

Jean-Louis Bourlanges was elected in 1989 on French Centre Party list led by Simone Veil. Chairman, budetary control committee during second half of 1984-9 Parliament. Member, EPP Group bureau in the outgoing Parliament. Member (on secondment), Court of Auditors. Regional councillor for Haute-Normandie. Former civil servant. Born May 13 1946.

Address: Rue du Colt Riviere, F-75008 Paris. Tel: (1) 42 25 94 32. Rue Marguerite Roll, F-76160 Varengeville sur Mer. Tel: 35 85 16 31.

BOWE, David — UK Cleveland and Yorkshire North PES (Lab)

David Bowe, a science teacher, won this seat in 1989. Chaired EP committee of inquiry into drugs. Served on Middlesbrough Borough Council. Northern regional secretary and Cleveland branch secretary, Socialist Educational Association. Former member, Northern regional executive of the Labour Party. Born July 19 1953.

Address: 10 Harris Street, Middlesbrough, Cleveland, TS1 5EF.
Tel: 0642 247722. Fax 0642 247804. 14 Thornfield Grove, Middlesbrough TS5 5LG. 0642 826078.

BREDIN, Frédérique — France PES (ES)

Frédérique Bredin was elected in 1994. Former minister of sport. Member of the National Assembly; member, Haute-Normandie regional council. Mayor of Fecamp. Inspector of finances. Born November 2 1956.

Address: 80 rue de Vaugirard, F-75006 Paris.

BRÉMOND D'ARS, Georges de — France EPP (UDF)

Georges de Brémond d'Ars was an MEP 1988-9 and returned in April 1993. Member UDF national council and political adviser. Farmer. Born April 20 1944.

Address: 50 rue Fabert, F-75007 Paris. Tel: (1) 47 05 83 58. F-40210 Commensalq. Tel: 58 07 07 59.

BREYER, Hiltrud   Germany Verts (Grüne)

Hiltrud Breyer was first elected in 1989. A political scientist and campaigner against nuclear pollution, she began her political career in the late Seventies with her fight against pollution at Saarland, near the French border. Local councillor. Born August 22 1957.

Address: Ormersheimer Strasse 3, D-66399 Mandelbachtal. Tel: (06803) 33 36.

BRINKHORST, Laurens-Jan   Netherlands LDR (D'66)

Laurens-Jan Brinkhorst became a member of the EP in January 1993 and was re-elected in 1994. Director-general of the environment at the European commission. Former Secretary of State for Foreign Affairs and a member of the second chamber of the national Parliament in 1977-82. Lawyer. Born March 18 1937.

Address: Wetstraat 236, B-1040 Brussel. Mallemolen 55/27, 2585 XH's Gravenhage Tel: (070) 360 55 75. Fax: (070) 360 55 75.

BROK, Elmar   Germany EPP (CDU)

Elmar Brok has been deputy chairman European Union of Christian Democratic Workers, since 1993; chairman, International Young Democratic Union, 1981-83. MEP since 1980. Chairman of several party organizations; deputy federal chairman, c Junge Union, 1977-81; chairman, CDU expert commitee on foreign policy; member, CDU North Rhine-Westphalia Land executive committee and CDU federal committee. A journalist. Born May 14 1946.

Address: Thomas-Mann-Strasse 15, D-3371 Bielefeld. Tel: (0521) 33 14 56. Fax: (0521) 17 7 27.

BURTONE, Giovanni — Italy EPP (PPI)

Giovanni Burtone was elected in 1994. Regional and local councillor. Doctor. Born August 4 1956.

Address: Via Monsignore, Ventimiglia 126 I-95135 Catania.

CABEZON ALONSO, Jésus — Spain PSE (PSOE)

Jesús Cabezon Alonso, a former senator and member of the Cantabria regional assembly, became an MEP in 1986. Former civil servant with special responsibility for social security. Born March 9 1946.

Addresses: Apartado de Correos 2211, E-39080 Santander. c/Ruiz Zorrilla, n 15-7 D, E-39009 Santander. Tel: (42) 31 18 14.

CABROL, Christian — France EPP (UDF/RPR)

Christian Cabrol, a surgeon, is President of "France Transplant". Elected in 1994. Local councillor. Born 1925.

Address: Hôpital de la Pitie, Service de chirurgie vasculaire, 83 bd de l'Hôpital, F-75013 Paris. tel: (1) 42 17 70 11. Fax: (1) 40 26 74 54. 36 rue Vivienne, F-75002 Paris. Tel: (1) 40 26 00 93. Fax: (1) 40 26 74 54.

CACCAVALE, Ernesto Italy FE (FI)

Ernesto Caccavale was elected in 1994. Journalist. Born August 22 1963.

Address: Via Stendhal 23, I-80193 Napoli. Tel: (081) 552 03 55. Fax: (081) 552 09 88. Via G. Ianelli 45 A, I-80131 Napoli. Tel: (081) 579 44 72.

CALIGARIS, Luigi Italy FE (FI)

Luigi Caligaris was elected in 1994. Former army general and television commentator on military issues. Born October 4 1931.

Address: Via Paisiello 26, I-00198 Roma. Tel (06) 69 94 13 94.

CAMPOS, António Portugal PES (PS)

António Campos was elected in 1994. A former secretary of state and member of the national Parliament. Engineer. Born July 4 1938.

Address: Av dos Bombeiros, P-3400 Oliveira Do Hospital. Travessa Henrique Cardoso 55-2-B, P-1700 Lisboa.

CAMPOY ZUECO, Luis — Spain EPP (PP)

Luis Campoy Zueco was elected in 1994. Local councillor and member of the Navarre regional assembly. Teacher. Born December 31 1938.

Address: Ugarte Dña Maria 14 A (3 A), E-31500 Tudela, Navarra. tel: 82 26 15.

CAPUCHO, Antonio — Portugal LDR (PSD)

Antonio Capucho became an MEP in 1989. A vice-president in the outgoing Parliament. Former member of the national Parliament and Minister for Parliamentary Affairs. A vice-chairman of the LDR Group. Business manager. Born January 3 1945.

Address: Parliamentio Europeu, Grupo LDR, 97-113 rue Belliard, B-1047 Bruxelles. Tel: 010 32 2 284 22 85.

CARNERO GONZALEZ, Carlos — Spain EUL (IU-IC)

Carlos Carnero Gonzalez was elected in 1994. Member of the Federal Council of the Izquierda Unida. Party official and has various posts in the Young Communists. Born 1961.

Address: General Rodrigo 6 6a Planta, E-28003 Madrid. Tel: 553 49 09. Fax: 534 97 47. Santa Hortensia 9 5 B, esc Isq, E-28002 Madrid. Tel: 519 18 55. Avenida Monte Igueldo 88, E-28018 Madrid. Tel: 519 17 55.

CARNITI, Pierre — Italy PSE (PDS)

Pierre Carniti was first elected in 1989. Former Secretary-General, Italian Confederation of Trade Unions; former vice-president of the European Confederation of Trade Unions. Journalist and trade unionist. Born September 25 1936.

Address: Via Oppido Mamertina 4, I-00178 Roma. Tel: (06) 718 73 10. Fax: (06) 718 73 10.

CARRÈRE d'ENCAUSSE, Hélène — France EPP (UDF/RPR)

Hélène Carrère d'Encausse was elected in 1994. She is a university lecturer and a member of the *Academie Française*. President of the committee on the science of man and society (Ministry of Culture). Born 1929.

Photograph unavailable

Address: 16 rue Raynouard, F-75016 Paris. Tel: (1) 42 88 67 75. Rue des Saint-Terres, F-75006 Paris.

CASINI, Carlo — Italy EPP (PPI)

Carlo Casini was first elected in 1984. Appointed chairman of the legal affairs and citizens' rights committee in 1994. Graduate in jurisprudence, he became a magistrate in Empoli and later assistant public prosecutor in Florence. In 1973 he was elected member of Law Council of Tuscany and became an appeal court judge 1977. Chairman, national federation of pro-life movements and life assistance centres. Born March 4 1935.

Address: Via Cavour 92, I-50129 Firenze. Tel (055) 571 754.

CASINI, Pierferdinando — Italy FE (FI)

Pierferdinando Casini was elected in 1994. Member of the Chamber of Deputies. Doctor of law and businessman. Born December 3 1955.

Address: Via di Ripetta 142,I-00186 Roma. Tel (06) 68 80 61 08/84/89. Fax: (06) 68 80 64 14. Strada Maggiore 71, I-40125 Bologna. Tel: (051) 34 26 64. Fax: (051) 34 39 36. Via dell'Osservanza 44, I-40136 Bologna. tel (051) 58 05 50.

CASSIDY, Bryan — UK Dorset and East Devon EPP (C)

Bryan Cassidy was first elected in 1984 as MEP for Dorset East and Hampshire West. Former European Democratic Group spokesman on external economic relations. Director-general, Cosmetic, Toiletry and Perfumery Association, 1981-4; previously with Ever Ready, Beecham's, Reed International (director, European associates). Contested Wandsworth Central in 1966 Westminster election. Member, council of Confederation of British Industries, 1981-4. Member, Greater London Council (for Hendon North), 1977-86. Born February 17 1934.

Address: 11 Esmond Court, Thackeray Street, London W8 5HB. Tel: 071 937 3558. Fax: 071 937 3558.

CASTAGNEDE, Bernard — France PES (ER)

Bernard Castagnede was elected in 1994. He is a member of the national committee of the *Mouvement des Radicaux de Gauches*. A lawyer and university lecturer. Born November 7 1944.

Address: 11 bis rue Jean Nicot, F-75007 Paris. Fax: 47 53 05 94. 5 bis rue Michelet, F66310 Estagel. Tel: 16 68 29 09 91.

CASTAGNETTI, Pierluigi   Italy EPP (PPI)

Pierluigi Castagnetti, a former member of the Chamber of Deputies, was elected to EP in 1994. Director of housing organisation. Born June 9 1945.

Address: Via IV Novembre 6, I-42100 Reggio Emilia. Tel (0522) 45 55 86. Fax: (0522) 413 02. Via L Ariosto 2, I-42100 Reggio Emilia. Tel: (0522) 419 17. Fax: (0522) 413 02.

CASTELLINA, Luciana   Italy EUL (RC)

Luciana Castellina is a founder member of the group responsible for reforming the Communist Party. She was first elected in 1979 on PDUP list and became a vice-chairman of CDI group for defence of independent groups. Elected in 1984 and 1989 on Communist list. Appointed chairman of the culture youth and media committee in 1994. Former member, Chamber of Deputies. A journalist, she served on committee on justice and the interparliamentary committee on general guidance and supervision of broadcasting services. Former member, PCI central committee. Born August 9 1929.

Address: Via San Valentino 32, I-00197 Roma. Tel: (06) 48 70 922-3. Fax: (06) 80 75 150.

CASTRICUM, Frits   Netherlands PES (ESD)

Frits Castricum was elected in 1994 when vice-president and member of the second chamber of the national Parliament. Former vice-president of his party. Journalist. Born April 14 1947.

Address: Albinonistraat 92, 5238 KT Boxtel. Tel: 4116 75 447.

CAUDRON, Gerard — France PES (ES)

Gerard Caudron was first elected in 1989. Mayor of Villeneuve-d'Ascq and vice-chairman of the Lille regional council. Former lecturer in business management. Born February 27 1945.

Address: Hotel de Ville, Place S. Allende, F-59650 Villeneuve d'Asq. Tel: 20 43 50 50. 45 rue de la Concorde, F-59650 Villeneuve d'Asq. Tel: 20 98 37 36.

CELLAI, Marco — Italy Ind (AN)

Marco Cellai, a former MEP, was re-elected in 1994. A former member of the Chamber of Deputies. A local councillor in Florence. Born March 5 1944.

Address: Via della Scala 25, I-50123 Firenze. Tel: (55) 21 89 65 / 0336 72 03 73. Fax: (055) 21 25 17. Piazza S.M. Movella 22, I50123 Firenze. Tel: 055 / 23 82 839. Fax: 055 / 238 28 39.

CHANTERIE, Raphael — Belgium EPP (CVP)

Raphael Chanterie has been an MEP since 1981. Vice-chairman, EPP Group, 1989-92. Secretary-General of European Union of Christian Democratic Workers (EUCDW), 1981-3. Adviser to Belgian Prime Minister, 1979, and to Minister for Co-operation with Developing Countries, 1981. Modern languages teacher, 1963-70. Born November 22 1942.

Address: Eikenlaan 26, B-8790 Waregem. Tel: (056) 60 35 87.

CHESA, Raymond   France EPP (UDF/RPR)

Raymond Chesa became an MEP in 1993. Mayor of Carcassonne and a regional councillor. RPR regional party secretary. A teacher. Born February 10 1937.

Address: Mairie de Carcassonne, Hotel de Ville, 32 rue A. Ramon, F-11000 Carcassonne. Tel: 68 77 70 78. Fax: 68 77 70 72. 16 Chemin Sainte Marie, F-11000 Carcassonne. Tel: 68 77 70 78.

CHICHESTER, Giles   UK Devon East and Plymouth PPE (C)

Giles Chichester won this seat in 1994. A publisher. Son of Sir Francis Chichester, the round-the-world yachtsman. Member, general council of Conservative Group for Europe, 1991-. Chairman, London West European constituency council 1987-8; and chairman, Hammersmith Conservative Association, 1984-7. Chairman, Carlton Club political committee, 1992- . Born 1946; ed Westminster School and Christ Church, Oxford.

Address: 9 St James's Place, London, SW1A 1PE. Tel: (071) 493 0931. Fax: (071) 409 1830. Constituency Office, 21 Waverley Road, Exmouth, Devon, EX8 3HL. Tel: 0395 264787. Longridge, West Hill, Ottery St Mary, Devon EX11 1UX. Tel: 0404 812889.

CHRISTODOULOU, Efthimios   Greece EPP (ND)

Efthimios Christodoulou was an MEP 1984-90 and was re-elected in 1994. Former head of the EPP Group Greek delegation. President and governor of the National Bank of Greece, 1979-81, and participated in many international conferences on economics and the work of international banking organisations such as the IMF and the OECD. Worked as a consultant director, director general and chairman of a number of major banks and enterprises, including the ETVA (Commercial Bank for Industrial Development), and for Olympic Airways. Born December 2 1932.

Address: Lamachou 3, GR 105 57 Athina. Tel: (1) 322 96 58. Louki Akrita 1B GR 152 37 Filothei. Tel: (1) 681 79 23/684 01 52.

CLERCQ, Willy de   Belgium LDR (VLD)

Willy de Clercq was Belgian Deputy Prime Minister and Minister for Finance and Foreign Trade, 1981-5; an EC Commissioner, 1985-9. Under-Secretary of State for the Budget, 1960-1; Deputy Prime Minister and Minister for the Budget, 1966-8; Deputy Prime Minister and Minister for Finance, 1973-4; Minister for Finance, 1974-7. Elected MEP, 1979-81, leaving to take ministerial office; re-elected 1989 and since then has been chairman of the external economic relations committee. Twice chairman, Interim Committee of International Monetary Fund. Born July 8 1927.

Address: Cyriel Buyssestraat 12, B-9000 Gent. Tel: 09 221 18 13. Fax: 09 220 07 77.

COATES, Kenneth   UK Nottingham PES (Lab)

Kenneth Coates won this seat in 1989 having contested it in 1984 and Nottingham South in the 1983 Westminster election. Joint secretary, European nuclear disarmament liaison committee, 1981-9. Member, Bertrand Russell peace foundation. Founder member, institute of workers' control. University lecturer and author; former miner. Born September 16 1930.

Address: 112 Church Street, Matlock, Derbyshire, DE4 3BZ. Tel: 0629 57159. Fax: 0629 580672.

COENE, Philippe de   Belgium PES (SP)

Philippe de Coene was elected in 1994. Member of the Bureau of the Socialist Party. A journalist. Born August 28 1960.

Address: Deken de Grijselaan 55, B-8500 Kortrijk.

COHN-BENDIT, Daniel   Germany Verts (Grüne)

Daniel Cohn-Bendit, who was elected in 1994, was a leading figure in the student protest movement in France in 1968. Appointed a vice-chairman of the culture, youth and media committee in 1994. Local councillor. Journalist. Born April 4 1945.

Address: European Parliament, 97-113 rue Belliard, B-1047 Brussels.

COLAJANNI, Luigi   Italy PES (PDS)

Luigi Colajanni was elected in 1989. Appointed vice-president of the PES after the 1994 election. Leader of the new European United Left (EUL) Group — Grupo por la Izquierda Unitaria Europea — and during the 1989-94 Parliament joined the Socialist Group, becoming one of its vice-chairmen. Former member, central committee and management caucus of Italian Communist Party (PCI) and Sicilian regional committee. Member, Sicilian Regional Assembly and local councillor at Palermo. Architect. Born October 2 1943.

Address: Parliamento Europeo, Bruxelles.

COLINO SALAMANCA, Jean Luis   Spain PES (PSOE)

Juan Luis Colino Salamanca has been an MEP since 1986. Former member of the Spanish Parliament. Lawyer and former civil servant. Born May 5 1947.

Address: Teresa Gill 12 2 izda, E-47002 Valladolid. Tel: (83) 30 38 31. Fax: (83) 30 36 45. Plaza de las Cortes 9, E-29014 Madrid. Tel: (1) 429 75 56. Fax: (1) 249 77 00. General Ruiz 1, E-47002 Valladolid. Tel: (83) 30 66 99/30 67 99.*

COLLI, Ombretta — Italy FE (FI)

Ombretta Colli was elected in 1994. A singer. Born September 21 1943.

Photograph unavailable

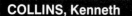

Address: Via Frescobaldi 25,I-20131 Milano.

COLLINS, Gerard — Ireland EDA (FF)

Gerard Collins was elected in 1994. Member of the Dail (Irish Parliament) since 1967. Minister for Foreign Affairs, 1989-92; Minister for Justice, 1987-9; Minister for Foreign Affairs, 1982; Minister for Justice 1977-81; Minister for Posts and Telegraphs 1970-3. Born October 1938.

Address: The Hill, Abbeyfeale, Co Limerick. tel: (068) 312 38.

COLLINS, Kenneth — UK Strathclyde East PES (Lab)

Kenneth Collins was elected in 1979 and was deputy leader Labour MEPs, 1979-84. Appointed chairman of the environment, public health and consumer protection committee in July 1994. Director, Institute for European Environmental Policy, London; Friends of the Earth (Scotland); vice-president, Royal Environmental Health Institute of Scotland; International Federation on Environmental Health; Institute of Trading Standards Administration. Member, East Kilbride Council, 1973-9; Lanark Council, 1973-5; East Kilbride Development Corporation, 1976-9. Born August 12 1939.

Address: 11 Stuarton Park, East Kilbride, Strathclyde, G74 4IA. Tel: 03552 37282. Fax: 03552 49670.

COLOMBO SVEVO, Maria Paloa — Italy EPP (PPI)

Maria Paloa Colombo Svevo was elected in 1994. A former senator and regional councillor. Born January 21 1942.

Address: Via Lecco 29 I-20052 Monza. Tel: (02) 67 07 10 15. Fax: (02) 67 07 10 37.

COLOM I NAVAL, Joan — Spain PES (PSOE)

Joan Colom i Naval has been an MEP since 1986. Former member of the national Parliament. Economist and university lecturer. Born July 5 1945.

Address: PSC-PSOE, Oficina Parlamentaria Europea, c/Nicaragua 75, E-08029 Barcelona. Tel: (3) 321 90 16. c/Napols 352 6*, E-08025 Barcelona. Tel: (3) 207 00 76.

CORNELISSEN, Petrus — Netherlands EPP (CDA)

Petrus Cornelissen was elected to EP in 1984. Member of the Dutch second chamber, 1967-81 (chairman of committee on housing and town and country planning and of his party's transport committee). Member of the Council of Europe and Western European Union; vice-president, WEU 1970-81. Former local and regional councillor. Civil engineer. Born January 13 1934.

Address: Willem-II-straat 47, NL-5682 AG Best. Tel: (4998) 72279.

CORRIE, John   UK Worcester and Warwickshire South PPE (C)

John Corrie won this seat in 1994. Appointed to ACP-EU joint assembly in 1994. An appointed member of European Assembly, 1975-6 and 1977-9. Westminster MP for Cunninghame North 1983-7 and Bute and North Ayrshire, 1974-83. Member, Council of Europe and WEU, 1983-7. A farmer and author of books on fish farming and on European rural policy. Born July 29 1935; ed George Watson's College, Edinburgh, and Lincoln Agricultural College, New Zealand.

Address: Park of Tongland, Kirkcudbright, DG6 4NE. Tel: 055 722232. Fax: 055 722211. 98 High Street, Evesham, Herford and Worcestershire. Tel: 0386 442469. Fax: 0386 40602.

COSTA NEVES, Carlos   Portugal PES (PSD)

Carlos Costa Neves was elected in 1994. Former member of the Azores regional assembly and secretary of state in several regional governments. Lawyer. Born June 16 1954 in the Azores.

Address: European Parliament, 97-113 rue Belliard, B-1047 Brussels.

COT, Jean-Pierre   France PES (ES)

Jean-Pierre Cot was leader of the Socialist group in the outgoing Parliament. First elected to the EP in 1984, having been a member of the nominated parliament, 1978-9. Member, central committee, French Socialist Party. From 1983 he chaired French Unesco delegation. Minister of Co-operation and Development, 1981-2; Savoie deputy, 1973-81; Mayor of Coise-St-Jean-Pied-Gauthier since 1971. Former lecturer at faculty of law in Amiens and Paris. Born October 23 1937.

Address: Coise-St-Jean-Pied-Gauthier, F-73800 Montmelian. Tel: (33) 79 28 80 31.

COX, Pat
Ireland LDR (Ind)

Pat Cox, a member of the Irish Parliament (Dail), was first elected to the EP in 1989. He is general secretary of the Progressive Democrats. He is a former presenter on Irish television and a former university lecturer in economics. He has been a member of the Parliament's economic and monetary affairs committee and its regional committee. Born November 28 1952 and educated in Limerick.

Address: 7 Maretimo Gardens East, Blackrock, co Dublin. Tel: (01) 880372.

CRAMPTON, Peter
UK Humberside PES (Lab)

Peter Crampton won the former Humberside seat for Labour in 1989; contested it, 1984. A vice-chairman, political affairs committee, 1989-92. Appointed the regional affairs committee in 1994. In the outgoing Parliament he was a member of the foreign affairs and security committee and its subcommittee on security and disarmament. Former chairman, European nuclear disarmament campaign; member, international committee, CND. Former lecturer and education officer in Uganda. Born June 10 1932.

Address: 135 Westbourne Avenue, Hull HU5, 3HU. Tel: 0482 449337. Fax: 0482 449403.

CRAWLEY, Christine
UK Birmingham East PES (Lab)

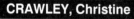

Christine Crawley was first elected for this seat in 1984. Appointed to women's rights committee in 1994; chair of the committee in the outgoing Parliament; a vice-chair, 1984-9. Member, Didcot Town Council and South Oxfordshire District Council, 1979-83; contested Staffordshire South East in 1983 Westminster election. Former teacher and part-time member, Manpower Services Commission. Born January 1 1950.

Address: Euro Office, Birmingham District Labour Party, 14/16 Bristol Street, Birmingham B5 7AF. Tel: 021 622 2270. Fax: (021) 622 7322. 50 Victoria Road, Harborne, Birmingham B17. Tel: (021) 428 1409.

CROWLEY, Brian — Ireland EDA (FF)

Brian Crowley, a member of the Irish Parliament since 1993, was elected to the EP in 1994. Born March 1964.

Address: 39 Sundays Well, Cork. Tel (021) 39 53 24. Fax: (021) 3958 31.

CUNHA, Arlindo — Portugal PES (PSD)

Arlindo Cunha was elected in 1994. Former Minister of Agriculture. Appointed to the agriculture and rural development committee in 1994. Agricultural economist. Born November 15 1950.

Address: Largo Jean Monet N 1-6, P-1200 Lisboa. Tel: 352 02 79. Fax: 352 02 80.

CUNNINGHAM, Tony — UK Cumbria and Lancashire North PES (Lab)

Tony Cunningham, a teacher, won this seat in 1994. Leader of Alderdale Borough Council and former Mayor of Workington. Aged 41. Educated at Workington Grammar School and Liverpool University.

Address: 17 Carlton Road, Workington, Cumbria, CA14 4BX.
Tel: 0900 605799.

CUSHNAHAN, John | Ireland EPP (FG)

John Cushnahan was elected to the EP in 1989. Leader, Alliance Party in Northern Ireland, 1984-7; chief whip of Alliance Party, 1982-4; general secretary of party, 1974-82. Former member, Northern Ireland Assembly and Belfast City Council. Since 1987 he has run a public relations and public affairs consultancy; member, Institute of Public Relations. Born July 23 1948; educated at St Joseph's College of Education, Belfast and Queen's University.

Address: Lisnagry, Co Limerick. Tel: 061 37 73 76.

D'ANDREA, Vittorio | Italy PPE (PPI)

Vittorio D'Andrea was elected in 1994. Former member of the Chamber of Deputies and former regional councillor. University lecturer. Born July 18 1948.

Address: Via del Gallitelli 68, I-85100 Potenza.

DANESIN, Alessandro | Italy FE (FI)

Alessandro Danesin was elected in 1994. Business consultant. Born March 3 1962.

Address: Cannaregio 5643, I-30131 Venezia.

DANKERT, Pieter

Netherlands PES (ESD)

Pieter Dankert was Dutch Secretary of State for Foreign Affairs when returned to the EP in 1994. President of the Parliament, 1982-4 and unsuccessfully contested the presidency in July 1984. Vice-president, 1987-89. Vice-chairman of the Socialist Group, 1984-9 and later a member of its bureau. He first became an MEP in 1977 and was first elected in 1979. Vice-president and member of the Dutch second chamber. Former vice-president of his party. He has served on the Council of Europe and the Western European Union. Born January 8 1934.

Address: Hoogstraat 1, 1135 BZ Edam. Tel: (02993) 716 68 (0031).

DARRAS, Danièle

France PES (ES)

Danièle Darras, a management secretary, was elected in 1994. Deputy mayor of Lievin. Local councillor and vice-chairman of Pas-de-Calais regional council. Born December 22 1943.

Address: 13 rue du 1er Mai, F-62800 Lievin. Fax: 21 44 89 88.

DARY, Michel

France PES (ER)

Michel Dary was elected in 1994. Local councillor. Vice-president, *Mouvement des Radicaux de Gauche.* Company director. Born 1945.

Address: Conseil Général des Bouches-du Rhône, 52 Avenue de Saint Just, F-13004 Marseille. Tel: 91 21 11 15. Fax: 91 69 20 40.

DASKALAKI, Katerina | Greece EDA (POLA)

Katerina Daskalaki was elected in 1994. A journalist and member of the administrative council of the European Journalists' Federation. Born 1944.

Address: Markissou 12, GR 176 75 Kallithea. Tel (01) 94 23 506.

DAVID, Wayne | UK South Wales Central PES (Lab)

Wayne David, who was first elected for Wales South in 1989, was appointed leader of the Labour MEPs after the 1994 election; a former vice-chairman. Part-time researcher and writer for Neil Kinnock, then Labour leader, 1984-9. Member, Welsh Labour Party executive, 1981-2 and 1986-9; Wales South Euro-constituency management committee, 1984-9; Labour Party executive working group on regional government, 1990-91; Cefn Cribwr Community Council, 1985-91. Born July 1 1957.

Address: South Wales Euro Office, 199 Newport Road, Cardiff CF2 1AJ. Tel: 0443 217810 or 0222 490215 or 0223 492560. 8 Bryn Rhedyn, Tonteg, Pontypridd, Mid-Glamorgan, CF38 1UY. Tel: (0443) 21 78 10.

DECOURRIÈRE, Francis | France EPP (UDF/RPR)

Francis Decourrière was elected in 1994. He is a businessman and president of a sports association. Born 1936.

Address: 29 rue Capron, F-59300 Valenciennes. Tel: 27 29 19 65. Fax: 27 36 05 42.

DE FRUTOS GAMA, Manuela — Spain PES (PSOE)

Manuela De Frutos Gama was elected in 1994. Mayor of Valverde de Merida and member of the Extremadura regional assembly. Teacher. Born July 18 1956.

Address: Gabriel y Galán 19, E-06890 Valverde de Merida. Tel: 32 18 70.

DE GIOVANNI, Biagio — Italy PES (PDS)

Biagio de Giovanni was elected in 1989. Member of the executive of the PDS. A university professor. Born December 21 1931.

Address: Via d'Isernia 57, I-80100 Napoli. Tel: (081) 761 20 31.

DE LA MERCED MONGE, Mercedes — Spain EPP (PP)

Mercedes De La Merced Monge was elected in 1994. Local councillor. Civil servant. Born October 31 1960.

Address: Génova 13 4a planta, E-28004 Madrid. Rel 319 20 27. Plaza de Chamberi, E-Madrid. Tel: 588 67 78. Fax: 58867 97.

DELL'ALBA, Gianfranco   Italy Ind (PR)

Gianfranco Dell'Alba was elected in 1994. Former joint general secretary of the Greens in the European Parliament. Born May 24 1955.

Address: Via Cassiodoro 14,I-001 193 Roma. Tel: (06) 689 65 51.

DE LUCA, Stefano   Italy FE (FI)

Stefano De Luca was elected in 1994. Former member of Chamber of Deputies and former secretary of state. Lawyer. Born April 7 1942.

Address: Via Libertà 159, I-90143 Palermo.

DELVAUX-STEHRES, Mady   Luxembourg PES (LSAP)

Mady Delvaux-Stehres was elected to EP in 1994 when secretary of state for health, social security and sports. Member of the Chamber of Deputies and a former local councillor. Member of the executive committee of the Socialist Workers Party. A former teacher. Born October 11 1950.

Photograph unavailable

Address: 75 route d'Arlon, L-1140 Luxembourg. tel: 44 98 03.

DE MELO, Eurico — Portugal PES (PSD)

Eurico De Melo was elected in 1994. Member of the national Parliament and a former Government minister. Civil Governor of Braga. Business manager. Born September 28 1925.

Address: Rua Largo Jean Monet 1-6, P-1200 Lisboa. Tel: 352 02 79. Fax: 352 02 80.

DEPREZ, Gerard — Belgium EPP (PSC)

Gerard Deprez was first elected in 1984. President of the party since 1981; former party political adviser. Served on staffs of ministers, 1979-81. Local councillor at Ottignies-Louvain-la-Neuve. A sociologist. Born August 13 1943.

Addresses: 25 Avenue des Combattants, B-1340 Ottignies. Tel: (010) 41 85 44. PSC, 45 rue des Deux Eglises, B-1040 Bruxelles. Tel: (2) 238 01 11.

DE SÁ, Luís — Portugal EUL (UDC)

Luís De Sá was elected in 1994. Member of the national Parliament. A lawyer. Born February 12 1952.

Photograph unavailable

Address: Soeiro Pereira Gomes No 3, P-1699 Lisboa Codex. Praceta Bombos Volentaries No 86- Dt, P-Fafundo. Tel: 419 40 80.

DESAMA, Claude   Belgium PES (SP)

Claude Desama became an MEP in 1988 and was re-elected in 1989 and 1994. Re-appointed chairman of the energy committee after the 1994 election. University lecturer. Born October 9 1942.

Address: 38 rue de la Banque, B-4800 Verviers. Tel: (087) 31 72 82. Fax: (087) 31 48 31. 161E rue du Paradis, B-4821 Dison. Tel: (087) 31 01 25.

DES PLACES, Edouard   France EDN (l'autre Europe)

Edouard Des Places is an agronomist and president of an agricultural organisation. First elected in 1994. Mayor of Vineuil. Born 1940.

Address: Le Coudray, F-36110 Vineuil. Tel: 54 36 60 43. Fax: 54 36 60 43.

DIEZ DE RIVERA ICAZA, Carmen   Spain PES (PSOE)

Carmen Diez de Rivera Icaza has been an MEP since 1987. Former head of the Spanish Prime Minister's office. Teacher. Born August 29 1942.

Address: Henares 10-A, E-28002 Madrid. Tel: (1) 411 51 51. Fax: 411 51 51.

DIJK, NEL van
Netherlands Verts (Green Left)

Nel van Dijk has been an MEP since 1987. Appointed chairman of the women's rights committee after the 1994 election. Former member of Communist Party. Former trade union activist in the steel industry. Born October 22 1952.

Address: Heistraat 14, 6136 Bd Sittard. Tel: (046) 51 17 68. Fax: (046) 51 35 15.

DILLEN, Karel
Belgium Ind (Far Right)

Karel Dillen was elected 1989, the first MEP from Vlaams Blok, the Flemish national party. Member of Volksunie until 1970; founder of Vlaams National Party in 1977, and Vlaams Blok in 1979. Former member, Belgian Chamber of Deputies and senator. Joined Technical Group of European Right, becoming a vice-chairman. An accountant formerly employed by Renault. Born October 16 1925.

Address: Colmastraat 3, D-2100 Antwerpen (Deurne). Tel: (03) 321 84 39. Fax: (02) 366 09 03.

DIMITRAKOPOULOS, Georgios
Greece EPP (ND)

Georgios Dimitrakopoulos was elected in 1994. Former adviser to the minister for foreign affairs. Director of the daily newspaper *Elefteria*. Political scientist and journalist. Born 1951.

Address: Papakyriazi 37-43, GR 412 22 Larissa. Tel: (041) 227 224. Fax: (041) 250 391.

DI PRIMA, Pietro — Italy FE (FI)

Pietro Di Prima was elected in 1994. A banker and director general of bank with the Italian banking association. Doctor of law. Born March10 1947.

Address: Via D Cirillo 18, I-92024 Canicatti (AG). Tel: (0922) 85 37 33. Fax: (0922) 73 104/73 12 82. Piazza Dante 16, I-92024 Canicatti (AG). Tel: (0922) 85 52 32.

DONNAY, Jacques — France EPP (UDF/RPR)

Jacques Donnay was elected in 1994. He is a local councillor and president of the Nord General Council. Born 1925.

Address: 2 rue Marquemars Giéké, Place de la Republique, F-59047 Lille Cedex. Tel: 20 63 50 70. Fax: 20 30 90 74. 12 Avenue du Maréchal Leclerc, F-59110 la Madeleine. Tel: 20 55 18 75.

DONNELLY, Alan — UK Tyne and Wear PES (Lab)

Alan Donnelly was elected for this seat in 1989. In the outgoing Parliament he was Labour spokesman on committee on economic and monetary affairs and industrial policy and member, subcommittee on monetary affairs. Chairman, delegation for relations with United States. Rapporteur for the Parliament's report on German unification. National finance manager for the general GMB union, 1987-9; previously union press liaison officer. South Tyneside councillor, 1980-3. Director, Unity Trust Bank, 1987-9. Born July 16 1957.

Address: Parliamentary Office, 1 South View, Jarrow, NE32 5JP. Tel: 091 489 7643. Fax: 091 489 0643. 1 Shearwater-Souter Point, Whitburn, Tyne and Wear.

DONNELLY, Brendan · UK Sussex South and Crawley PPE (C)

Brendan Donnelly won this seat in 1994. Special adviser to Sir Christopher Prout, former Conservative leader in the European Parliament. Private secretary to Lord Plumb when he was chairman of the European Conservatives, 1983-6 and political adviser to Lord Cockfield when EC commissioner, 1986-7. On the Foreign Office staff, 1976-82, including a period as first secretary in Bonn. Contested London West in 1989 Euro election. European Community specialist with public affairs consultancy, 1986-90. Born 1950; educated at St Ignatius College, Tottenham, and Christ Church, Oxford.

Address: 61 Leopold Road, London, N2 8BG. Tel (081) 444 0154. Fax: (081) 833 5273.

DUHRKOP DUHRKOP, Barbara · Spain PES (PSOE)

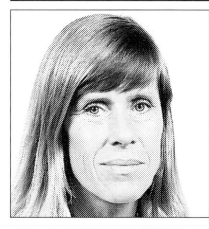

Barbara Duhrkop Duhrkop has been an MEP since 1987. Member of the PES bureau. A teacher and translator. Born July 27 1945.

Address: Plaza de las Cortes 7, E-28014 Madrid.

DURY, Raymonde · Belgium PES (PS)

Raymonde Dury first became an MEP in 1982. Appointed vice-president of the PES after the 1994 election. A former vice-chairman of Socialist Group and leader of the Belgian delegation. Press attaché to Socialist Group of EP, 1976-82. Sociologist. Born July 22 1947.

Address: 33-45 rue Uyttenhove, B-1090.

123

DYBKJAER, Lone   Denmark LDR (RLP)

Lone Dybkjaer, a former minister of the environment, was elected in 1994. A member of the Folketing since 1973. An engineer. Born May 25 1940.

Address: Allégade 6 A 2, DK-2000 Frederiksberg.

EBNER, Michael   Italy EPP (SV)

Michael Ebner was elected in 1994. Former member of the Chamber of Deputies. Doctor of law and journalist. Born September 20 1952.

Address: Lauben 41, I-39100 Bolzano. Tel: (0471) 92 52 59. Fax: (0471) 92 52 29.

EISMA, Doeke   Netherlands LDR (D'66)

Doeke Eisma was an MEP in 1981 4 and was re-elected to the EP in 1994. Former member of both chambers of the national Parliament and a former civil servant. Sociologist. Born December 30 1939.

Address: Ruychrocklaan 36, 2597 En Den Hag. Tel: (070) 324 15 43. Fax: (070 324 15 43.

ELLES, James   UK Buckinghamshire and Oxfordshire East EPP (C)

James Elles was first elected in 1984 as MEP for Oxford and Buckinghamshire. Member, budgets committee in outgoing Parliament and in 1984-89. Served in external relations directorate of European commission, 1976-80 with responsibility for fisheries negotiations, 1976-7; participated in Tokyo Round multilateral trade negotiations in Gatt, 1977-80; assistant to deputy director general of agriculture, EC Commission, 1980-3. Founder, EC baroque orchestra. Born September 3 1949.

Address: Aylesbury Conservative Association, 100 Walton Street, Aylesbury, Bucks HP21 7QP. Tel: 0296 82102.

ELLIOTT, Michael   UK London West PES (Lab)

Michael Elliott was first elected for this seat in 1984. Labour representative on British section of international union of local authorities. Contested Bedfordshire in first Euro elections in 1979, and Wembley South in 1970, 1966 and 1964 Westminster elections. Member, Ealing Council, 1964-86. Member, CND and Friends of the Earth. Former executive and scientist in food industry. Born June 3 1932.

Address: 358 Oldfield Lane North, Greenford, Middlesex, UB6 8PT. Tel: 081 578 1303. Fax: 081 575 5007.

ELMALAN, Mireille   France EUL (PCF)

Mireille Elmalan was first elected in 1989. Deputy mayor of Pierre-Bénite (Rhône). Former member, central committee of PCF. Born January 8 1949.

Address: Federation du P.C.F., 2 av. Maurice Thorex, F-69200 Venissieux. Tel: 78 70 18 93. Fax: 78 70 95 89. 28 Allee de la Claveliere, F-69310 Pierre-Benite. Tel: 72 39 08 33.

EPHREMIDIS, Vassilis — Greece EUL (KKE)

Vassilis Ephremidis has been an MEP since 1981. Became a vice-chairman, Coalition des Gauches (Left Unity) group, after 1989 election; group treasurer; a vice-chairman, Communist and Allies Group, during the 1984-9 Parliament. World War Two resistance veteran. Elected to Greek national assembly during the Fifties. Former member of his party's central committee. Editor of *Avgi*, 1952-6. A lawyer. Born December 31 1915.

Address: Kentriki Epitropi tou KKE, Leoforos Irakleiou 145, GR-142 31 New Ionia. Tel: (1) 25 22 591. Ithakis 41, GR-112 51 Athina. Tel: (1) 884 33 20.

ESCUDERO LOPEZ, Jose Antonio — Spain EPP (PP)

Jose Antonio Escudero Lopez was an MEP from 1987-9 and returned to the EP in November 1989. Senator during Spain's first democratic Parliament. Former director-general of immigration; member, board of directors, Spanish national radio and television (RTVE). Professor at Complutense University, Madrid; honorary professor, University of Lisbon; former secretary-general and vice-rector, Menendez Pelayo International University, Santander. Full member, Royal Academy of Jurisprudence and Legislation. Born October 12 1936.

Address: Instituto de Historia de la Inquisicion, Facultad de Derecho, Ciudad Universitaria, E-28040 Madrid. Tel: (1) 394 57 20.

ESTEBAN MARTIN, Laura Elena — Spain EPP (PP)

Laura Elena Esteban Martin was elected in 1994. Member of the Madrid regional assembly. Vice-president of the International Youth Democratic Union. Born August 8 1962.

Address: Gaztambide 64, E-28015 Madrid. Tel 543 40 51. Fax: 543 40 51.

ESTEVAN BOLEA, Maria Teresa — Spain EPP (PP)

Maria Teresa Estevan Bolea was elected in 1994. Former member of the national Parliament. Engineer and civil servant with the Ministry of Industry and Energy. Born October 26 1936.

Address: Guzmán el Bueno 135 4-D, E-28003 Madrid. Tel (1) 533 28 47. Fax: 544 69 35.

EVANS, Robert — UK London North West PES (Lab)

Robert Evans won this seat in 1994. Contested London South and Surrey in the 1989 Euro election and Uxbridge in 1992 and East Berkshire in 1987 in the Westminster elections. Member, Fabian Society; League Against Cruel Sports; and Co-operative Party. A primary school head teacher and member, national executive of the Socialist Educational Association. Born October 1956; ed County School, Ashford, Middlesex, Shoreditch College of Education, and Institute of Education, London.

Address: Flat 3 Oatlands Court, St Marys Road, Weybridge, Surrey, KT13 9QE. Tel: 0932 848810

EWING, Winifred — UK Highlands and Island RBW (SNP)

Winifred Ewing, president of the Scottish National Party since 1989, was first elected for this seat in 1979, having been a nominated MEP, 1975-9. Joined the Arc-en-Ciel (Rainbow) group in 1989. Group representative in many international meetings and member of ACP-EEC assembly; member, Parliament's committee on development and co-operation. Rapporteur on EC fisheries agreements with developing countries. Former chairman, committee on youth, culture, education, information and sport. Former member, regional and legal affairs committees. B July 10 1929.

Address: 52 Queen's Drive Glasgow, G42 8DD. Tel: 041 423 1765. Goodwill, Miltonduff, Elgin, IV30 3TL.

FABRA VALLES, Juan Manuel   Spain EPP (PP)

Juan Manuel Fabra Valles was elected in 1994. Member of the national Parliament and the parliamentary assembly of the Council of Europe and the Western European Union. President of the local party in Tarragona. Businessman. Born 1950.

Address: Simpática 2 E-43500 Tortosa. Tel: (77) 44 00 16. Fax: (77) 50 48 52.

FABRE-AUBRESPY, Hervé   France EDN (l'autre Europe)

Hervé Fabre-Aubrespy was elected in 1994. Civil servant, Council of State (Petitions). Former secretary of the RPR. Born 1956.

Address: 15 cours de la République, F-13120 Gardanne. Tel: 42 65 84 06. Fax: 42 51 32 48.

FALCONER, Alexander   UK Mid Scotland and Fife PES (Lab)

Alexander Falconer was first elected in 1984. Appointed to external economic relations committee after the 1994 election. In the outgoing Parliament he was a member of the regional committee and delegation for relations with South America. Former engineer and trade union official. Served in the Royal Navy for nine years. Born April 1 1940.

Address: 25 Church Street, Inverkeithing, Fife KY11 1LH. Tel: 0383 419330 Fax: 0383 417957.

FANTUZZI, Giulio — Italy PES (PDS)

Giulio Fantuzzi was first elected in 1989. Former Mayor of Reggio Emilia. Vice-president of agricultural co-operative organization. An engineer. Born September 17 1950.

Address: Federazione PDS, Via S. Girolamo 9, I-42100 Reggio Emilia. Tel: (0522) 45 81. Fax: (0522) 45 82 50. Via Panisi 30, I-42015 Correggio (RE). Tel: (0522) 64 13 76. Fax: (0522) 63 21 42.

FARASSINO, Gipo — Italy Ind (Lega Nord)

Gipo Farassino was elected in 1994. Former senator, regional and local councillor. A musician. Born March 11 1944.

Address: Via Cernaia 24, I-10122 Torino. Tel: (011) 562 17 20. Fax: (011) 562 17 23.

FASSA, Raimondo — Italy Ind (Lega Nord)

Raimondo Fassa was elected in 1994. Mayor of Varese. Solicitor. Born July 18 1959.

Address: Via Agnelli 3, I-21013 Gallarate (VA). Tel: (0331) 78 08 25. Fax: (0331) 78 05 21.

FERBER, Markus  Germany EPP (CSU)

Markus Ferber was elected in 1994. Active in the Young CSU movement. Engineer in the private sector. Born January 15 1965.

Address: Peutinger Strasse 11, D-86152 Ausburg. Tel: 0821 15 41 90. Fax: 0821 350 20.

FERET, Daniel   Belgium Ind (NF)

Daniel Feret, a doctor and surgeon, was elected in 1994. A founder-member of the National Front. Born August 7 1944.

Address: 12/8 Clos du Parnasse, B-1050 Bruxelles.

FERNANDEZ ALBOR, Gerardo   Spain EPP (PP)

Gerardo Fernandez Albor, a medical practitioner and surgeon, is former chairman of Santiago School of Medicine and Surgery and of Board of Santiago University. Elected to EP in 1989. Chairman of Spanish Alianza Popular; chairman, Galician Partido Popular; Former president of the regional government of Galicia and former member of the regional assembly. Born September 7 1917.

Address: Calle Orense 8, E-15701 Santiago de Compostela. Tel: (81) 56 66 50.

FERNANDEZ MARTIN, Fernando — Spain EPP (PP)

Fernando Fernandez Martin was elected in 1994. Former president of the regional assembly for the Canaries and member of the regional assembly. Doctor and neurologist. Born May 29 1943.

Address: Calle Manzanilla 26, La Laguna E-Tenerife. Tel: (22) 25 77 96/28 60 06.

FERRAZ MENDONÇA, Nélio — Portugal PES (PSD)

Nélio Ferraz Mendonça was elected in 1994. Former member of the Madeira regional assembly and regional secretary of the Madeira regional government. A doctor. Born July 22 1930.

Address: Rue Tenente Coronel Larmento, Bloc Residencial dis Ihens 10 A, P-9000 Funchal. Tel: 74 31 60.

FERRER I CASALS, Concepcio — Spain EPP (CiU-UDC)

Concepcio Ferrer i Casals was elected to the EP in 1987. Former member and former first vice-president of the of the Catalonian regional assembly and a local councillor. Former secretary-general of the Democratic Union of Catalonia. Chairman, Union of Christian-Democratic Women; vice-president, European Union of Christian Democrats. Teacher. Born January 27 1938.

Address: Diagonal 461, E-08036 Barcelona. Tel: (3) 410 92 79. Fax: (3) 410 67 74.

FERRI, Enrico | Italy PES (PSDI)

Enrico Ferri, a former minister for public works, was first elected in 1989. Member of the bureau of PES in the outgoing Parliament. Former vice-chairman, Committee on Institutional Affairs. Former member, Council of Magistrates and former president, National Association of Magistrates. University professor Born February 17 1942.

Address: Via Tellini 26, I-54027 Pontremoli (MS). Tel: 0187 83 08 70. Fax: (0187) 83 12 84.

FILIPPI, Livio | Italy EPP (Patto Segni)

Livio Filippi was elected in 1994.

Address: *Via Emilia Ovest 108, I-41100 Modena. Tel (059) 33 45 35. Fax: (059) 82 79 41.*

FINI, Gianfranco | Italy Ind (AN)

Gianfranco Fini was first elected in 1989. Elected in 1994 in five constituencies. Member of the Chamber of Deputies. Leader of the National Alliance. Former secretary general of the MSI movement. Journalist. Born January 3 1952.

Address: Segreteria Nazionale, Via della Scrofa 30, 00186 Roma. Tel: (06) 654 51 26.

FITZSIMONS, Jim   Ireland EDA (FF)

Jim Fitzsimons was elected to the EP in 1984. Minister of State, Department of Industry and Energy, 1982. Member of the Irish Parliament (Dail) 1977-89. Born December 16 1936.

Address: Ardsion, Dublin Road, Navan, Co Meath. Tel: 046 21540.

FLORENZ, Karl-Heinz   Germany EPP (CDU)

Karl-Heinz Florenz was first elected in 1989. Spokesman of CDU group on Neukirchen-Vluyn Town Council since 1984. Member, North Rhine-North Westphalia Land expert committee. chairman, Lower Rhine district committee on agriculture since 1987. A farmer. Born October 22 1947.

Address: Gross-Opholt 1, D-47506 Neukirchen-Vluyn. Tel: (02845) 274 34. Fax: (02845) 109 95.

FLORIO, Luigi   Italy FE (FI)

Luigi Florio was elected in 1994. Former local councillor. Lawyer and journalist. Born April 7 1953.

Address: Puazza Astesano 10, I-14100 ASTI. Tel: (0141) 332 22. Fax: (0141 332 22.

FONTAINE, Nicole — France EPP (UDF/RPR)

Nicole Fontaine was elected in 1984. A vice-president of the outgoing Parliament. Former chairman, the EPP Group working party on political affairs. Member, EPP Group Bureau. Former member, Economic and Social Council. Member of the UDF political bureau and the National Education Council. Adviser to the Catholic Education Secretariat. A teacher and lawyer. Born January 16 1942.

Address: 45 rue du Bois de Bologne, F-92200 Neuilly-sur-Seine. Tel: (1) 47 47 22 24. Fax: (1) 46 41 04 21. Villa Mirasol, Pont St. Jean. F-06310 Villefranche sur Mer.

FONTANA, Alessandro — Italy FE (FI)

Alessandro Fontana, a former minister for agriculture and research, was elected to the EP in 1994. Former senator. Teacher. Born August 18 1936.

Address: Via Boifava 17/A, I-25100 Brescia. Tel: (030) 375 03 14. Fax: (030) 375 03 34.

FORD, Glyn — UK Greater Manchester East PES (Lab)

Glyn Ford was leader of the Labour group of MEPs (EPLP), 1989-93 and subsequently deputy leader. Former senior vice-chairman, Socialist Group. First elected in 1984. Chairman, EP committee of inquiry into growth of racism and fascism in Europe, 1984-6. Member, Tameside Council, 1978-86. Contested Hazel Grove in 1987 Westminster election. Senior research fellow, Manchester University, 1980-4; visiting research fellow since 1984; visiting professor, Tokyo university, 1983. Born January 28 1950.

Address: 46 Stamford Road, Mossley, Lancashire OL5 0BE. Tel: 04578 36276. Fax: 04578 34927.

FORMENTINI, Marco — Italy Ind (Lega Nord)

Marco Formentini was elected in 1994. Mayor of Milan. Former member of the Chamber of Deputies. Born April 14 1930.

Address: Via Cosimo del Fante 14, I-20122 Milano. Tel: (02) 89 31 94 94.

FOUQUE, Antoinette — France PES (ER)

Antoinette Fouque was elected in 1994. Co-founder of the women's liberation movement and *Femmes d'Europe*. A psychiatrist. Born October 1 1936.

Photograph unavailable

Address: 4 rue de Verneuil, F-75007 Paris.

FRAGA ESTEVEZ, Carmen — Spain EPP (PP)

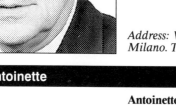

Carmen Fraga Estevez was elected in 1994. Former civil servant and official with the EPP Group in the European Parliament. Born October 19 1948.

Address: 8 Avenue Penaissance, B-Bruxelles. Tel: 735 98 61.

FRIEDRICH, Ingo — Germany EPP (CSU)

Ingo Friedrich, vice-president of the CSU, was first elected to the EP in 1979. Member, EPP bureau. Chairman of the European Small Business Forum. Executive in electrical industry, 1970-80; on staff of Institute for Politics and Communications, University of Erlangen-Nuremberg, 1967-70. Vice-president, Pan-European Union. Member, CSU Land Executive Bureau, 1989- . Born January 24 1942.

Address: Albert-Schweitzer-Strasse 61, D-91710 Gunzenhausen. Tel: (09831) 74 47. Fax: (09831) 43 30.

FRUTOS Gama, Manuela — Spain PES (PSOE)

Manuela Frutos Gama was elected in 1994. Mayor of Valverde de Merida and member of the Extremadura regional assembly. Born August 18 1956.

Photograph unavailable

Address: Gabriel y Galán 19, E-06890 Valverde de Merida. Tel: 32 18 70.

FUNCK, Honor — Germany EPP (CDU)

Honor Funck, a member of the Bundestag 1981-9, was first elected to the EP in 1989. Local councillor in Gutenzell, 1962-89; Biberach district councillor, 1969-89. Chairman, South Wurttemberg area agriculture committee; supervisory board, South West Karlsruhe central milk co-operative, 1975- ; Biberach District Farmers' Association, 1981- ; advisory board, Central Agricultural Co-operative, Stuttgart. Agricultural engineer and farmer. Born June 27 1930.

Address: Siechberg 2, D-88416 Ochsenhausen. Tel: (07352) 24 03. Fax: (07352) 93 231/233.

GALEOTE QUECEDE, José Gerardo   Spain EPP (PP)

José Gerardo Galeote Quecede was elected in 1994. Former official with the EPP group in the Parliament. Lawyer and university lecturer. Born January 27 1957.

Address: Alcala Galiano 4, E-28010 Madrid. Tel: 31020 53. Fax: 310 22 51.

GALLAGHER, Pat   Ireland EDA (FF)

Pat Gallagher was elected to the EP in 1994. Minister of state successively at the departments if the marine (1987-9 and 1992-3), Gaeltacht (1989-93), and at the department of arts, culture and Gaeltecht since 1993. Appointed a vice-chairman of the EP fisheries committee in 1994. Born March 1948.

Address: Dungloe, Co Donegal. Tel: (045) 212 76/ 213 64. Fax: (045) 211 33.

GALLAND, Yves   France EPP (UDF/RPR)

Yves Galland, a former government minister, unsuccessfully contected the presidency of the Parliament in July 1994. He was leader of the Liberal, Democratic and Reformist Group of the Parliament, 1992-4; a vice-president of EP, 1989-92. First elected in 1979; re-elected 1984 until 1986 and re-elected again in 1989. Chairman, Radical Party. Deputy mayor of Paris and former Paris deputy. Former national secretary and former vice-president of UDF (Union for French Democracy). Businessman. Born March 8 1941.

Address: 6 rue des Haudriettes, F-75004 Paris. Tel: (1) 42 78 62 02.

137

GALLOU, Jean-Yves Le
France Ind (FN)

Jean-Yves Le Gallou was elected in 1994. A local councillor and regional councillor for Ile-de-France. Born 1948.

Address: 57 Rue de Babylon, F-75007, Paris. Tel: (1) 40 43 89 90. Fax (1) 40 43 89 83.

GARCIA ARIAS, Ludivina
Spain PES (PSOE)

Ludivina Garcia Arias has been an MEP since 1986. Former member of the Spanish Parliament. Former local councillor and member of Asturias regional assembly. A teacher. Born December 13 1945.

Address: FSA-POSE, Santa Teresa N 20, E-28004 Madrid. Tel: (1) 85 25 65 99.

GARCIA MARGALLO, José Manuel
Spain EPP (PP)

José Manuel Garcia Margallo was elected in 1994. Member of the national Parliament. Tax inspector and university lecturer. Born August 13 1944.

Address: Velázquez 15, E-28001 Madrid.

GAROSCI, Riccardo — Italy FE (FI)

Riccardo Garosci was elected in 1994. He is a businessman and owner of a chain of supermarkets. Former director general of Federcom, a business organisation. Born July 5 1955.

Address: Piazza S Marco 1, i-Milano.

GARRIGA POLLEDO, Salvador — Spain EPP (PP)

Salvador Garriga Polledo, an MEP in 1987-9, was re-elected in 1994. Former member of the national Parliament. Economist. Born August 6 1957.

Address: Géova 13, E-28014 Madrid. Tel: (1) 319 20 27.

GASOLIBA I BOHM, Carles Alfred — Spain LDR (CDC-CiU)

Carles Alfred Gasoliba i Bohm became an MEP in 1986. Former member of the Spanish Parliament. Economist. Born November 22 1945.

Address: Valencia 231 atic, E-08007 Barcelona. Tel: (3) 487 01 11. Fax: (3) 487 12 09.

GAULLE, Charles de — France EDN (l'autre Europe)

Charles de Gaulle became an MEP during in 1993 and was elected in 1994 on the de Villiers list of Majorité pour l'autre Europe. An international lawyer. Born September 25 1948.

Address: 1 avenue du President Wilson, F-75116 Paris. Tel: (1) 47 20 85 49. Fax: (1) 49 52 00 81.

GEBHARDT, Evelyne — Germany PES (SPD)

Evelyne Gebhardt was elected in 1994. Member of the executive committee of the SPD for Baden-Württemberg. Involved with the Friedrich Ebert Foundation. A translator. Born January 19 1954.

Address: Tiefenbachstrasse 91,D-70329 Stuttgart. Tel: 0711 420 48 88. Fax: 0711 42 89 59.

GHILARDOTTI, Fiorella — Italy EUL (PDS)

Fiorella Ghilardotti was elected in 1994. Former president of Lombardy regional council. Member of the EU committee of the regions. Trade unionist. Born June 25 1946.

Address: Via Enrico Nöe 22, I-20133 Milano. Tel: (02) 70 63 15 94. Fax: (02) 70 63 15 97.

GILLIS, Alan — Ireland EPP (FG)

Alan Gillis was elected in 1994. A farmer and president of the Irish Farmers' Association, 1990-4. Elected senior vice-president of COPA in January 1993.

Address: Ballyhook House, Grangecon, Co Wicklow. Tel: (0508) 812 29. Fax (0508) 812 29.

GIL-ROBLES GIL-DELGADO, Jose Maria — Spain EPP (PP)

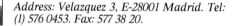

Jose Maria Gil-Robles Gil-Delgado was elected in 1989 and is a member of the EPP group bureau. Chairman of the institutional affairs committee of the outgoing Parliament. Member of the thought and action committee of European Union of Christian Democrats; founder member, People's Democratic Federation with Federation of Christian Democrats. Lawyer and former legal official of the Spanish Parliament. Born June 17 1935.

Address: Velazquez 3, E-28001 Madrid. Tel: (1) 576 0453. Fax: 577 38 20.

GIRÃO PEREIRA, José — Portugal EPP (CDSP)

José Girão Pereira was elected in 1994. A former member of the national Parliament. A lawyer. Born March 1 1938.

Address: Rua de Sao Sebastiao 118-2 dt, P-3800 Aveiro. Tel: 24 680. Fax: 38 25 31.

GLANTE, Norbert — Germany PES (SPD)

Norbert Glante was elected in 1994. An administrator in the Potsdam region 1990-4. Worked in computers and electrical engineering. Born August 8 1952.

Address: 216 rue Stevin, B-1040 Bruxelles. Siegfriedstrasse 5, D-14542 Werder. Tel: (03327) 45359. Fax: (03327) 3132 (4-3132)

GLASE, Anne-Karin — Germany EPP (CDU)

Anne-Karin Glase, a former member of the Volkskammer and a former observer from East Germany, was elected in 1994. Member of the executive committee of the Europa Union. A nurse. Born July 24 1954.

Address: Am Wald 22a, D-16816 Wustrau.

GOEPEL, Lutz — Germany EPP (CDU)

Lutz Goepel, a former member of the Volkskammer and a former observer from East Germany, was elected in 1994. Agricultural engineer. Born October 10 1942.

Address: Gartenstrasse 6, D-04720 Mochau. Tel: (03431) 3443. Fax: 03431 2971.

GOL, Jean — Belgium LDR (PVV)

Jean Gol, a former minister, was first elected in 1994. President of the Liberal Reformist Party. A doctor of law. Born February 2 1942.

Address: 16 rue des Genets, B-4052 Beaufays.

GOLDSMITH, Sir James — France EDN (l'autre Europe)

Sir James Goldsmith, president of l'autre Europe, is a businessman and financier. Anti-free trade campaigner. First elected in 1994. President of the Goldsmith foundation for the environment. Born February 2 1933.

Address: 13 rue Monsieur, F-75007 Paris. BP No 18, F-71401 Autun Cedex. Tel: (85) 86 33 54. Fax: (85) 86 33 52.

GOLLNISCH, Bruno — France Ind (FN)

Bruno Gollnisch, a vice-president of the National Front, was first elected in 1989. Member, Rhône-Alpes regional council; former deputy for Rhône. Doctor of international law and professor of Japanese at Lyon university; member of the EP delegation for relations with Japan in the outgoing Parliament. Born January 28 1950.

Address: Conseil Regional Rhone-Alpes BP 19, 78 route de Paris, F-69751 Charbonnieres-les-Bains Cedex. Tel: 78 92 41 07. Fax: 78 92 43 66.

GOMOLKA, Alfred — Germany EPP (CDU)

Alfred Gomolka was the former Prime Minister for Mecklenburg-Vorpommern and a former member of the Volkskammer. Elected to the EP in 1994. Member of regional assembly. A lecturer. Born July 21 1942.

Photograph unavailable   *Address: Ahornweg 3 D-17493 Greifswald.*

GONZALES ALVAREZ, Laura — Spain EUL (IU-IC)

Laura Gonzales Alvarez became an MEP in January 1993. Member of the Asturias regional assembly and former president of the regional council. Social worker and care assistant. Born July 9 1941.

Address: Plaza de America 10-4, E-33005 Oviedo. Tel: 525 39 00/ 525 30 78. Fax: 25 92 96. Calle Magdalena 32-7 C, E-33400 Aviles. Tel: 554 22 13.

GONZALEZ TRIVIÑO, Antonio — Spain PES (PSOE)

Antonio Gonzalez Triviño was elected in 1994. Mayor of Zaragoza. Member of the Aragon regional assembly. Factory manager. Born March 5 1951.

Address: Alcaldia Ayuntamiento, Plaza del Pilar, E-50001 Zaragoza. Tel: (3476) 39 58 77. Fax: (3476) 29 00 84.

144

GÖRLACH, Willi — Germany PES (SPD)

Willi Görlach, was elected in 1989. Former member of Hesse regional assembly and minister for agriculture and the environment in the Hesse region. A teacher. Born December 17 1940.

Address: SPD/Europaburo, Fischerfeldstrasse   7-11,   D-60311 Frankfurt/Main. Tel: (069) 29 98 88 43/42. Oberpforte 2, D-35510 Butzbach. Tel: (06033) 602 92. Fax: 06033/60292.

GRAEFE ZU BARINGDORF, Friedrich Wilhelm — Germany Verts

Friedrich Wilhelm Graefe zu Baringdorf was an MEP 1984-7 and returned in 1989. Reappointed vice-chairman of agriculture and rural development committee after the 1994 election. Former co-chairman of ARC (Rainbow) Group. Former member, Evangelical Young Farmers of Westphalian/Lippisch Young Farmers. Teacher and organic farmer. Born November 29 1942.

Address: Europagruppe Die Grunen, Agrarburo — Bundehaus, Hochhaus Tulpenfeld Zi 217, D-53113 Bonn. Tel: (0228) 16 74 13. Fax: (0228) 16 90 90. Telex: 88 65 29. Am Berningshof 2, D-32139 Spenge, Tel: (05225) 1744.

GRAZIANI, Antonio — Italy EPP (PPI)

Antonio Graziani was elected in 1994. Appointed a vice-president of the EPP Group after the 1994 election. A former senator and a former director of *Il Popolo* newspaper. Journalist. Born August 15 1930.

Address: Via I Bonomi 173, I-00193 Roma.

GREEN, Pauline · UK London North PES (Lab)

Pauline Green became president of the Socialist Group after the 1994 elections. Former leader of the Labour Group. Member of the national executive committee of Labour Party. First elected in 1989. Leading campaigner on consumer issues and chairman of the EP inter-group on consumer affairs. Former assistant parliamentary secretary, Co-operative Union Ltd, responsible for European affairs. Born December 8 1948.

Address: Gibson House, 800 High Road, Tottenham, London N17 0DH. Tel: 081 365 1892. Fax: 081 365 1894. Mobile 0850 584234. 8 Normandy Avenue, Barnet, Herts EN5 2JA, Herts. Tel (081) 449 4885. Fax: (081) 449 48 85.

GRÖNER, Lieselotte · Germany PES (SPD)

Lissy Gröner has held several posts in SPD organization. First elected to EP in 1989. Former vice-chairman of women's rights committee. Telecommunications official. Born May 31 1954.

Address: Parkstrasse 15, D-91413 Naustadt/Aisch. Tel: (09161) 10 76. Fax: (09161) 1068.

GROSCH, Mathieu · Belgium EPP (CD)

Mathieu Grosch, mayor of Kelmis and president of the council of the Germany-speaking community, was first elected in 1994. Born September 14 1950.

Address: Albert I Strasse 34, B-4720 Kelmis. Tel: (087) 65 91 53.

GROSSETÊTE, Françoise — France EPP (UDF/RPR)

François Grossetête was elected in 1994. A Rhône Alpes regional councillor and local councillor. A political adviser. Born 1946.

Address: Hotel de Ville, F-42007 Saint-Etienne Cedex. Tel: 77 42 87 39. Fax: 77 42 88 89.

GUIGOU, Elisabeth — France PES (ES)

Elizabeth Guigou is a former adviser to Jacques Delors and President Mitterand. Former minister of European affairs. First elected to EP in 1994. Regional councillor and president *l'Association Femmes d'Europe*. Appointed a vice-chairman of the institutional affairs committee in 1994. Born August 6 1946.

Address: 168 Bd du Montparnasse. F-75014 Paris.

GUINEBERTIÈRE, Armelle — France EPP (UDF/RPR)

Armelle Guinebertière was elected in 1994. A local councillor and vice-president of Poitou-Charentes regional council. Born 1944.

Address: 25 Avenue du Général Marigny, F-79140 Cerizay, Tel: (16) 49 80 02 34. Fax: (16) 49 80 05 96.

GÜNTHER, Maren   Germany EPP (CSU)

Maren Günther, who became an MEP in 1993, has been active in the European Union for Women. Teacher. Born June 18 1931.

Address: Rosenstrasse 1, D-85540 Haar. Tel/Fax: (089) 688 39 41. Rechnerstrasse 51, D-95540 Haar. Tel: (089) 460 51 40.

GUTIERREZ DIAZ, Antoni   Spain EUL (IU)

Antoni Gutierrez Diaz was first elected in 1987. Former member of the national Parliament and regional government of Catalonia. Former secretary general of the Catalonia Socialist Party. Chairman of the regional committee of the outgoing Parliament. A doctor. Born January 19 1929.

Address: Ciutat n⁰ 7, Comite Central PSUC, E-08002 Barcelona. Tel: (3) 302 74 40. Fax: (3) 412 07 38. Balmes n⁰ 349 2⁰ 4⁰, E-08006 Barcelona. Tel: (3) 417 33 62.

GYLDENKILDE, Lilli   Denmark Verts (SF)

Lilli Gyldenkilde was elected to the EP in 1994. A member of the Volketing since 1977. A former unskilled worker. Born February 12 1936.

Address: Emil Mollersgade 13, DK-8700 Horsens. Tel: 75 61 78 08.

HAARDER, Bertel — Denmark LDR (V)

Bertel Haarder, a former minister of education and research, was elected to the EP in 1994. Member of the Folketing since 1975. Born September 7 1944.

Address: AL Drewsensvej 4, DK-2100 Koben-havn 0. Tel: 31 38 13 23. Fax: 33 91 44 15.

HALLAM, David — UK Hereford and Shropshire PES (Lab)

David Hallam runs a publicity business and is a member of the Chartered Institute of Marketing. Contested Shropshire and Stafford in 1989 and 1984 Euro elections. Contested Solihull in the 1979 Westminster election. Former member of Sandwell Borough Council. Methodist lay preacher. Member of Evangelical Christians for Racial Justice; Child Poverty Action Group; supporter of Keep Sunday Special Campaign. Born June 1948; educated at Sussex University.

Address: 4 Wigorn Road, Smethwick, Warley, West Midlands, B67, 5HN. Tel: 021 429 4207. Fax: 021 429 42 07.

HÄNSCH, Klaus — Germany PES (SDP)

Klaus Hänsch was elected President of the Parliament in July 1994. First elected to EP in 1979. He has played a prominent role in foreign affairs and was chairman of the EP delegation for relations with the United States. He has lectured on foreign affairs at Duisberg University. Journalist and lecturer. Born December 15 1938.

Address: Europa-Abgeordnetenburo, Kavalleriestrasse 22/V, D-40213 Dusseldorf. Tel: (0211) 13 29 12. Fax: (0211) 13 43 30.

HANSEN, Eva Kjer | Denmark LDR (V)

Eva Kjer Hansen, a member of the Folketing since 1990, was elected to the EP in 1994. Born August 22 1964.

Address: Gl Kongevej 33, DK-6200 Abenra. Tel: 74 62 81 18. Fax: 74 62 81 16.

HAPPART, Jose | Belgium PES (PS)

Jose Happart was first elected in 1984. Former Mayor of Furons. Founder-President of movement Wallonie region d'Europe. Appointed a vice-chairman of the agriculture and rural development committee after the 1994 election. Farmer. Born March 14 1947.

Address: 23 En Feronstree, B-4000 Liege 1. Tel: (041) 23 06 69. Fax: (041) 21 15 65. 63a Rullen, B-3792 Fouron-Saint-Pierre. Tel: (041) 81 06 56.

HARDSTAFF, Veronica | UK Lincolnshire and Humberside South

Veronica Hardstaff is a French and German teacher in Sheffield. Former Sheffield councillor. Former Christain Aid organiser. Member, World Development Movement and United Nations Association. B October 1941; educated at Manchester and Cologne Universities.

Address: 64 Linaker Road, Sheffield, S6 5DT. Tel: 0742 335414.

HARRISON, Lyndon   UK Cheshire West and Wirral PES (Lab)

Lyndon Harrison was returned for this seat in 1994; gained Cheshire West for Labour in 1989. In the outgoing Parliament he was Labour spokesman and former vice-chairman of committee on rules of procedure, verification of credentials and immunities; member of committee on economic and monetary affairs and industrial policy. Former member, committee on regional policy and regional planning. Secretary, Labour group of MEPs (EPLP). Deputy chairman, North West Tourist Board, 1987-9. Member, Cheshire Council, 1982 and 1984-9. Born September 28 1947.

Address: The Labour Party, 2 Stanley Street, Chester CH1 2LB.
Tel: 0244 320623/343826. Fax: 0244 350355.

HATZIDAKIS, Constantinos   Greece EPP (ND)

Constantinos Hatzidakis was elected in 1994. President of the party's youth organisation. A lawyer. Born 1965.

Address: Ellanikou 3, GR 116 35 Athina.

HAUG, Jutta   Germany PES (SPD)

Jutta Haug, who was elected in 1994, has been an adviser to members of the Bundestag since 1987. Financial adviser. Born October 8 1951.

Address: Snirgelskamp 12c, D-45699 Herten.

151

HEINISCH, Renate — Germany EPP (CDU)

Renate Heinisch was elected in 1994. President of a local education committee. Chemist. Born December 15 1937.

Address: Kurpfaizstrasse 37, D-97944 Boxberg. Tel: (07930 2051/8851. Fax: (07930) 1797/8852.

HENDRICK, Mark — UK Lancashire PES (Lab)

Mark Hendrick was elected in 1994. A chartered electrical engineer having worked for Ministry of Defence, AEG Telefunken, and the Science and Engineering Research Council. Former lecturer. Alternate director of Manchester Airport. Salford councillor since 1987. B November 1958; educated at Salford Grammar School, Liverpool Polytechnic, and Manchester University.

Address: 20 Milton Avenue, Weaste, Salford, M5 2HG. Tel: 061 743 1648.

HERMAN, Fernand — Belgium EPP (CVP)

Fernand Herman was first elected in 1979. Minister for Economic Affairs, 1975-7; Senator for Brussels, 1977-8, and deputy for Brussels, 1978-80. Former secretary-general, Cercles populaires europeens (European people's movement). Director, National Society for Investment (SNI), 1964-75. Vice-chairman, PSC and member, EPP bureau. Former university lecturer. Born January 23 1932.

Address: 28 rue Franklin, B-1040 Bruxelles 4. Tel: 2 735 87 91. Fax: 2 736 56 45.

HERMANGE, Marie-Thérèse — France EPP (UDF/RPR)

Marie-Thérèse Hermange was elected in 1994. She is deputy mayor of Paris and vice-president of Ile-de-France regional council. Born 1947.

Address: Hotel de Ville de Paris, F-75004 Paris. Tel: (1) 42 76 57 71. Fax: (1) 42 76 65 60. 13 rue Saint-Louis en L'Isle, F-75004 Paris

HERSANT, Robert — France EPP (UDF/RPR)

Robert Hersant is the founder-president of the Hersant newspaper group which publishes *Le Figaro* and *France Soir*. He also has television interests. In 1972 he became vice-president of the National French Press Federation. First elected to EP in 1984. He was a Oise deputy, 1956-7; Mayor of Ravenel, 1953-9, and Liancourt, 1967-74; county councillor, 1954-73. Born January 31 1920.

Address: 32 rue du Calvaire, F-92210 Saint-Cloud.

HERZOG, Philippe — France EUL (PCF)

Philippe Herzog was first elected in 1989. Member, political bureau of PCF and Economic and Social Council. An economist and university professor. Born March 6 1940.

Address: 10 rue Colmet Lepinay, Appartement 111, F-93100 Montreuil. Tel: 42 87 42 11. Fax: 42 87 02 43.

153

HINDLEY, Michael   UK Lancashire East PES (Lab)

Michael Hindley was elected to the EP in 1984. Re-appointed a vice-chairman of the external economic relations committee. Co-ordinator of the former Socialist group on trade matters and former member of group bureau. Member, delegation for relations with China in the outgoing Parliament. Member, Hyndburn District Council, 1979-84 (leader, 1981-4). Contested Blackpool North in 1983 Westminster election. Former teacher in Poland and East Germany. Born April 11 1947.

Address: Old Municipal Offices, Bury Road, Haslingden BB4 5PG.
Tel: 0706 830013. Fax: 0706 830536. 27 Commercial Road, Great Harwood, Lancashire BB6 7HX. Tel: (0254) 887017.

HOFF, Magdalene   Germany PES (SDP)

Magdalene Hoff was elected in 1979. Appointed vice-president of the group after the 1994 election. Member, federal executive of SPD. Former Hagen municipal councillor. Civil engineer and lecturer on industrial safety and accident prevention. Born December 29 1940.

Address: Riegestrasse 8-10, D-58091 Hagen. Tel: (02331) 763 33. Telex: 823 132 euro d. Fax: (02331) 758 49. Zur Hohe 72A, D-58091 Hagen. Tel: (02331) 756 61.

HOPPENSTEDT, Karsten   Germany EPP (CDU)

Karsten Hoppenstedt was elected in 1989. Former Mayor of Burgwedel; district administrator, Hannover; chairman, NDR Broadcasting Council, 1988-91. Veterinary surgeon. Born April 6 1937.

Address: Hannoversche Strasse 21b, D-30938 Burgwedel. Tel: (05139) 5093/5094. Fax: (05139) 889 98. Bruchholzwiesen 21, D-30938 Burgwedel. Tel: (05139) 5332.

HORY, Jean-Francois

France PES (ER)

Jean-Francois Hory was first elected to the EP in 1989. President, *Mouvement des Radicaux de Gauche.* Town councillor at Venarey-les-Laumes (Cotes-d'Or); former deputy for Mayotte. Born May 15 1949.

Address: 50 rue du Disque, F-75013 Paris. Tel: (1) 44 24 06 13. Hotel de Ville, F-21150 Venarey les Laumes. 2 rue de l'Hopital, F-97600 Mamoudzou (Mayotte). Tel: (269) 61 12 28.

HOWITT, Richard

UK Essex South PES (Lab)

Richard Howitt was elected in 1994. A specialist in community care for the disabled. Assists voluntary groups campaigning for European funds. Chair, South East Economic Development Strategy think-tank. Leader of Harlow Council for three years. Contested Billericay in the 1987 Westminster election. B April 5 1961; educated at comprehensive school and Oxford University.

Address: 141 Guilfords, Harlow, Essex CM17 0HZ. Tel: 0459 843071; pager 0279 445370. Fax: 0279 445370.

HUGHES, Stephen

UK Durham PES (Lab)

Stephen Hughes was first elected in 1984. Appointed chairman of the social affairs and employment committee after the 1994 election. Chairman, EP all-party inter-group on peace and nuclear disarmament. Member, Amnesty International and Coalfield Communities Campaign. Vice-president of the Association of District Councils and the Federation of Industrial Development Authorities. Former local government officer and former research assistant to MEP. Former executive member, Northern Regional Labour Party. Born August 19 1952.

Address: Room 1/76, County Hall, Durham DH1 5UR. Tel: 091 384 9371. Fax: 091 384 6100. 79 Greenbank Road, Darlington, DL3 6EN. Tel: 0325 480975.

HUME, John
UK Northern Ireland PES (SDLP)

John Hume is a founder member of the SDLP and has been leader since 1979. Deputy leader, 1970-9. First elected to the EP in 1979 and is a member of the PES Group bureau and a member of the former Socialist group bureau. Won Westminster seat of Foyle in 1983 election. MP for Foyle, Northern Ireland Parliament, 1969-73. Elected for Londonderry in Northern Ireland Assembly, 1973-5; NI Constitutional Convention, 1975-6; NI Assembly, 1982-6. Member, NI Forum, 1983-4. Minister for Commerce in NI power-sharing executive, 1974. Born January 18 1937.

Address: 5 Bayview Terrace, Derry, Northern Ireland. Tel: 0504 265340. 6 West End Park, Derry, Northern Ireland. Tel: (0504) 265321.

HYLAND, Liam,
Ireland EDA (FF)

Liam Hyland was elected to the EP in 1994. Minister of State at the Department of Agriculture since 1992. A member of Dail (Irish Parliament) since 1981 and a senator 1977-81.

Address: Fearagh, Ballacolla, Portlaoise, Co Laois.

IMAZ SAN MIGUEL, Josu Jon
Spain EPP (NC)

Josu Jon Imaz San Miguel was elected in 1994. Local councillor. Chemist. Aged 30.

Address: Ibanez de Bilbao 16, Edificio Sabin Etxea, E-48001 Bilbao.

IMBENI, Renzo — Italy EUL (PDS)

Renzo Imbeni was elected in 1989. Former Mayor of Bologna. Former member of central committee and management caucus of Italian Communist Party. Born October 12 1944.

Address: Gruppo per la Sinistra Unitaria Europea, Ufficio di Bologna, Via Barbaria 4, I-40123 Bologna. Tel: (051) 29 12 96. Fax: (051) 29 12 78.

IZQUIERDO COLLADO, Juan de Bois — Spain PES (PSOE)

Juan de Bois Izquierdo Collado was elected in 1994. Former senator and member of the national Parliament. University lecturer. Born September 29 1947.

Address: Avenida del Arte 54, E-02006 Albacete. Tel: (967) 23 02 55. Fax: (967) 23 02 55.

IZQUIERDO ROJO, Maria — Spain PES (PSOE)

Maria Izquierdo Rojo, a former member of the Spanish national Parliament and Secretary of State for the regions, was elected to EP in 1989. University professor. Born November 13 1946.

Address: Vereda de Pinchos 9, E-18010 Granada. Tel: (58) 22 52 48. Fax: (58) 22 23 15.

JAC

JACKSON, Caroline   UK Wiltshire North and Bath EPP (C)

Caroline Jackson was elected for this seat in 1994; first elected MEP for Wiltshire in 1984. Appointed vice-chairman of the environment, public health and consumer protection committee in 1994. Member EPP group bureau in the outgoing Parliament and a former member of the European Democrat group bureau. Head of London office, ED (Conservative) Group, 1979-84; on the staff of the secretariat of Conservative Group, EP, Luxembourg, 1974-6. Born November 5 1946.

Address: 74 Carlisle Mansions, Carlisle Place, London SW1P 1HZ.
Tel: 071 828 6113. Fax: 071 233 5244. New House, Hanney Road, Southmoor, Abingdon, Oxon OX13 5HR. Tel: (0865) 821243.

JACOB, Christian   France EPP (UDF/RPR)

Christian Jacob, a farmer and former president of the young farmers organisation, was elected in 1994. Appointed chairman of the agriculture and rural development committee. Born 1959.

Address: 123 rue de Lille, F-75340 Paris. Tel (1) 49 55 63 00. Germe de la Berge, F-77141 Vaudoy en Brie. tel 64 07 51 22. Fax: 64 07 51 85.

JANSSEN van RAAY, James   Netherlands EPP (CDA)

James Janssen van Raay was an MEP in 1979-84 and returned in 1986. Chairman, International Federation of Professional Footballers. Vice-chairman, CDA, 1975-80; member, Rotterdam council, 1977-80. Honorary consul, Republic of Singapore. Lawyer and public prosecutor. Born June 1 1932.

Address: Postbus 4402, 3006 AK Rotterdam. Tel: 31 10 4042 538. fax: (010 404 24 60). Westzeedijk 200, 3016 AM Rotterdam. Tel: (010) 436 44 38.

158

JARZEMBOWSKI, Georg   Germany EPP (CDU)

Georg Jarzembowski has been an MEP since September 1991. Former member of Hamburg regional assembly. Member, CDU Hamburg regional executive; member, CDU national foreign policy committee; member Hamburg city council, 1979-91; expert adviser to Hamburg judiciary, 1979-91; deputy chairman, central Hamburg CDU. Lawyer and civil servant. Born February 3 1947.

Address: CDU-Europaburo, Poststrasse 11, D-20354 Hamburg. Tel: (40) 36 81 24 72. Fax: (40) 36 81 25 27. Parkallee 43, D-20144 Hamburg. Tel: (40) 45 45 37.

JEAN PIERRE, Thierry   France EDN (l'autre Europe)

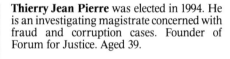

Thierry Jean Pierre was elected in 1994. He is an investigating magistrate concerned with fraud and corruption cases. Founder of Forum for Justice. Aged 39.

Address: 19 rue Abraham, F-72000 Le Mans. Tel: (1) 43 76 69 12. Fax: 43 76 69 12.

JENSEN, Kirsten   Denmark PES (S)

Kirsten Jensen was first elected in 1989. Former member, Socialist group bureau. Chairman, delegation for relations with Estonia, Latvia and Lithuania in the outgoing Parliament. A journalist. Born March 3 1961.

Address: Socialdemokratiet, Thorvaldensvej 2, DK-1780 Kobenhavn V. Tel: 31 39 15 22. Fax: 31 39 40 30.

JENSEN, Lis — Denmark EDN (Anti-EU)

Lis Jensen, a social worker with a trade union, was elected in 1994. Born July 6 1952.

Address: Norregade 33, DK-9490 Pandrup. Tel: 98 24 01 65.

JÖNS, Karin — Germany PES (SPD)

Karin Jöns was elected in 1994. Head of the Bremen-EU liaison office. Journalist. Born April 29 1953.

Address: SPD Europanüro, Findorffstrasse,106, D-28215 Bremen. Tel: 0421 350 1817. Fax: 0421 74189.

JOVE PERES, Salvador — Spain EUL (IU-IC)

Salvador Jove Peres was elected in 1994. Head of an agricultural company. Economist. Born December 28 1941.

Address: General Rodrigo 6 6a planta, E-28003 Madrid. Tel: 55 34 909. Fax: 53 49 747.

JUNCKER, Jean-Claude — Luxembourg PES (CSV)

Jean-Claude Juncker was elected to the EP in 1994 but was re-appointed to the Government and did not take his seat. Former minister of finance and employment and member of the Chamber of Deputies. President of the Christian Social Party. Lawyer. Born December 9 1954.

Photograph unavailable

Address: 37 route d'Arlon, L-8310 CAP.

JUNKER, Karin — Germany PES (SPD)

Karin Junker was first elected to EP in 1979. Appointed vice-chairman of the ACP-EU assembly after the 1994 election; a former member. Member of the SPD executive. Member of the Council of West German radio. Journalist. Born December 24 1940.

Address: Feldstrasse 82, D-40479 Dusseldorf. Tel: (0211) 498 31 84. Fax: (0211) 491 18 30.

KAKLAMANIS, Nikitas — Greece EDA (POLA)

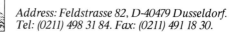

Nikitas Kaklamanis was elected in 1994. Former member of the national Parliament. Doctor and university professor. Born 1947.

Address: Loukianou 25, GR-106 75 Athina. Tel: (01) 72 93 234 - 72 14 026. Fax (01) 72 93 235.

KATIFORIS, Georgios   Greece PES (PASOK)

Georgios Katiforis was elected in 1994. Former adviser to the prime minister. Former professor at University College, London. Economist. Born 1935.

Address: Alopekis 51, GR-106 76 Athina, Tel (01) 72 29 408.

KELLETT-BOWMAN, Edward   UK Itchen, Test and Avon EPP (C)

Edward Kellett-Bowman, who won this seat in 1994, was MEP for Lancashire East, 1979-84, and for Hampshire Central, 1988-94. Treasurer of Conservative MEPs since 1992. He is married to Dame Elaine Kellett-Bowman, Conservative MP for Lancaster and former MEP for Cumbria. Business and management consultant; Freeman, City of London; liveryman, Worshipful Company of Wheelwrights. Born February 25 1931.

Address: 18A Bargates, Christchurch, Dorset BH23 1QL. Tel 0202 473500. Fax: 0202 474949. Naishes Barn, Newnham, Basingstoke, Hampshire, RG27 9AF. Tel: 0256 766103. Fax: 0256 763333.

KEPPELHOFF-WIECHERT, Helwig   Germany, EPP (CDU)

Helwig Keppelhoff-Wiechert was elected in 1989. President and former chairman of the Deutscher Landfrauenverband, the German federation of women farmers. Member, bureau, Westphalia-Lippe Agricultural Association. Member, general assembly of Westphalia-Lippe Chamber of Agriculture; North Rhine-Westphalia Land CDU directoral committee. Chairman, National Farm Holidays Co-operative. Born May 31 1939.

Address: Bienwall 81, D-46325 Borken. Tel (02861) 650 61. Fax: (02861) 643 75. Coesfelderstrasse 104, D-46342 Velen. Tel: (02863) 12 44.

KERR, Hugh   UK Essex West and Hertfordshire East PES (Lab)

Hugh Kerr is a university lecturer specialising in European social policy. Visiting professor in United States and Canada. Harlow councillor and member, West Essex Community Health Council. Director of Harlow Playhouse. Aged 49.

Address: 14 Home Close, Harlow, Essex, CM20 3PD. Tel: 071 607 2789. Fax: 0279 414464

KESTELYN-SIERENS, Mimi   Belgium LDR (PVV)

Mimi Kestelyn-Sierens, a former member of the Chamber of Deputies, was elected to the EP in 1994. President of the Flemish Institute for the self-employed. Has worked in the field of economics and health care. Born May 28 1945.

Address: Bisschopsdreef 40, B-8310 Sint Kruis (Brugge). tel: 050/35 13 25. Fax: 050/35 86 99.

KILLILEA, Mark   Ireland EDA (FF)

Mark Killilea, a former farmer, became an MEP in 1987 and was re-elected in 1989 and 1994. Dail deputy for Galway West, 1981-2 and Galway East, 1977-81. Minister of State, Department of Posts and Telegraphs, 1979-81. Senator, Labour panel, 1982-7 and 1969-77. Born September 1939; educated at St Jarlath's Coll, Tuam, Co Galway.

Address: Caherhugh House, Belclare, Tuam, Co Galway. Tel: (093) 55414. Fax: (093) 55386.

KINDERMANN, Heinz   Germany PES (SPD)

Heinz Kindermann was elected in 1994. A veterinary surgeon. Born June 20 1942.

Address: Jüterizer Strasse 13, D-17336 Strasbourg. Tel: (039753) 217 37.

KINNOCK, Glenys   UK South Wales South PES (Lab)

Glenys Kinnock won this seat in 1994. She is the wife of the former Labour Party leader, Neil Kinnock. She is a teacher specialising in reading development. Chair and co-founder of One World Action, a development agency. Appointed vice-chairman of the ACP-EU joint assembly. On the UK executive of Unicef and trustee of Canon Collins Trust. Vice-president of Council of University of Wales, Cardiff. Special interests include overseas development and women's rights. Member of Co-operative Party, Amnesty and Anti-Apartheid. B July 1944.

Address: 8 Mount Avenue, London, W5 2RG. Tel: 0495 225974. 28 Sir Ivors Road, Blackwood NP2 2JH. Tel: 0495 225974. Fax: 0495 225974.

KITTELMANN, Peter   Germany EPP (CDU)

Peter Kittelmann, a member of the Bundestag since 1976, was elected to the EP in 1994. Vice-president of the CDU in Berlin. Member of the Council of European and Western European Union. A Lawyer. Born July 17 1936.

Address: Im Dol 15, D-14195 Berlin.

KLASS, Christa   Germany EPP (CDU)

Christa Klass was elected in 1994. Local councillor and president of the Rheinland-Nassau country women's association. Teacher. Born November 7 1951.

Address: Moselstrasse 35, D-54518 Osann Monzel. Tel: 06535 1446.

KLIRONOMOS, Constantinos   Greece PES (PASOK)

Constantinos Klironomos was elected in 1994. Mayor of Heraklion and a member of the EU committee of the regions. A lawyer. Born 1940.

Address: Pl Kallergon 11, GR 712 01 Iraklio Kritis. Tel: (081) 33 08 98. Fax: (081) 33 08 87.

KOCH, Dieter-Lebrecht   Germany EPP (CDU)

Dieter-Lebrecht Koch, a former member of the Volkskammer and East German observer at the EP, was elected in 1994. Architect. Born January 7 1953.

Address: Rembrandtweg 1, D-99423 Weimar. Tel: (03643) 646 16. Fax: (03643) 646 16.

KOFOED, Niels Anker   Denmark LDR (V)

Niels Anker Kofoed, former Danish Minister of Agriculture and Fishing, and a member of Folketing (Danish Parliament), was a member of the nominated European Parliament 1975-78 and was elected in 1989. A vice-president of the Parliament, 1989-92. Former vice-chairman, LDR Group. A farmer. Born February 21 1929.

Address: Folketinget, Christiansborg, DK-1240 Kobenhavn K. Tel: 33 37 55 00. Knarregard, DK-3730 Nekso. Tel: 56 49 21 04.

KOKKOLA, Angela   Greece PES (PASOK)

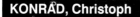

Angela Kokkola was elected in 1994. Founder-member of PASOK and a member of its central committee. Former political adviser to the Prime Minister. Born 1932.

Address: Lykavittou 39, GR 106 72 Athina.

KONRÅD, Christoph   Germany EPP (CDU)

Christoph Konrad was elected in 1994. President of local association of small businesses. Manager of a travel company. Born August 28 1957.

Address: Harpener Hellweg 12, D-44791 Bochum. Tel: 0234 59 11 06. Fax: 0234 50 30 90.

KOUCHNER, Bernard   France PES (ES)

Bernard Kouchner, who was elected in 1994, is founder and president of the aid organisations *Médecins Sans Frontières* and *Médecins du Monde.* Appointed chairman of the development and co-operation committee in 1994. Former health minister, social affairs secretary and foreign affairs secretary. A gastro-enterologist. Born November 1 1939.

Address: 4 rue Guyemer, F-75006 Paris.

KRARUP, Ole   Denmark END (Anti-EU)

Ole Krarup, a lawyer and university lecturer, was elected in 1994. Born March 17 1935.

Address: Det Retsvidenskabelige Institut B, Studiestraede 6, DK-1455 Kobenhavn K. Tel: 35 22 31 05. Fax: 35 32 32 01.

KREHL, Constanze   Germany PES (SDP)

Constanze Krehl, a former member of the Volkskammer and the Bundestag and a former East German observer at the EP, was elected in 1994. Computer worker. Born October 14 1956.

Address: Herlossohnstrasse 12, D-04155 Leipzig.

KREISSL-Dörfler, Wolfgang   Germany Verts (Grüne)

Wolfgang Kreissl-Dörfler was elected in 1994. Agricultural specialist and overseas aid worker. Born December 1 1950.

Address: Faberstrasse 13, D-81373 München. tel 089 769 54 75.

KRISTOFFERSEN, Frode   Denmark EPP (KF)

Frode Kristoffersen, an MEP in 1988-9, was re-elected in 1994. A television journalist with spells in various European capitals. Born August 9 1931.

Address: Haderslevvej 94, DK-6200 Abenra. Tel: (74) 63 13 73.

KUCKELKORN, Wilfried   Germany PES (SDP)

Wilfried Kuckelkorn was elected in 1994. Car worker and trade union official. Born August 30 1943.

Address: Hohe Strasse 83, D-50129 Bergheim-Glessen. Tel: (02238) 438 41. Fax: (0221) 901 28 78.

168

KUHN, Annemarie — Germany PES (SPD)

Annemarie Kuhn has been an MEP since 1990. Former local councillor. Holds a variety of posts in the party. Trade union official. Born May 9 1937.

Address: Kaiserstrasse 26-30, D-55116 Mainz. Tel: (06131) 23 81 59. Fax: (06131) 287 28 25. Eichendorfstrasse 59, D-55122 Mainz, Tel: (06131) 38 75 58.

KUHNE, Helmut — Germany PES (SPD)

Helmut Kuhne was elected in 1994. Local councillor. Member of the Council of West German radio. Sociologist. Born September 6 1949.

Address: Akazienstrasse 1, D-59505 Bad Sassendorf.

LAGE, Carlos — Portugal PES (PS)

Carlos Lage was elected in 1994. Former member of the national Parliament. Teacher. Born November 21 1944.

Address: Rua Monte dos Burgos 161-11, P-4200 Porto. tel (02) 81 47 02.

LAIGNEL, André — France PES (ES)

André Laignel, a former secretary of state for vocational training and planning and a former member of the National Assembly, was elected to the EP in 1994. Mayor of Issoudun. Doctor of law. Born December 12 1942.

Address: 4 Place du Marché anx Légumes, F-36100 Issoudin. Tel 54 21 31 55. Fax: 54 03 36 30.

LALUMIÈRE, Catherine — France PES (ER)

Catherine Lalumière was elected in 1994. Former minister and former member of the National Assembly. Outgoing secretary-general of the Council of Europe. Local councillor. Born August 3 1935.

Address: 65 rue Notre Dame des Champs, F 75006 paris. Tel: 43 25 77 32.

LAMBRAKI, Irini — Greece PES (PASOK)

Irini Lambraki was elected in 1994. Former member of the national Parliament and a member of the Council of Europe. Lawyer. Born 1949.

Address: Omirou 60, GR-106 72 Athina. Tel 01 36 05 381. Fax: 01 36 19 248.

LAMBRIAS, Panayotis — Greece EPP (ND)

Panayotis Lambrias is a journalist, lawyer and former secretary-general, Greek National Tourist Office. First elected to EP in 1984. Re-appointed a vice-president of the EPP Group after the 1994 election. Member of national Parliament and state secretary attached to president's office, 1974-7; secretary of state for tourism, 1977-81. Translated and supplemented Unesco's three-volume dictionary of social sciences. Responsible for Greek edition of General de Gaulle's memoirs and Greek edition of Time-Life Science Library. Born September 1 1926.

Addresses: Akadimias 35, GR-106 72 Athina. Tel: (1) 364 16 11. Neophytou Vamva 10, GR-106 71 Athina. Tel: (1) 723 04 89.

LA MALFA, Girogio — Italy LDR (PRI)

Girogio La Malfa was first elected in 1989. Former minister and member of the Chamber of Deputies. Former leader of the Italian republican party. Doctor of law and university lecturer. Born October 13 1939.

Address: Via del Tritone 46, I-00187 Roma. Tel (06) 678 67 55. Fax: (06) 678 16 67.

LANG, Carl — France Ind (FN)

Carl Lang, who was elected in 1994, is secretary-general of the National Front. Member of Nord Pas de Calais regional council. Physiotherapist. Born March 20 1957.

Address: 8 rue de Général Clergerie, F-27200 Vernon. Tel: 32 21 58 87.

LANG, Jack — France PES (ES)

Jack Lang is a former minister of culture and education and a former member of the National Assembly. Elected to EP in 1994. Mayor of Blois. Born September 2 1939.

Address: 3 Places de Vosges, F-75004 Paris. Tel: 42 74 55 15.

LANGE, Bernd — Germany PES (SPD)

Bernd Lange was elected in 1994. Leader of local party. Teacher. Born November 11 1955.

Address: Odeonstrasse 15/16, D30159 Hannover. tel (0511) 1674 210/269. Fax: (0511) 167 42 63.

LANGEN, Werner — Germany EPP (CDU)

Werner Langen was elected in 1994. Local councillor. Member of the Rheinland-Pfalz regional assembly and former agricultural minister for the region. Former president of the party in Rheinland-Pfalz. Economist. Born November 27 1949.

Address: Müdenerberg 17, D-56254 Muden (Mosel).

LANGENHAGEN, Brigitte — Germany EPP (CDU)

Brigitte Langenhagen became an MEP in November 1990. Chairman, Cuxhaven district party; member, regional executive, Europa-Union Deutschland, Lower Saxony. Former member, Cuxhaven town council, Cuxhaven district assembly and deputy chief administration officer of district until 1991. Deputy chairman, CDU regional association, Stade. Former regional chairman of FU (the CDU women's union) Stade; member, regional executive, Lower Saxony FU, and until 1991 chairman of FU Cuxhaven; now a co-opted member. Worked in the food industry. Born December 8 1939.

Addresses: Heinrichstrasse 8, D-27472 Cuxhaven. Tel: (04721) 527 44. Fax: (04721) 527 45.

LANGER, Alexander — Italy Verts (Verdi)

Alexander Langer, a founder of the Green movement in Italy, was elected to EP in 1989. Former co-president of the Green Group. Former member, Trentine regional council; member South Tyrol regional council, 1978-81 and 1983-8. A director of league for the environment. Campaigner to unite linguistic groups of Alto Adige and for an inter-ethnic alternative to German/Italian problems in his native South Tyrol. Teacher, university professor, translator and journalist. Born February 22 1946.

Address: Gruppo Verde/Fraktion die Grunen, Via Crispi 9, I-39100 Bolzano/Bozen.
Tel: (0471) 99 30 15. Fax: (0471) 97 84 44.

LANNOYE, Paul — Belgium Verts (Green)

Paul Lannoye is a founder member of the Belgian Green Party, Ecolo, and of Friends of the Earth in the Seventies. First elected in 1989. Joint chairman of the Green group. Former federal secretary of Ecolo. Councillor in Namur, 1982-8. A research scientist at University of Namur. Born Jun 22 1939.

Address: 28 Rue Basse-Marcelle, B-5000 Namur. Tel: (081) 22 78 71. Fax: (081) 23 06 03. 81 rue des Nobles, B-5003 Saint-Marc (Namur). Tel: (081) 73 21 17.

LARIVE, Jessica — Netherlands LDR (VVD)

Jessica Larive was elected in 1984 and is a former vice-chairman of the LDR Group. International civil servant, 1973-8. Member of the staff of EP Liberal and Democratic Group, 1979-84. A lawyer. Born November 24 1945.

Address: Europees Parlement, Van Maerlantgebouw, Burau 9-24, B-1047 Brussel. Tel: (2) 284 56 06. Fax: (2) 284 96 06.

LE CHEVALLIER, Jean-Marie — France Ind (FN)

Jean-Marie le Chevallier was first elected in 1984 when Jean-Marie Le Pen's principal private secretary. Former treasurer of Technical Group of European Right (DR). Former member, Economic and Social Council. Municipal councillor, Toulon; former deputy for Var. President of *Toulon Ecologie*. Director general, Rennes Chamber of Commerce and Industry, 1965-76; administrator, Pinault-Investments Society. Born November 22 1936.

Address: 1 rue Silvain, BP 564, F-83054 Toulon Cedex. Tel: 94 31 05 38.

LEHNE, Klaus-Heiner — Germany EPP (CDU)

Klaus-Heiner Lehne, a member of the Bundestag since 1992, was elected to the EP in 1994. A lawyer. Born October 28 1957.

Address: Ziegeleiweg 52, D-40591 Düsseldorf.

LENZ, Marlene — Germany EPP (CDU)

Marlene Lenz was elected in 1979. President of the European section of the CDU/CSU women. Chairman, EP committee on women's rights, 1984-7, A vice-chairman in 1979-84 Parliament of committee of inquiry into situation of women in Europe. Chairman, political committee, European Union of Women. General secretary, European Women's Union, 1967-71; adviser to external relations office, CDU federal headquarters, 1972-5. Member, Bundestag committee for EC affairs. Translator and EC Commission official, 1958-68. Born July 4 1932.

Address: Burgstrasse 102, D-53177 Bonn. Tel: (0228) 31 38 45.

LEOPARDI, Giacomo — Italy FE (FI)

Giacomo Leopardi was elected in 1994. A chemist and university lecturer. President of the national federation of chemistry. Member of the national health committee and training committee for pharmacists in the European Union. Born December 19 1928.

Address: Via F Martini 16, I-00137 Roma. Tel (06) 827 03 85. Fax: (06) 87 19 35 37.

LE PEN, Jean-Marie — France Ind (FN)

Jean-Marie Le Pen has been president of the National Front since 1972. First elected to EP in 1984 and was leader of the European Right Group in the outgoing Parliament. Contested French presidential election in 1974 and in 1989 he unsuccessfully stood for Presidency of the Parliament. Former member of the National Assembly and member of Provence-Côte d'Azur regional council. Paratroop officer in Indo-China in 1954. Born June 20 1928.

Address: 8 Parc de Montretout, F-92210 Saint Cloud. Tel: (1) 46 02 50 40. Fax: (1) 46 02 20 74.

LE RACHINEL, Fernand   France Ind (FN)

Fernand Le Rachinel was elected in 1994. Member, Basse Normandie regional council. Born 1942.

Address: La Chevalerie, BP 403, F-50003 Saint Lo Cedex. Tel: 33 05 67 67. Fax: 33 57 83 54.

LIESE, Hans-Peter   Germany EPP (CDU)

Hans-Pieter Liese was elected in 1994. Local councillor. Doctor. Born May 20 1965.

Address: Haupstrasse 23, D-59909 Bestwig.

LIGABUE, Giancarlo   Italy FE (FI)

Giancarlo Ligabue was elected in 1994. Businessman and explorer. Chairman of a travel company. Adviser to the World Wildlife Fund. Born January 30 1931.

Address: San Marco 3319, I-30124 Venezia. Tel: (041) 528 61 34. Fax: (041) 270 56 61.

LINDEPERG, Michèle — France PES (ES)

Michèle Lindeperg was elected in 1994. A local councillor. Teacher. Born October 20 1941.

Address: 3 rue Camelinat, F-42000 Saint Etienne. tel: 77 38 09 51. fax: 77 47 26 26.

LINKOHR, Rolf — Germany PES (SPD)

Rolf Linkohr was first elected in 1979. A physicist who worked as a physics engineer with an oil company, and author of publications on science and technology. Re-appointed to EP energy and research committee after 1994 election. Chairman of Stuttgart SPD from 1977, member since 1972. Born March 11 1941.

Address: Asangstrasse 219a, D-70329 Stuttgart. Tel: (0711) 32 49 45. Werastrasse 10, D-70182 Stuttgart. Tel: (0711) 23 24 65. Fax: (0711) 60 82 67.

LOMAS, Alfred — UK London North East PES (Lab)

Alfred Lomas was first elected in 1979 and was leader of British Labour Group, 1985-7; former deputy leader. Secretary, London Co-operative Political Committee, 1965-79, and member, London regional executive, Labour Party. Vice-president, institute for workers' control and British peace assembly. Railway signalman, 1951-9; Labour Party secretary/agent, 1959-65. Born April 30 1928.

Address: Suite 2, 2nd Floor, 78/102 The Broadway, Stratford, London E15 1NL. Tel: (081) 519 8114. Fax: 081 503 0028. 28 Brookway, London SE3 9BJ.

LUCAS PIRES, Francisco   Portugal EPP (PSD)

Francisco Lucas Pires has been an MEP since 1986. Former minister for culture and former member of the national Parliament. Former vice-president of the EP. Member of EPP bureau in the outgoing Parliament. Former member of the Council of Europe. Former vice-president of the European Union of Christian Democrats and former president of the CDS. Lawyer and professor at University of Coimbra. Born September 15 1944.

Address: Rua Joaquim Antonio de Aguiar 27-5, P-1000 Lisboa. Tel: (1) 38 60 584/38 60 468 and (1) 38 61 472/38 64 084. Fax: (1) 38 64 061.

LÜTTGE, Gunter   Germany PES (SPD)

Gunter Lüttge was elected in 1989. Mayor of Ihlow; member, regional government of Mieder-Saxony. Teacher. Born July 8 1938.

Addresses: Ringstrasse 44, D-26721 Emden. Tel: (04921) 290 17/18. Fax: (04921) 323 93.

MACARTNEY, Allan   UK Scotland North East ERA (SNP)

Allan Macartney won this seat from Labour in 1994 having contested it in 1989. Senior vice-convenor of the SNP and spokesman on foreign affairs. A staff tutor with the Open University, freelance broadcaster and author. Born in Ghana, the son of a Church of Scotland minister, he spent some years teaching in Africa. Speaks German, French and Dutch as well as a number of African languages. Member of the executive, European Movement in Scotland and president, United Nations Association in Edinburgh. Born February 1941.

Address: SNP Rooms 78 Menzies Road, Aberdeen, AB1. Tel 0226 899010. 15 Clarence Street, Edinburgh, EH3 5AE. Tel 031 556 7619.

McCARTHY, Arlene °
UK Peak District PES (Lab)

Arlene McCarthy is head of European affairs for Kirklees Council. Campaigner for European funds for areas facing decline in their coal and textile industries. Has a degree from Manchester University in French/German and international politics and a PhD; former lecturer on European policy at the Free University of Berlin. Vice-chair, national group of European officers. Born October 10 1962.

Address: 19 Queen Street, Glossop, Derbyshire, SK13 8EL. Tel: 0484 442359 or 0457 857090.

McCARTIN, John Joseph
° Ireland EPP (FG)

Joe McCartin was first elected in 1979. Leader of the Irish delegation within the EPP Group and member of EPP bureau. Member of the Dail 1981-9; senator, 1973-81 (vice-president of Senate, 1977-81). Former member Leitrum County Council. Former member of the general council of committees of agriculture (chairman, 1970-2). Former farmer and businessman. Born April 24 1939.

Address: Mullyaster, Newtowngore, Carrick-on-Shannon, Co Leitrum. Tel: 049 33490 (home); 049 33395 (office).

McGOWAN, Michael
UK Leeds PES (Lab)

Michael McGowan was first elected in 1984. Former journalist, television and radio producer. Former member, Leeds City Council; West Riding County Council; and Spenborough Council. Contested Brighouse and Spenborough in 1979 Westminster election, and Ripon in 1966. Born May 19 1940.

Address: Civic Hall, Leeds, West Yorkshire LS1 1UR. Tel: 0532 476961. Fax: 0532 442163. 3 Grosvenor Terrace, Otley, West Yorkshire LS21 1HJ. Tel: 0943 462864.

McINTOSH Anne   UK Essex North and Suffolk South EPP (C)

Anne McIntosh won this seat in 1994; MEP for Essex North East, 1989-94. Contested Workington in 1987 Westminster election. Political adviser with European Democratic (Conservative) Group in EP, 1983-9. Admitted to Faculty of Advocates in 1982; practised European law in Community Law Office, Brussels, 1982-3. Member, executive council, Conservative Association in Belgium. Born September 20 1954.

Address: Conservative Office, The Old Armoury, Museum Street, Saffron Walden, Essex, CB10 1JN. Tel: 0799 523631. Fax: 0799 523631.

McKENNA, Patricia   Ireland Verts (Green)

Patrica McKenna was elected in 1994. Founding member of the Women's Environmental Network. Co-secretary of the European Greens. Led a High Court challenge to the Government on the funding of the Maastricht referendum campaign. Born March 13 1957.

Address: 12 Heytesbury Street, Dublin 8.

McMAHON, Hugh   UK Strathclyde West PES (Lab)

Hugh McMahon was first elected in 1984. Vice-chairman of the social affairs, employment and working environment committee in the outgoing Parliament. Contested Angus North and Mearns in 1979 Westminster election. Member, Scottish executive, Labour party, 1980-3. Chairman, Scottish council, Fabian Society, 1979-84; socialist education association of Scotland, 1978-82. Former teacher. Born June 17 1938.

Address: Constituency Office, 9 Low Road, Paisley, PA2 6AQ. Tel: 041 889 9990. Fax: 041 889 4790.

McMILLAN-SCOTT, Edward   UK Yorkshire North EPP (C)

Edward McMillan-Scott won this seat in 1994; MEP for York, 1984-94. Conservative spokesman on foreign affairs and security committee and its subcommittee on security and disarmament in the outgoing Parliament. Member, general council, Conservative group for Europe. Political consultant, 1976-84; political adviser to Falkland Islands Government, London Office, 1983-4; tour director in Europe, Scandinavia, Africa and USSR, 1968-75 and tourism campaigner; coordinator of campaign against timeshare fraud. Born August 15 1949.

Address: Wick House Farm, Wick, Pershore, Worcestershire, WR10 3NU. Tel: 0386 552366. Fax: 0386 556038.

McNALLY, Eryl   UK Bedfordshire and Milton Keynes PES (Lab)

Eryl McNally was elected in 1994 and appointed a vice-chairman of the energy, research and technology committee. Deputy leader of Hertfordshire County Council. Member, Amnesty International, Friends of the Earth, Fabian Society. Former school inspector for foreign languages. Born April 1942; educated at Newbridge Grammar School, Gwent and Bristol and Swansea Universities.

Address: 146 Abbots Road, Abbots Langley, Hertfordshire, WO5 0BL. Tel: 0923 264525. Fax 0923 270608.

MAIJ-WEGGEN, Hanja   Netherlands EPP (CDA)

Hanja Maij-Weggen was Minister of Transport when she was re-elected in 1994. MEP in 1979-89 when she resigned on becoming Minister for Communications. Former vice-chairman of EPP Group with responsibility for international relations and links with Christian Democrat International and European organizations. She has held various posts in the Anti-Revolutionary Party and CDA. Former member of the executive of the Dutch Women's Council. A nurse. Born December 29 1943.

Photograph unavailable

Address: Aquariuslaan 53, 5632 BB Eindhoven. Tel: (040) 41 63 10. Fax: (040) 48 24 58.

MALANGRE, Kurt — Germany EPP (CDU)

Kurt Malangre was elected in 1979. Joined Aachen municipal council in 1969; Burgomaster of Aachen, 1971-3, and Chief Burgomaster, 1973-89. Chairman, Aachen district CDU, since 1989. A lawyer. Born September 18 1934.

Address: Wilhelmstrasse 2, D-52070 Aachen. Tel: (0241) 44802/24243. Fax (0241) 40 36 85.

MALERBA, Franco — Italy FE (FI)

France Malerba, an astronaut and researcher at the European Space Agency, was elected in 1994. Born October 10 1946.

Address: Via Cantore 10, I-16149 Genova. Tel: (0330) 25 20 86. Fax: (010) 42 19 19.

MALONE, Bernie — Ireland PES (Lab)

Bernie Malone became a member of the EP in February 1994 and was re-elected in June 1994. Appointed vice-president of the PES after the 1994 election. Former leader of Dublic County Council and a county councillor 1979-94. Born March 26 1948.

Photograph unavailable

Address: Elmhill, 18 Grove Road, Malahide, Co Dublin. Tel (1) 845 30 85. Fax: (1) 661 03 91.

MAMÈRE, Noël   France PES (ER)

Noël Mamère was elected in 1994. Mayor of Bègles and a regional councillor. Vice-president of *Generation Ecologie* movement. Born December 25 1948.

Address: 16 rue Béranger, F-75003 Paris. 14 rue St Louis en l'Ile, F-75004 Paris. Tel (1) 44 41 62 12/13/15/16. Fax: 40 46 05 12.

MANISCO, Lucio   Italy EUL (RC)

Lucio Manisco was elected in 1994. Former member of the Chamber of Deputies. Journalist. Born February 16 1928.

Address: Via C Beccaria 88, I-00196 Roma. Tel: 06 361 33 42. Fax: 06 361 33 42.

MANN, Erika   Germany PES (SPD)

Erika Mann was elected in 1994. A local councillor in Nordheim. Educationist. Born November 2 1950.

Address: Klostergut Schachtenbeck, D-37581 Bad Gandersheim, Tel: (05382) 26 67. fax: (05382) 26 41.

183

MANN, Thomas   Germany EPP (CDU)

Thomas Mann was elected in 1994. Former president of Young Workers' Association and local party office holder. Works in advertising. Born January 28 1946.

Address: Württemberger Strasse 11, D-65824 Schwalbach am Taunus.

MANZELLA, Andrea   Italy PES (PDS)

Andrea Manzella was elected in 1994. University lecturer. Born December 8 1933.

Address: Centro Studi NR, Corso Vittorio Emanuele 269, I-00186 Roma. tel: 68 75 00. Fax: 68 80 56 96.

MARIN, Marilena   Italy Ind (Lega Nord)

Marilena Marin was elected in 1994. Member of the Chamber of Deputies. Secretary of the Veneta branch of the Lega Nord movement. Former regional councillor. Teacher. Born July 24 1947.

Address: Piazza Calvi 90 I-31015 Conegliano Veneto (TV). Tel: (0438) 32301

MARINHO, Luis Portugal PES (PS)

Luis Marinho was elected in 1987. Appointed a vice-president of the PES Group after the 1994 election. Deputy in the Portuguese national assembly, 1976-86. Lawyer. Born June 5 1949.

Address: Rua Antonio Feliciano de Castiho, 111 D-9* Dt, P-3000 Coimbra. Tel: (39) 71 66 93.

MARINUCCI, Elena Italy PES (PSI-AD)

Elena Marinucci was elected in 1994. Former senator. Journalist. Born August 18 1928.

Address: Via F Crispi 3, I-67100 L'Aquila. Tel 41 34 05. Fax: 42 00 28.

MARRA, Alfonso Italy FE (FI)

Alfonso Marra was elected in 1994. A lawyer and writer. Born December 18 1947.

Address: Centro Direzionale, Edifico G1,I-80143 Napoli. Tel (081) 787 91 66. Fax: (081) 787 90 05.

MARSET CAMPOS, Pedro · Spain EUL (IU-IC)

Pedro Marset Campos was elected in 1994. Member of the federal council of the Izquierda Unida party and the Communist Party. Doctor and university lecturer. Born September 11 1941.

Address: Princesa 3, E-30002 Murcia. Tel: (68) 21 34 35.

MARTENS, Wilfried · Belgium EPP (CD)

Wilfried Martens, Belgian Prime Minister, 1979-91, and a member of the Chamber of Deputies since 1974, was first elected to the EP in 1994. Appointed new leader of the EPP Group after the 1994 election. A lawyer. Born April 19 1936.

Address: Overwinningstraat 16, B-1060 Brussel. Tel (02) 537 86 06. Fax: (02) 354 66 76.

MARTIN, David · UK Lothians PES (Lab)

David Martin, who was first elected in 1984, was a vice-president in the outgoing parliament and was re-elected a vice-president in July 1994. Leader of British Labour MEPs, 1987-8. Member, Lothian Regional Council, 1982-4. He formerly worked in accountancy and finance. Born August 26 1954.

Address: 4 Lothian Street, Dalkeith, Midlothian, EH22 1DS. Tel: 031 654 1606 Fax: 031 654 1607.

MARTIN, Philippe   France EDN (l'autre Europe)

Philippe Martin was elected in 1994. Former member of the national assembly, local councillor and Mayor of Cumières A wine grower and vice-president of the local wine growers' organisation. Aged 45.

Address: Hotel de Ville, F-51200 Cumieres.

MARTINEZ, Jean-Claude   France Ind (FN)

Jean-Claude Martinez became an MEP during 1989-94 Parliament. Former member of the national assembly. Member, Languedoc Rousillon regional council. President of farmers' organisation. University lecturer. Born July 30 1945.

Address: Enclos Fontaines, Batiment Ivoire, rue du Curat, F-34000 Montpellier.
Tel: 67 72 84 44.

MATHER, Graham   UK Hampshire North and Oxfordshire EPP (C)

Graham Mather, who won this seat in 1994, has been president of the European Policy Forum since 1992. Director general, Institute of Economic Affairs, 1987-92; head of policy unit, Institute of Directors, 1980-86. Member, European manifesto sub-group, 1992. Member, Monopolies and Mergers Commission. Contested Blackburn in the 1983 Westminster election. Member, Westminster Council, 1982-6. Visting fellow, Nuffield College, Oxford. Editor, *Europe's Constitutional Future,* 1991. B October 23 1954; ed Hutton Grammar School and New College, Oxford.

Address: European Policy Forum, 20 Queen Anne's gate, London SW1H 9AA. 20 Archery Close Street, London W2 2CE. Tel 071 723 3903.

MATUTES JUAN, Abel — Spain EPP (PP)

Abel Matutes, a former member of the European Commission with responsibility for energy and transport, was elected in 1994. Appointed chairman of the foreign affairs and security committee. Former senator and member of the national parliament. University lecturer and businessman. Born October 31 1941.

Address: Genova 13, E-28004 Madrid. Tel 319 20 27. fax; 308 15 12.

MAYER, Franz Xaver — Germany EPP (CSU)

Franz Xaver Mayer was elected in 1994. An agricultural specialist who is active in farming groups. Born November 11 1938.

Address: Landauer Strasse 9, D94431 Pilsting. Tel and fax 099531275.

MEDINA ORTEGA, Manuel — Spain PES (PSOE)

Manuel Medina Ortega became an MEP in 1986. A vice-president in the outgoing Parliament. Former member of the Spanish parliament for Lanzarote. University professor. Born December 15 1935.

Address: Uga (Yaiza), E-35340 Lanzarote, Islas Canarias. Tel: (28) 83 00 63.

MEGAHY, Thomas   UK Yorkshire South West PES (Lab)

Thomas Megahy has been an MEP since 1979. Vice-President of the Parliament, 1987-9; leader, Labour group, 1984-5 and deputy leader, 1985-7. Leader, Kirklees Council, 1973-6; opposition leader, 1976-8; member, Mirfield Council, 1963-74. Vice-president, Association of Municipal Authorities since 1979. Member, Yorks and Humberside Development Association. Lecturer and former railway signalman. Born July 16 1929.

Address: 3 Burton Street, Wakefield, West Yorkshire WF1 2DD. Tel: 0924 382396. Fax: 0924 366851. 6 Lady Heton Grove, Mirfield, West Yorkshire WF14 9DY. Tel: 0924 492680.

MEGRET, Bruno   France Ind (FN)

Bruno Megret, a former member of the national assembly for l'Isere, was elected to EP in 1989. Member, Provence-Côte d'Azur regional council. Civil engineer. Born April 4 1949.

Address: Mas les Césaires, 1273 avenue des Muriers, F-13340 Rognac.

MENDEZ DE VIGO, Inigo   Spain EPP (PP)

Inigo Mendez de Vigo became an MEP in 1992. Formerly with the Council of Europe. Visiting professor, International Institute of Human Rights, Strasbourg. Professor of EC law, Complutense University, Madrid. Born January 21 1956.

Address: Velazquez 15, E-28001 Madrid, tel (1) 575 06 67. Fax: (1) 578 29 92.

MENDILUCE PEREIRO, Jose María   Spain PES (PSOE)

Jose María Mendiluce Pereiro was elected in 1994. An official with the United Nations High Commission for Refugees with experience of aid programmes in Namibia, Nicaragua, and the Balkans. Born April 14 1951.

Address: Abescal 52 E-Madrid. Tel: 441 36 54.

MENRAD, Winfried   Germany EPP (CDU)

Winfried Menrad was elected in 1989. President of Nordwürtemberg Christian Democrat workers and holder of various party offices. Local councillor. Teacher. Born February 10 1939.

Address: Sudetenweg 55, D-74523 Schwabisch Hall. Tel: 0791 520 30. Fax: (0791) 520 21.

METTEN, Alman   Netherlands PES (SD)

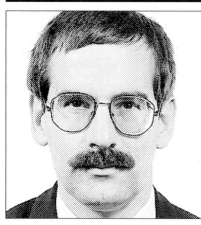

Alman Metten was elected in 1984. Sociologist and scientific adviser at University of Amsterdam. Trade unionist activist. Born October 9 1948.

Address: Bloemendaalseweg 184, 2051 GK Overveen. Tel: (023) 25 19 77. Fax: (023) 27 60 90.

MEZZAROMA, Roberto — Italy FE (FI)

Roberto Mezzaroma was elected in 1994. Businessman and architect. Born August 11 1946.

Address: Via Nepal 16, I-00144 Roma.

MILLER, Bill — UK Glasgow PES (Lab)

Bill Miller was elected in 1994. Strathclyde regional councillor since 1986 and chairman of economic and industrial development committee. Campaigner to save the Ravenscraig steelworks. A chartered survey-or. B July 1954.

Address: 131 Clarkson Road, Glasgow, G44 3BN. Tel: 041 637 3845.

MIRANDA DA SILVA, Joaquim Antonio — Portugal EUL (PCP)

Joaquim Miranda Da Silva has been a member of the EP since 1986 and was leader of the Left Unity Group in the outgoing Parliament. Member of the central committee of the PCP. Deputy in Portuguese national assembly 1980-6. Former member of the Council of Europe. Economist. Born September 7 1950.

Address: Rua Soeiro Pereira Gomes, PCP, P-1699 Lisboa Codex. Tel: (1) 793 62 72. Fax: (1) 793 91 62.

MIRANDA DE LAGE, Ana — Spain, PSE (PSOE)

Ana Miranda de Lage has been an MEP since 1986. Former senator. Party administrator. Born May 8 1946.

Address: Plaza de les Cortes 9, E-28014 Madrid. Tel (1) 424 75 56.

MOMBAUR, Peter-Michael — Germany EPP (CDU)

Peter-Michael Mombaur was elected in 1994. Former member of the German federation of towns and districts and European branch. A lawyer. Born December 12 1938.

Address: Am Ideck 8, D-42781 Haan. Tel 02129 21 84.

MONIZ, Fernando — Portugal PES (PS)

Fernando Moniz was elected in 1994. Deputy mayor of Vila Nova de Famalicao. A financial adviser. Born July 29 1963.

Address: Partico Socialista, Largo do Rato, P-1200 Lisboa.

MONTEIRO, Manuel   Portugal EDA (CDSP)

Manuel Monteiro, a member of the national Parliament, was elected to the EP in 1994. President of the Central Democratic and Social Party. A lawyer. Born April 1 1962.

Address: Largo Adelino Amaro da Costa, P-1196 Lisboa Codex. Tel: (01) 886 97 35.

MONTESANO, Enrico   Italy PES (PDS)

Enrico Montesano was elected in 1994. A local councillor in Rome. Actor. Born June 7 1945.

Address: Gruppo Consiliare PDS, Via S Marco 8, I-00186 Roma. Tel (06) 679 52 30. Fax: (06) 679 53 42.

MOORHOUSE, James   UK London South and Surrey East EPP (C)

James Moorhouse was first elected in 1979. Member, UK parliamentary and scientific committee and adviser and member of organisations concerned with the protection of the environment. Group environmental affairs adviser, Rio Tinto Zinc Corporation, 1973-80; technical adviser, 1953-68, and environmental conservation adviser, 1968-72, Shell International Petroleum. Chartered engineer and consultant on transport, energy and environmental affairs. Born January 1 1924.

Address: 1 Dean Farrar Street, London SW1H 0DY. Tel: 071 416 0093.

MORAN LOPEZ, Fernando — Spain PES (PSOE)

Fernando Moran Lopez first became an MEP in 1987. Appointed vice-president of the PES after the 1994 election and chairman of the institutional affairs committee. Former senator and deputy in the Spanish parliament and minister for foreign affairs, 1982-5. Spanish Ambassador to United Nations, 1985-7. Member of the EP Socialist group bureau in the outgoing Parliament. Born March 25 1926.

Address: Calle I. Antonio 16, Casa de la Reina pral. 2, E-San Lorenzo de El Escorial. Tel: (1) 890 41 98.

MOREAU, Gisèle — France EUL (PC)

Gisèle Moreau, a former member of the National Assembly, was elected to the EP in 1994. A local councillor. Bank employee. Born June 19 1941.

Address: 2 Place Colonel Fabien, F-Paris 19ème. Tel: (1) 40 41 12 25. Fax: 40 40 13 56.

MORETTI, Luigi — Italy Ind (Lega Nord)

Luigi Moretti was first elected in 1989. Provincial secretary of the Bergamo branch of the Lega Nord movement. Sponsor and founder of the Lega Lombardy regional party. Surveyor. Born June 6 1944.

Address: c/o Lega Lombarda Piazza Umberto I,, I-24027 Nembro (BG). Tel: (035) 47 03 37.

MORGAN, Eluned   UK Wales Mid and West PES (Lab)

Eluned Morgan won this seat in 1994 at the age of 27 and was then the youngest MEP. She was a television documentary researcher for BBC Wales and has worked as a researcher for the Labour group in Brussels. She speaks fluent French, Spanish, German and Welsh. Member of the European Movement and Amnesty International. B February 1967; educated at Atlantic College and Universities of Hull, Madrid, Strasbourg and Bogota.

Address: 17 Barn Road, Carmarthen, Dyfed, SA3 1DD. Tel: 0267 222205. 4 Felin Wynt, St Davids, Dyfed, SA62 6QS.

MORRIS, David   UK Mid and West Wales PES (Lab)

David Morris was first elected in 1984. Contested Brecon and Radnor in 1983 Westminster election. Former Newport councillor. Former foundry worker, Presbyterian minister and educational adviser to Gwent County Council. Born January 28 1930.

Address: 39 St James Crescent, Swansea SA1 6DR. Tel: 0792 643542. Fax: 0792 646430. 65 Harlech Crescent, Tycoch, West Glamorgan. Tel: 0792 206968.

MOSCOVICI, Pierre   France PES (ES)

Pierre Moscovici was elected in 1994. A local councillor. Former adviser to the ministries of education and planning. Teacher. Born September 16 1957.

Address: 13 rue de Seine, F-75006 Paris. tel: (1) 46 34 29 87. Fax: 46 34 11 24.

MOSIEK-URBAHN, Marlies   Germany EPP (CDU)

Marlies Mosiek-Urbahn was elected in 1994. Magistrate at local, regional and federal level. Born August 9 1946.

Address: Wendelsteinstrasse 9. D-65199 Wiesbadn. Tel 0611/46 16 93.

MOUSKOURI, Nana   Greece EPP (ND)

Nana Mouskouri, the singer and entertainer, was elected in 1994. She is ambassador to Unicef. Appointed to the ACP-EU joint assembly and committee on women's rights in July 1994.

Address: Perikleous 2A, GR 166 71 Vouliagmeni.

MULDER, Jan   Netherlands LDR (VVD)

Jan Mulder was elected in 1994. European Commission official specialising in agriculture in developing countries. Agricultural engineer. Born October 3 1943.

Address: Ambiorixsquare 18 bus 9, B-1049 Brussel. Tel: (2) 735 71 91.

MÜLLER, Edith — Germany Verts (Grüne)

Edith Müller was elected in 1994. Founder-member of the Greens and a party worker. Lawyer. Born March 3 1949.

Address: Stadtwaldgürtel 2, D-50931 Köln.

MURPHY, Simon — UK Midlands West PES (Lab)

Simon Murphy won this seat in 1994. He was research assistant and press officer to John Bird, the outgoing MEP for this seat, who stood down at the 1994 election. Former university lecturer. Contested Wolverhampton South West in the 1992 Westminster election. Born February 1962; ed University College of Wales, Aberystwyth, where he studied political science and international politics.

Address: Rooms 2/3 Gresham Chambers, 14 Lichfield Street, Wolverhampton, WV1 1DP. Tel: 0902 712366 or 0902 334114. Fax: 0902 20276.

MUSCARDINI, Cristiana — Italy Ind (AN)

Cristiana Muscardini was elected in 1989. Former member, Chamber of Deputies. Local councillor in Milan. Former member of the national executive of the MSI. Journalist and writer. Born November 6 1948.

Address: Via P. Sotto Corno 5, I-20129 Milano. Tel: (02) 79 61 75. Via Donizetti 34, I-20122 Milano. Tel: (02) 76 00 10 50.

MUSUMECI, Nello — Italy Ind (AN)

Nello Musumeci was elected in 1994. President of Catania province and a local and regional councillor. Banker and journalist. Born January 21 1955.

Photograph unavailable

Address: c/o Federazione MSI/AN, I-Catania.

NASSAUER, Hartmut — Germany EPP (CDU)

Hartmut Nassauer was elected in 1994. Member and vice-president, Hesse regional assembly. Former minister for the interior for Hesse. Born October 17 1942.

Address: Wieselweg 5, D-34466 Wolfhagen. Tel: 05692 23 66. Fax: 05692 50 34.

NEEDLE, Clive — UK Norfolk PES (Lab)

Clive Needle is a Labour Party organiser in Norfolk. Former community councillor. B September 1956; educated Southend High School and Aston University.

Address: 21 Damgate Street, Wymondham, Norfolk, NR18 0BA. Tel: 0953 603220. Fax: 0953 606119.

NENCINI, Riccardo — Italy PES (PSI-AD)

Riccardo Nencini was elected in 1994. Former member of the Chamber of Deputies and a regional councillor. Journalist. Born October 19 1959.

Address: Via Castellare 6, I-50031 Barberino di Mugello (FI).

NEWENS, Stanley — UK London Central PES (Lab)

Stanley Newens was first elected in 1984. Deputy leader, Labour Group of MEPs, 1988-9; group chairman, 1985-7. Labour MP for Epping, 1964-70, and Harlow, 1974-83; contested Harlow, 1987 Westminster election. Labour spokesman, EP committee for foreign affairs and security and member of subcommittee on human rights in the outgoing Parliament. Chairman, Tribune Group of Labour MPs, 1982-83. Director, London Co-operative Society, 1971-7, and president, 1977-81. Former teacher and miner. Born February 4 1930.

Addresses: Basement Office, 92 Ladbroke Grove, London W11 2HE. Tel: 071 221 0092. Fax: 071 792 3691. The Leys, 18 Park Hill, Harlow, Essex CM17 0AE. Tel: (0279) 420108.

NEWMAN, Edward — UK Greater Manchester Central PES (Lab)

Edward Newman was first elected in 1984. Appointed chairman of the committee on petitions after the 1994 elections. Labour spokesman and PES co-ordinator on the committee in the outgoing Parliament. Treasurer, British Labour Group of MEPs, 1988-9. Member, Manchester City Council, 1979-85. Former semi-skilled manual worker in light engineering and cable-making and later a postal worker in Manchester. Born May 14 1953.

Address: 7th Floor, Graeme House, Wilbraham Road, Chorlton cum Hardy, Manchester, M21 1AQ. Tel: 061 881 2144. Fax: 061 771 5041. 234 Ryebank Road, Chorlton cum Hardy, Manchester M21 1LU. Tel: 061 881 9641.

NEYTS-UYTTEBROECK, Annemie — Belgium LDR (PVV)

Annemie Neyts-Uyttebroeck, a former secretary of state for the Brussels region, was elected in 1994. Member of the Chamber of Deputies since 1981. Former teacher and party worker.

Address: L Lepagestraat 9, B-1000 Brussel.

NICHOLSON, James — UK Northern Ireland EPP (UUP)

James Nicholson, was elected to the European Parliament in 1989 and until 1992 was United Kingdom's sole representative in EPP Group; bureau member since 1989. Westminster Ulster Unionist MP for Newry and Armagh, 1983-6, losing his seat in the by-election forced by the Unionist protest at the Anglo-Irish Agreement. Vice-President, Ulster Unionist Council. Official Unionist member, Northern Ireland Assembly, 1982-6. Farmer. Born January 29 1945.

Address: European Office, 3 Glengall Street, Belfast, BT12 5AE. Tel: 0232 439431. Fax: 0232 246738. 147 Keady Road, Ballyards, Armagh BT60 3AE. Tel/Fax: 0861 523307.

OCCHETTO, Achille — Italy PSE (PDS)

Achille Occhetto was elected in three constituencies in 1994; first elected in 1989. Member of the Chamber of Deputies. Former secretary general of the PDS. Journalist. Born March 3 1936.

Address: Direzione Naziobale PDS, Via delle Botteghe Oscure 4, I-00186 Roma. Tel: (06) 671 11. Via Tribune Campitelli 23, I-00186 Roma.

ODDY, Christine — UK Coventry & Warwickshire North PES (Lab)

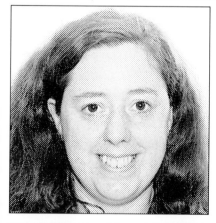

Christine Oddy won the seat for Labour in 1989. Secretary, Labour group working party on ethnic minorities. Solicitor; lecturer in law, City of London Polytechnic, 1984-9. Worked in general secretariat, European Commission, 1980, and in a law firm in Paris in 1982. Former member, regional executive, National Association of Teachers in Further and Higher Education. Born September 20 1955.

Address: 3 Copthall House, Station Square, Coventry CV1 2FZ. Tel: 0203 552328. Fax: 0203 551424.

OOMEN-RUIJTEN, Maria — Netherlands EPP (CDA)

Maria Oomen-Ruijten, a former member of the second chamber in the national parliament, has been an MEP since 1989. Appointed a vice-president of the EPP Group after the 1994 election. Former vice-chairman and bureau member of EPP group. Public relations consultant and specialist on environment, consumer protection and social affairs. Born September 6 1950.

Address: Postbus 7174, 6051 Ad Maasbracht. Julianalaan 55, 6051 As Maasbracht. Tel: (04746) 23 23.

OOSTLANDER, Arie   Netherlands EPP (CDA)

Arie Oostlander was first elected in 1989. Member, Muiden local government council. CDA group chairman, Gooi and Vechtstreek Regional Council. Psychologist and lecturer in experimental psychology. Director of the party's scientific institute. Born March 28 1936.

Address: Gentiaanveld 19, 7006 TB Doetinchem. Tel: (08340) 62 223. Fax: (08340) 72 117.

ORLANDO, Leoluca   Italy Verts (La Rete)

Leoluca Orlando was elected in 1994. Mayor of Palermo. Former member of the Chamber of Deputies. Lawyer. Born August 1 1947.

Address: Via Principe Paternò 70, I90144 Palermo. Tel: (091) 30 27 69.

PACK, Doris   Germany EPP (CDU)

Doris Pack was first elected to the European Parliament in 1989. Member of the Bundestag, 1974-83 and 1985-9. Former member, Council of Europe and Western European Union. Chairman, CDU Women's Union for the Saar; deputy federal chairman of CDU Women's Union bureau; vice-chairman, CDU federal expert committee on European policy; vice-president, German Council of European Movement in Saarland. Headmistress. Born March 18 1942.

Address: Bei der Weiss Eich 1, D-66129 Saarbrücken/Bübingen. Tel: (06805) 16 54. Fax: (06805) 2 15 80.

PAILLER, Aline — France EUL (PC)

Aline Pailler was elected in 1994. A journalist. Born 1955.

Address: 160 rue d'Aubervilliers, F-75019 Paris. Tel: (1) 40 37 56 90.

PAISLEY, The Rev Ian — UK Northern Ireland Ind (DUP)

The Rev Ian Paisley, leader of the Democratic Unionist Party, was first elected as an MEP in 1979. Westminster MP for Antrim North since 1970, sitting as Protestant Unionist, 1970-4. Stormont MP and leader of the Opposition, 1970-2; Democratic Unionist member for North Antrim in Northern Ireland Assembly, 1973-5, and UUUC member, Northern Ireland Constitutional Convention, 1975-6. Member, Northern Ireland Assembly, 1982-6.
Born April 6 1926.

Address: 256 Ravenhill Road, Belfast BT6 8GJ. Tel: 0232 454255/458900. Fax: 0232 457783. The Parsonage, 17 Cyprus Avenue, Belfast BT5 5NT. Tel: 0232 650150. Fax: 0232 651574.

PALACIO VALLERSUNDI, Ana Isabel — Spain EPP (PP)

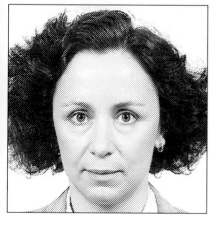

Ana Isabel Palacio Vallersundi was elected in 1994. Vice-president of the legal committee of the European Union of Women. Lawyer and former university lecturer. Born 1949.

Address: Plaza Salesas 3, E-28004 Madrid. Tel: 31 95 895. Fax: 30 81 463.

PANAGOPOULOS, Stylianos Greece PES (PASOK)

Stylianos Panagopoulos was elected in 1994. Former governor of the National Bank of Greece and president of the union of Greek banks. Born 1939.

Address: Valaoritou 9, GR-106 71 Athina. Tel (01) 36 03 555. Fax: (01) 36 41 392.

PANNELLA, Marco Italy EDA (PR)

Marco Pannella was elected in two constituencies in 1994. First elected to the EP in 1979. Former member of the Chamber of Deputies. Former chairman, parliamentary group of Partito Radicale. One of party's founders and a former secretary general. Chairman, league of conscientious objectors. Journalist. Born May 2 1930.

Address: Gruppo Parlamentare Radicale, Camera dei Deputati, Via Uffici del Vicario 21, I-00186 Roma. Tel: (06) 67 17 92 97.

PAPAKYRIAZIS, Nikolaos Greece PES (PASOK)

Nikolaos Papakyriazis was re-elected in 1994. MEP 1986-9. Doctor and university professor. Born 1940.

Address: Anaximandrou 100, GR-542 50 Thessaloniki. Tel (030) 30 30 78. Fax: (031) 264 467.

PAPAYANNAKIS, Mihail — Greece EUL (SYN)

Mihail Papayannakis was first elected in 1989 on the Greek Communist Alliance list SAP (Synaspismos). Member of the executive of the central committee of the EAR party (Greek Left). Economics journalist. Born August 19 1941.

Address: Galinou 29, GR-117 41 Athina. Tel: (01) 92 48 734.

PAPOUTSIS, Christos — Greece PES (PASOK)

Christos Papoutsis became an MEP in 1984. Appointed a vice-president of the PES Group after the 1994 election. Former vice-chairman of Socialist Group and leader of its Greek delegation. Member, group bureau; member, Pasok's central committee. Economist. Born April 11 1953.

Address: Merlin 11, GR-106 74 Athina. Tel: (1) 360 17 40. Fax: (1) 364 04 58. Sokratous 59, GR-155 62 Holargos. Tel: (1) 653 29 62.

PARIGI, Gastone — Italy Ind (AN)

Gastone Parigi was elected in 1994. Member of the Chamber of Deputies. Member of the national executive of the MSI-DN. Business adviser. Born August 10 1931.

Address: Vicolo S Rocco 1, I-33170 Pordenone.

PARODI, Eolo — Italy FE (FI)

Eolo Parodi was an MEP in 1984-89 and returned to the Parliament in 1990. Surgeon. President of the national federation of doctors and dentists. Member, national health board; national Aids committee. Chairman, joint standing committee of professional bodies and colleges, and of Genoa scientific institute for tumours, 1982-4. May 21 1926.

Address: Via Mameli, 2A/16,I-16122 Genova. Tel: (010) 81 27 50. Fax: (010) 29 67 56.

PASTY, Jean-Claude — France EPP (UDR/RPR)

Jean-Claude Pasty was elected in 1984. Political adviser and former director at the agriculture ministry. Technical adviser in private office of Robert Boulin (Minister of Agriculture), Bernard Pons (Secretary of State for Agriculture) and Jacques Chirac (Minister of Agriculture), 1968-73. Director of social affairs, Ministry of Agriculture, 1973-8. Member of the national council of the RPR. Former member of the national assembly. Civil administrator; conseiller general, Creuse; conseiller regional, Limousin. Creuse deputy (RPR), 1978-81; national secretary of RPR. Born June 15 1937.

Address: 128 Boulevard Saint-Germain, F-75066 Paris. Tel 43 54 40 08 08.46 33 40 69. Fax: 40 46 07 15.

PEIJS, Karla — Netherlands EPP (CDA)

Karla Peijs was first elected in 1989. Member Utrecht regional council. Professor of economic science at Utrecht University and the International College of Business Administration, Zeist. She has held various offices in the CDA at central and local level. Born September 1 1944.

Address: Achtersloot 53, 3401 NS Ijsselstein. Tel: (03408) 885 56. Fax: (03408) 701 40.

PÉREZ ROYO, Fernando — Spain PES (PSOE)

Fernando Pérez Royo was returned to the EP in 1994. MEP 1987-93 and a former vice-president. Former member of the national Parliament. Former member of the left-wing Izquierda Unida party before standing for the Socialists. A lawyer. Born January 25 1943.

Address: Grupo Parlemntario IU-CA, Reyes Católicos 21, E-41001 Sevilla. Tel: (5) 421 84 14.

PERRY, Roy — UK Wight and Hampshire South PPE (C)

Roy Perry won this seat in 1994. A senior lecturer in politics at Southampton University. Leader, Test Valley Council since 1985 and member since 1979. Member, Wessex area executive council since 1985. Contested Swansea West in the 1992 Westminster election. Chairman, Romsey and Waterside Conservative Association, 1982-5. Director, Test Valley Development Ltd and former executive of Marks and Spencer plc. Born April 7 1938; educated at Manchester and Swansea Universities.

Address: Tarrants Farmhouse, Maurys Lane, West Wellow, Romsey, Hampshire, SO51 6DA.

PÉRY, Nicole — France PES (ES)

Nicole Péry, an MEP since 1979, was a senior vice-president of the outgoing Parliament. Appointed a vice-president of the PES Group after the 1994 election. Member, bureau of PES group. First elected in 1979. Former national committee member and party secretary for women's rights organisation. Regional councillor, d'Aquitaine; municipal councillor, Bayonne (Pyrenees-Atlantiques); deputy mayor, Ciboure. Born May 15 1943.

Address: 63 rue Bourg-Neuf, F-64100 Bayonne. Tel: 59 59 48 47. Fax: 59 59 71 49. Villa "Xori-Kanta", 40 rue Massy, F-64500 Ciboure. Tel: 59 47 28 92.

PETER, Helwin   Germany PES (SDP)

Helwin Peter, a former member of the Bundestag, was first elected to the Parliament in 1989. Trade union leader and factory foreman. Born July 18 1941.

Address: Fliederstrasse 3, D-66649 Oberthal. Tel and Fax: (06854) 369.

PETTINARI, Luciano   Italy EUL (RC)

Luciano Pettinari was elected in 1994. Born March 18 1950.

Address: Direzione Nazionale Rifondazione Communista, Via Barberni 11, I-00187 Roma. Tel: (06) 487 08 71. Fax: (06) 489 32 52.

PEX, Peter   Netherlands EPP (CDA)

Peter Pex was elected in 1994. Consultant and manager. Born June 5 1946.

Address: Verdilaan 6, 3055 SM Rotterdam. Tel: 461 22 64. Fax: 461 39 27.

PIECYK, Wilhelm Ernst   Germany PES (SPD)

Wilhelm Ernst Piecyk became an MEP in 1992. Leader of the SPD in Schleswig-Holstein. Policeman. Born August 11 1948.

Address: Kleiner Kuhberg 28-30, D-24103 Kiel. Tel: (0431) 90 60 622/21. Fax: (0431) 90 60 641. Schauberg 23, D-23858 Reinfeld. Tel: (04533) 43 17.

PIMENTA, Carlos   Portugal LDR (PSD)

Carlos Pimenta, a member of the national parliament and a former secretary of state, became an MEP in 1987. Electronics engineer. Born May 7 1955.

Address: Parliamento Europeu, Grup LDR, Bruxelles.

PIQUET, René-Emile   France EUL (PC)

René-Emile Piquet, first elected an MEP in 1979, became chairman of the Coalition des Gauches (Left Unity) Group after the 1989 elections and a vice-chairman in 1992; a vice-chairman of Communist and allies group in 1984-9 Parliament. Former metal worker. Member, PCF political bureau, having been secretary, central committee, French Communist Party. Born October 23 1932.

Address: Comite Central du Parti Communiste Francais, 2 place du Colonel Fabien, F-75940 Paris Cedex 19. Tel: (1) 40 40 12 54. Fax: (1) 40 40 13 56. 16 rue les Terres Blanches, F-41120 Chailles. Tel: 54 79 48 47.

PLOOIJ-VAN GORSEL, Elly   Netherlands LDR (VVD)

Elly Plooij-van Gorsel was elected in 1994. An academic and company sales director. Born March 20 1947.

Address: Plantage 9, 2377 AA oude Wetering. Tel (01713) 14 510. Fax: (01713) 17 248.

PLUMB, Lord   UK Cotswolds EPP (C)

Lord Plumb became leader of the Conservative MEPs and a vice-president of the EPP Group after the 1994 election. Appointed chairman of the ACP-EU assembly in July 1994. President of the Parliament, 1987-9; leader, European Democratic (Conservative) Group, 1982-7; chairman, agriculture, fisheries and rural development committee, 1979-82. Member, EPP bureau. First elected, in 1979. President, National Farmers' Union, 1970-9; chairman, British Agricultural Council, 1975-9. Born March 27 1925.

Address: Maxstoke, Coleshill, Warwickshire B46 2QJ. Tel: 0675 463133 (home); 0675 464156 office. Fax: 0675 464156.

PODESTA, Guido   Italy FE (FI)

Guido Podesta was elected in 1994. Architect. Born April 1 1947.

Address: Residenza Andromeda 8, Via Vivaldi, I-20080 Basiglio (MI).

POETTERING, Hans-Gert Germany EPP (CDU)

Hans-Gert Poettering was first elected in 1979. Appointed a vice-president of the EPP Group after the 1994 election. Active in Europa Union. Spokesman on European policy for Junge Union, Lower Saxony, 1974-80; assistant to CDU/CSU Bundestag group, 1976-9; Land chairman, Lower Saxony branch of Europa Union, 1981-91; member, bureau, German Europa Union; Osnabruck district chairman, CDU. A lawyer. Born September 15 1945.

Address: Sophienstrasse 8, D-49186 Bad Iburg. Tel: (05403) 48 55. Europaburo, Schepeler Strasse 18, D-49074 Osnabruck. Tel: (0541) 570 60. Fax: (0541) 57 32 83.

POGGIOLINI, Danilo Italy EPP (Patto Segni)

Danilo Poggiolini was elected in 1994. Born September 15 1932.

Address: Corso Racconigi 239, I-Torino. (011) 58 17 138.

POISSON, Anne-Christine France EDN (l'autre Europe)

Anne-Christine Poisson was elected in 1994. Involved in farming and rural organisations. Born 1956.

Address: 52 Grand Rue, F-91150 Marolles-en-Beauce. Tel: 69 95 41 02. Fax: 69 95 40 56.

POLLACK, Anita   UK London South West PES (Lab)

Anita Pollack gained this seat for Labour in 1989 having contested it in the 1984 election. Political researcher for Barbara Castle, then an MEP, 1981-9. Labour spokesman on the environment, public health and consumer protection committee and women's rights committee in the outgoing Parliament. President, Parliament's animal welfare committee. Chairman, EP delegation for relations with countries of South Asia and the South Asian association for regional co-operation. Contested Woking in 1987 Westminster election. Born June 3 1946.

Address: 199 Lavender Hill, London SW11 5TE. Tel: 071 228 0939. Fax: 071 228 0916. 139 Windsor Road, London E7 0RA. Tel: (081) 552 2625. Fax: (081) 552 2625.

POMPIDOU, Alain   France EPP (UDF/RPR)

Alain Pompidou, the son of the former President of France, was elected in 1989. Former adviser to ministries for higher education and for health. Doctor and professor of medicine. Born April 5 1942.

Address: Faculté de Médecine Cochin, 24 rue du Faubourg Saint Jacques, F-75014 Paris. Tel: (1) 44 41 23 50. Fax: (1) 40 51 09 46.

PONS GRAU, Josep Enrique   Spain PES (PSOE)

Josep Enrique Pons Grau became an MEP in 1986. Former member of the Spanish Parliament. University professor of history and geography. Born June 19 1948.

Address: c/Jurista n 11 pt 4, E-46001 Valencia. Tel: (6) 331 89 80.

POOS, Jacques — Luxembourg PES (LSAP)

Jacques Poos was Deputy Prime Minister and Minister for Foreign Affairs at the time of his election to the EP in 1994. Member of the Chamber of Deputies. Vice-president of the Socialist Workers Party. Former banker and newspaper director. Born June 3 1935.

Address: 45 Squarw Emile Mayrisch, L-4240 Esch/Alzette.

PORTO, Manuel — Portugal PES (SD)

Manuel Porto was first elected to EP in 1989 and was elected a quaestor in 1992. A vice-chairman of Liberal and Democratic Reformist Group (LDR). Economist and chairman of the National Planning Council. University professor. Born June 15 1943.

Address: Pátio da Universidade, P-3049 Coimbra Codex. Tel: 39 22 113. Fax: 39 23 353.

POSSELT, Bernd — Germany EPP (CSU)

Bernd Posselt was elected in 1994. Vice-president of the Pan European Union. Journalist and former assistant to an MEP. Born June 4 1956.

Address: Paneuropa-Union, Karlstrasse 57, D-80333 München. Tel: 089 55 46 83. Fax: 089 59 47 68.

PRADIER, Pierre
France PES (ER)

Pierre Pradier, a doctor, is a co-founder and outgoing director-general of *Médecins du Monde.* Elected to EC in 1994. Born 1933.

Address: 14 bd St Germain, F-750057 Paris. Tel (1) 46 34 53 83.

PRONK, Bartho
Netherlands EPP (CDA)

Bartho Pronk became an MEP in November 1989. International relations co-ordinator for the National Federation of Protestant Trade Unions. Member of the European Movement in the Netherlands. Member of the CDA committee on foreign policy. Born September 28 1950.

Address: Copijlaan 27, 3737 AV Groenekan. Tel: (03461) 2291. Fax: (03461) 1502.

PROVAN, James
UK South Downs West EPP (C)

James Provan, a farmer, was returned for this seat in 1994. MEP for North East Scotland, 1979-89. Former area chairman of NFU; former manager of a farming newspaper; former member, UK agriculture and food research council. Former executive director and consultant promoting Scottish finance. Born December 19 1936; educated at Oundle and Royal Agricultural College, Cirencester.

Address: 30 West Street, Chichester, Sussex, PO19 1 RP. Newton of Balcanquhal, Glenfarg, Perthshire, PH 29 QD. Tel: 0577 830 777. Fax: 0577 830 733.

PUERTA GUTIERREZ, Alonso Jose   Spain EUL (IU-IC)

Alonso Jose Puerta Gutierrez, a former member of the Spanish Parliament, was elected to the EP in 1987. Secretary-general of the Socialist Action Party. Municipal councillor in Madrid. Civil engineer. Born March 24 1944.

Address: Comision Ejecutiva Federal del PASOC, Plaza de Canalejas 6 3, E-28014 Madrid. Avda. de la Albufera 133-135, E-28038 Madrid. Tel: (1) 477 01 05.

PUTTEN, Maartje van   Netherlands PES (ESD)

Maartje van Putten was first elected in 1989. President, national movement for road safety. Research worker, journalist and film maker. Born July 5 1951.

Address: Roemer Visscherstraat 21, 1054 EV Amsterdam. Tel: (020) 612 81 55. Fax: (020) 616 45 69.

QUISTHOUDT-ROWOHL, Godelieve   Germany EPP (CDU)

Godelieve Quisthoudt-Rowohl was first elected 1989. Head of institute of applied linguistics, Hildesheim, 1979-89. Former professor (physics and chemistry) at University of Louvain, Belgium. Member of CDU district board, Hildesheim. Born June 18 1947.

Address: Goschenstrasse 80, D-31134 Hildesheim. Tel: (05121) 14 292. Fax: 05121 39 748.

215

RAFFARIN, Jean-Pierre — France EPP (PR)

Jean-Pierre Raffarin was first elected in 1989. Political adviser and member of the bureau of the Republican party. Local councillor and leader of Poitou-Charentes Regional Council. Born August 3 1948.

Address: 7 rue de Saint Georges, F-86360 Chasseneuil. Tel: 49 52 70 61.

RANDZIO-PLATH, Christa — Germany PES (SPD)

Christa Randzio-Plath was first elected in 1989. Vice-president, international union of socialist women. Former adviser to finance department, Hamburg Council. Lawyer and writer. Born October 29 1940.

Address: Europa-Buro, Alter Fischmarkt 11, D-20457 Hamburg. Tel: (040) 33 17 44. Fax: (040) 32 25 88. Hadermannsweg 23, D-22459 Hamburg. Tel: (040) 551 83 64. Fax: (040) 555 39 86.

RAPKAY, Bernhard — Germany PES (SDP)

Bernhard Rapkay was elected in 1994. Leader of local party in Dortmund. Works in public relations. Born January 8 1951.

Address: Kurler Strasse 64a, D-44319 Dortmund.

RAUTI, Pino — Italy Ind (AN)

Giuseppe Rauti was first elected to EP in 1989. Former national secretary of the Italian Social Movement (MSI-DN). Former member of the Chamber of Deputies. Journalist. Born November 19 1926.

Address: Via Stresa 133, I-00135 Roma. Tel: (06) 30 145 65. Fax: (06) 32 00 286.

READ, Imelda Read — UK Leicester PES (Lab)

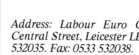

Mel Read was elected to EP in 1989 and elected as a quaestor in 1992. Former employment officer for Nottingham Community Relations Council; former laboratory technician with Plessey Telecommunications and a former lecturer and researcher at Trent Polytechnic. Contested Leicestershire North West in the 1983 Westminster election and Melton in 1979. Member, Trades Union Council Women's Advisory Committee and chair of regional TUC Women's Committee. Born January 8 1939.

Address: Labour Euro Office, 81 Great Central Street, Leicester LE1 4ND. Tel: 0533 532035. Fax: 0533 532038.

REDONDO JIMENEZ, Encarnación — Spain EPP (PP)

Encarnción Redondo Jimenez was elected in 1994. Civil servant, agricultural engineer and university lecturer. Born April 18 1944.

Address: Fueros 4, E-42003 Soria. Tel: (975) 22 54 01. Fax: (975) 22 54 01.

REHDER, Klaus   Germany PES (SPD)

Klaus Rehder was elected in 1994. Teacher and former trade union leader. Born July 12 1943.

Address: Dr Dessauer Strasse 9, D86609 Donauworth. Tel: 0906 1859. Fax: 0906 23 867.

RIBEIRO, Sergio   Portugal EUL (UDC)

Sergio Ribeiro became an MEP in 1990. Former member of the national Parliament. Former director general in the Ministry of Employment. Economist. Born December 21 1935.

Address: Zambujal, P-2490 Ourém. Tel: (049) 59 11 20.

RIIS-JORGENSEN, Karin   Denmark LDR (V)

Karin Riis-Jorgensen, head of an international accountancy office, was elected in 1994. Born November 11 1952.

Address: Brodeerskabsvej 27, DK-2000 Frederiksberg.

RINSCHE, Günter   Germany EPP (CDU)

Günter Rinsche was first elected to EP in 1979; leader, German delegation in EPP group and member of group bureau. Member, Bundestag, 1965-72; former member, North Rhine-Westphalia Land assembly, being CDU group spokesman on economic affairs. Mayor of Hamm, 1964-79; on North Rhine-Westphalia Europa Union Land executive and German Council of European Movement; chaired planning committee, Institute for International Solidarity; on executive of Konrad Adenauer Foundation; member, North Rhine-Westphalia convention of municipal authorities, 1975-80. Born July 13 1930.

Address: Feldgarten 15, D-59063 Hamm. Tel: (02381) 523 30. Fax: (02381) 579 99.

RIPA DI MEANA, Carlo   Italy Verts (Verdi)

Carlo Ripa di Meana, a former MEP, was re-elected in 1994 in two constituencies. Former minister for the environment and former EC commissioner. Born August 15 1929.

Address: c/o Federazione dei Verdi, Via Catalana 1/A, I-00186 Roma.

ROBLES PIQUER, Carlos   Spain EPP (PP)

Carlos Robles Piquer, who was Spanish foreign secretary, 1979-81, has been an MEP since 1986; first elected in 1987. Appointed a vice-president of the EPP Group after the 1994 election. Diplomat and senator representing Grupo Popular in the Madrid Assembly. At Spanish Embassy, Bogota, 1955-9; consul, Nador, Morocco, 1959-62; secretary, Spanish Embassy, London, 1962; Ambassador to Libya and Chad, 1973; Rome and La Valetta, 1976. Was managing director of information and of popular culture and entertainment, 1962-69; minister of education and science, 1975-6. Born October 13 1925.

Address: Calle Monte Alto 42, E-28223 Pozuelo (Madrid). Tel: (1) 352 38 79. Fax: 715 60 45.

ROCARD, Michel — France PES (ES)

Michel Rocard, the former French Prime Minister, was elected in 1994 when leader of the French Socialist Party but was forced to resign as leader within weeks of the election when he lost of vote of confidence from the party's council. He had been party leader for 14 months. Mayor of Conflans-Sainte-Honorine. Born August 23 1930.

Address: Mairie, 54 Rue Maurice Berteaux, F-78700, Conflans-Sainte-Honorine. Tel: 34 90 89 89.

ROSADO FERNANDES, Raúl — Portugal EDA (CDSP)

Raúl Rosado Fernandes, was elected in 1994. Former rector of Lisbon University. President of the Portuguese Confederation of Farmers. Vice-president of COPA since 1987. Member of the Economic and Social Committee. Farmer. Born July 11 1934.

Address: Av Colégio Militar Lote 1786, P-1500 Lisboa. Tel (1) 710 00 00. fax: (1) 716 61 22.

ROSE, Marie-France de — France EDN (l'autre Europe)

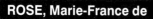

Marie-France de Rose was elected in 1994. A media executive in a private company. Born 1943.

Address: Ugine-Paris la Defense, Immeuble Ile de France, Cedex 33, F-92070 Paris la Defense 9. Tel: 41 25 55 16. Fax: 41 25 55 34.

ROTH, Claudia   Germany Verts (Grüne)

Claudia Roth is a former press spokesman for the Greens in the Bundestag and a former joint vice-chairman of the EP Verts Group. First elected to EP in 1989. Began career in political drama in Swabian State Theatre in 1974. Later, at Buhnen Dortmund and with Hoffman Comic Theatre, associated with politically oriented rock band Ton Steine Scherben. Born May 15 1955.

Addresses: Hochhaus Tulpenfeld Bundeshaus, D-53113 Bonn. Tel: (0228) 16 31 38. Fax: (0228) 16 86 642. An der Steinbrucke 19, D-53119 Bonn. Tel: (0228) 66 60 13. Fax: (0228) 66 64 02.

ROTH-BEHRENDT, Dagmar   Germany PES (SPD)

Dagmar Roth-Behrendt was elected in 1989. Vice-president of Europa Union. Member of the ÖTV trade union. Lawyer working in Berlin. Born February 21 1953.

Addresses: Reichstag, Scheidemannstrasse 2, D-10557 Berlin. Tel: (030) 39 77 3228/3229. Fax: (030) 394 74 11. Weinmeisterhornweg 39, D-13595 Berlin. Tel: (030) 361 89 66.

ROTHE, Mechtild   Germany PES (SPD)

Mechtild Rothe was first elected to the EP in 1984 and has served on the agriculture, fisheries and rural development committee Former vice-chairman of EP/Cyprus delegation. Former member of the SPD federal council and of town council of Bad Lippspringe. Member of party council. Teacher. Born August 10 1947.

Addresses: Europaburo, Am Steintor 2, D-33175 Bad Lippspringe. Tel: (05252) 518 88. Fax: (05252) 10 99. Karlstrasse 5, D-33175 Bad Lippspringe. Tel: (05252) 516 17.

ROTHLEY, Willi
Germany PES (SDP)

Willi Rothley was first elected to the EP in 1984. Former member, Rheinland-Pfalz regional assembly; deputy state chairman of SDP and holder of other party posts. Lawyer. Born December 15 1943.

Address: Europa-Buro, Ringstrasse 2a, D-67806 Rochenhausen. Tel: (06361) 34 38/16 83. Fax: (06361) 51 19.

ROUBATIS, Ioannis
Greece PES (PASOK)

Ioannis Roubatis was elected in 1994. Journalist and former government press spokesman. Born 1948.

Address: Kypselis 2A, GR-113 62 Athina.

ROVSING, Christian
Denmark EPP (KF)

Christian Rovsing, a former deputy in the Danish Parliament, was first elected to EP in 1989. Member, EPP bureau. Chairman, Copenhagen industrial development board; vice-chairman, Esprit advisory board; member, Danish space board; British academy of technical science. Member, Copenhagen county council, 1974-8. Engineer. Born November 2 1936.

Address: Christians Brygge 28, DK-1559 Kobenhavn V. Tel: 33 93 64 64. Fax: 33 93 64 60.

SAI

RUFFOLO, Giorgio — Italy PES (PDS)

Giorgio Ruffolo, a former member of the EP, was re-elected in 1994. Former minister and former member of the Chamber of Deputies. University lecturer and journalist. Born August 14 1926.

Address: c/o CER, Via Luigi Luciani, 1, I-00197 Roma.

SAINJON, Andre — France PES (ER)

Andre Sainjon, former secretary general of French metalworkers union, was first elected to EP in 1989. Former member, central committee of Communist Party (PCF). Born July 23 1943.

Address: 9 rue Lagrange, F-75005 Paris. Tel: (1) 40 51 70 00. Fax: (1) 40 51 09 94.

SAINT-PIERRE, Dominique — France PES (ER)

Dominique Saint-Pierre, a former member of the National Assembly, was elected in 1994. Vice-president *Mouvement des Radicaux de Gauche*. Regional councillor. Lawyer. Born November 10 1940.

Address: 2 rue Guichenon, F-01000 Bourg-en-Bresse. Tel: 74 45 19 20.

SAKELLARIOU, Jannis — Germany PES (SPD)

Jannis Sakellariou was first elected in 1984. Engineer and economist. Scientific director of German army academy in Munich. Spokesman for Munich Young Socialists, 1972-4, becoming deputy chairman, local SDP, Sendlingnen. Born November 12 1939.

Address: Oberanger 38/IV, D-80331 München. Tel: (089) 26 63 47/23 17 11 52. Fax: (089)23 17 11 47.

SALAFRANCA SANCHEZNEYRA, José Ignacio — Spain EPP (PP)

José Ignacio Salafranca Sanchezneyra was elected in 1994. A lawyer and civil servant formerly with the European Commission. Born May 31 1955.

Address: Plaza de la Castellana, 199, E-28046, Madrid. Tel: (3) 15 44 79.

SALISCH, Heinke — Germany PES (SPD)

Heinke Salisch was first elected to the EP in 1979. Former member, Karlsruhe municipal council. Leader of local party. An interpreter. Born August 14 1941.

Address: Sonntagsstrasse 2, 7500 Karlsruhe. Tel: 0721 81 88 88. Fax: 0721 81 57 00.

SAMLAND, Detlev — Germany PES (SPD)

Detlev Samland was elected in 1989. Appointed chairman of the budgets committee after the 1994 elections. Spokesman for young socialists Planning engineer and former director of advertising agency. Born May 1 1953.

Address: Frankenstrasse 143, D-45134 Essen. Tel: (0201) 147 10 30. Fax: (0201) 47 38 29. Holunderweg 35a, D-45133 Essen. Tel: (0201) 41 10 59.

SANCHEZ GARCIA, Isidoro — Spain EPP (Nat Co)

Isidoro Sanchez Garcia was an MEP in 1991-3 and was re-elected in 1994. Senator and member of the Canaries regional assembly. Former director general of national parks in the Canary Islands. Born January 29 1942.

Address: c/Rodriguez Figueroa 9, E-38400 Puerto de la Cruz, Tenerife. Tel: (22) 38 03 69. Fax: (22) 37 13 68.

SANDBAEK, Ulla — Denmark EDN (June Mov)

Ulla Sandbaek, a minister in the Danish state chruch, was first elected in 1989. Re-appointed member of the ACP/EU assembly after 1994 election. Born April 1 1943.

Address: Gongehusvej 288, DK-2970 Horsholm. Tel: 45 66 18 48. Fax: 42 89 07 18.

225

SANTER, Jacques   Luxembourg PES (CSV)

Jacques Santer was Prime Minister of Luxembourg at the time of his re-election to the EP in 1994. He was then appointed President of the European Commission and was due to succeed Jacques Delors on January 1 1995 and therefore did not take his seat. He has held various government posts including minister of finance. He was vice-president of the EP, 1975-79. Former Mayor of Luxembourg. Born May 18 1937.

Address: 69 rue Jean-Pierre Huberty, L-1742 Luxembourg. Tel: 22 20 59.

SANTINI, Giacomo   Italy FE (FI)

Giacomo Santini was elected in 1994. A television sports presenter, journalist and writer. Born November 10 1941.

Address: Via delle Case Longhe 2, I-38060 Mattarello di Trento.

SANZ FERNANDEZ, Francisco Javier   Spain PES (PSOE)

Francisco Javier Sanz Fernandez, a former member of the Spanish Parliament, has been an MEP since 1986. Agricultural engineer and university professor. Born January 13 1949.

Address: Presidente del Consejo Social Universidad Politecnica, Camino de Vera s/n, E-46022 Valencia. Pza. José Maria Orense 5, E-46022 Valencia. Tel: (6) 372 77 88.

SARLIS, Pavlos   Greece EPP (ND)

Pavlos Sarlis became an MEP in 1989. Member, Greek Parliament for Piraeus and the Islands, 1981-9; member, Greek delegation to Council of Europe, 1985-9. Secretary-General, Ministry of Merchant Shipping, 1977-81; secretary, Greek Chamber of Shipping, 1975-7. Born August 18 1932.

Address: Karaiskou 117, GR-185 35 Pireas. Tel: (1) 417 01 73. Fax: (1) 41 29 232.

SAUQUILLO PEREZ del ARCO, Francisca   Spain PES (PSOE)

Francisca Sauquillo Perez del Arco was elected in 1994. Senator and member of the Madrid regional assembly. President of peace movement. Member of the European Union inquiry into women in Bosnia. Winner of "Women of Europe" prize in 1994. A lawyer. Born July 31 1943.

Address: Narvaez 28, E-28009 Madrid. Tel: 431 13 24.

SCAPAGNINI, Umberto   Italy FE (FI)

Umberto Scapagnini was elected in 1994. Director of pharmacy institute at the University of Catania. Doctor and university lecturer. Born October 16 1941.

Address: Via dei Belfiore 140, I-95028 Valverde.

SCHÄFER, Axel   Germany PES (SPD)

Axel Schäfer was elected in 1994. Head of SPD European office in East Westphalia. Vice-president of local party. Former local government official. Born August 3 1952.

Address: Auf dem Aspei 60, D-44801 Bochum.

SCHAFFNER, Anne-Marie   France EPP (UDF/RPR)

Anne-Marie Schaffner was elected in 1994. Deputy mayor of Fontenay Trésigny. Ile-de-France regional councillor. Born 1945.

Address: 18 rue Leclerc, F-77610 Fontenay Tresigny. Tel: 64 25 93 24. Fax: 64 42 63 12.

SCHIEDERMEIER, Edgar Josef   Germany EPP (CSU)

Edgar Josef Schiedermeier became an MEP in July 1993. Senior official in postal service. Former town and district councillor. Upper Palatinate area chairman of CSA trade union. Diocesan chairman, Catholic workers' union, Regensburg. Head of administration, CSU area committee. Born November 8 1936.

Address: Fichtenstrasse 7, D-93413 Cham. Tel: (09971) 20 892. Fax: (09971) 55 85.

SCHLEICHER, Ursula — Germany EPP (CSU)

Ursula Schleicher, a member of the Bundestag, 1972-80, was elected to the EP in 1979. Member EPP Group bureau. President of Pan-European Union for Bavaria. President of the Union of European Women. Former chairman, Bundestag committee on problems of women and society. CSU adviser on women's rights, 1965-75; president, European Union of Women, 1983-7. Has served as praesidium member, German council of the European Movement, and been deputy federal chairman, German Catholic Workers' Movement. Harpist. Born May 15 1933.

Address: Bundeshaus, D-53113 Bonn. Tel: (0228) 16 77 45. Fax: (0228) 168 60 38. Backoffenstrasse 6, D-63739 Aschaffenburg. Tel: (06021) 92 09 01.

SCHLÜTER, Poul — Denmark EPP (KF)

Poul Schlüter, was Danish Prime Minister, 1982-93 and has been a member of the Folketing since 1964. He was elected to the EP in 1994. A lawyer. Born April 3 1929.

Address: Frederiksberg Alle 66, DK-1820 Frederiksberg C.

SCHMID, Gerhard — Germany PES (SPD)

Gerhard Schmid has been an elected MEP since 1979. Member, Niederbayern-Oberpfalz SPD district executive; district chairman, Young Socialists, 1972-5; member, SPD district management in Lower Bavaria-Upper Palatinate from 1975. Chemist and research fellow, Institute of Biochemistry, Regensburg. Born May 5 1946.

Address: Richard Wagner Strasse 4, D-93055 Regensburg. Tel: (0941) 79 38 01. Fax: (0941) 79 41 29. Altdorfstrasse 13a, D-93049 Regensburg. Tel: (0941) 266 19.

SCHMIDBAUER, Barbara — Germany PES (SPD)

Barbara Schmidbauer has been an MEP since 1987. Vice-chairman, Europa Union, Hesse. Former member, Darmstadt council. Former bank employee. Born November 15 1937.

Address: Jahnstrasse 1, D-64285 Darmstadt. Tel: (06151) 66 30 92. Fax: (06151) 63 725.

SCHNELLHARDT, Horst — Germany EPP (CDU)

Horst Schnellhardt was elected in 1994. Member of Sachsen-Anhalt regional assembly. Member of regional party executive. Veterinary surgeon. Born July 12 1946.

Address: Maxim Gorky Strasse 27, D-38820 Halberstadt. Tel: 03941 24 783. Fax: 03941 27 510.

SCHRÖDER, Jürgen — Germany EPP (CDU)

Jürgen Schröder was elected in 1994. Former member of the Volkskammer and East German observer at the EC. President of CDU regional committee. Translator. Born September 15 1940.

Address: Mendelsohnalle 19, D-01309 Dresden. (0351) 35 219.

SCHROEDTER, Elisabeth   Germany Verts (Grüne)

Elisabeth Schroedter was elected in 1994. Environmental adviser and party worker. Born March 1 1959.

Address: Lindesnstrasse 53, D-14467 Potsdam. Tel: 49 331 28 00 580.

SCHULZ, Martin   Germany PES (SDP)

Martin Schulz was elected in 1994. Mayor of Würselen and a local councillor. Leader of local party. A bookseller. Born December 20 1955.

Address: Dobacher Strasse 15, D-52146 Würselen. Tel: 02405 94 628. Fax: 02405 18 762.

SCHWAIGER, Konrad   Germany EPP (CDU)

Konrad Schwaiger was elected in 1994. A senior official with the Economic and Social Committee. Born April 25 1935.

Address: Stadtgrabenstrasse 17, D-76646 Bruchsal.

231

SEAL, Barry — UK Yorkshire West PES (Lab)

Barry Seal was first elected in 1979. Leader of British Labour MEPs, 1988-9 and a vice-chairman of the Socialist Group. Former member of group bureau and former chief whip of Labour group. Contested Harrogate in the Westminster election in October 1974. Bradford councillor, 1971-9. Chemical engineer and computer consultant with leading British manufacturers before becoming an MEP. Born October 28 1937.

Addresses: City Hall, Bradford, West Yorkshire BD1 1HY. Tel: 0274 752091. Fax: 0274 752092. Brookfields Farm, Brookfields Road, Wyke, Bradford BD12 9LU.

SECCHI, Carlo — Italy EPP (PPI)

Carlo Secchi was elected in 1994. Former local councillor. Economist, journalist and university lecturer. Born February 4 1944.

Address: Via Parodi 23, I-22054 Mandello Del Lario (Lecco). Tel: 0341 735 072.

SEGNI Mario — Italy EPP (Patto Segni)

Mario Segni was elected in 1994 in three constituencies. Former secretary of state. University lecturer and lawyer. Born May 16 1939.

Address: Largo Nazareno 3, I-00187 Roma. tel: (06) 678 34 70. Fax: (06) 678 98 90.

SEILLIER, Françoise — France EDN (l'autre Europe)

Françoise Seillier was elected in 1994. Member of the education committee of the confederation of family organisations in the European Community. Born 1945.

Address: La Châtaigniers, F-12620 Saint Beauzely. Tel: 65 62 01 65. Fax: 65 62 03 99.

SIERRA GONZALEZ, Angela de Carmen — Spain EUL (IU-IC)

Angela de Carmen Sierra Gonzalez was elected in 1994. Active in the feminist movement. University lecturer. Born 1945.

Address: General Mola 18, 1 Deha, E38006 Santa Cruz de Tenerife. tel: 922 28 61 54. Fax: 922 60 31 02.

SIMPSON, Brian — UK Cheshire East PES (Lab)

Brian Simpson won this seat in 1989. Merseyside city councillor, 1981-6, serving on Merseyside Police Authority and being deputy chairman of Liverpool Airport, 1981-6. Member, Warrington Council, 1987-91. Member, League Against Cruel Sports. Teacher in Liverpool, 1974-89. Born February 6 1953.

Addresses: Gilbert Kakefield House, 67 Bewsey Street, Warrington WA2 7JQ. Tel: 0925 654074 Fax: 0925 240799. 28 Walkers Lane, Warrington WA5 2PA. Tel: (0925) 728093.

SINDAL, Niels   Denmark PES (SDP)

Niels Sindal, a deputy mayor, was elected in 1994. A physiotherapist. Born April 29 1959.

Address: Thorvaldsensvej 2, DK-1780 Koben-havn V. Tel: 31 39 15 22. fax: 31 39 40 30.

SISO CRUELLAS, Joaquin   Spain EPP (PP)

Joaquin Siso Cruellas was first elected to the EP in 1989. Former Spanish deputy, being elected in 1982 and 1986. Became programme director, Ministry of Planning and Development, in 1974; later head of construction and infrastructure department, Ministry of Economic Affairs. Author of Government's economic plans for basic infrastructure for 1977-82. Member, executive committee, Alianza Popular. Engineer and architect. Born June 6 1931.

Address: c/los Ciruelos 3, Urb. Monteprincipe, E-28668 Boadilla Del Monte, Madrid. Tel and Fax: 352 44 95.

SKINNER, Peter   UK Kent West PES (Lab)

Peter Skinner won the seat for Labour in 1994. A lecturer and author and at the time of his election was course director for Higher National Certificate in business and finance at a North Kent college. B June 1959; ed Bradford and Warwick Universities.

Address: 69 Holland Road, Maidstone, Kent, ME 14 1UN. Tel: 0622 763679.

SMITH Alex   UK Scotland South PES (Lab)

Alex Smith, former gardener and factory worker, gained this Euro seat for Labour in 1989. Labour Group whip. Chairman, Cunninghame South Labour Party, 1983-7 and constituency trade union liaison officer, 1986-8. Member of the Transport and General Workers' Union's regional and public services and political committees; former convenor of shop stewards committee. Former chairman, Irvine and district trades council. Member of Amnesty International and CND. Born December 2 1943.

Address: 35 Kersland Foot, Girdle Toll, Irvine, Scotland KA11 1BP. Tel: (0294) 216704. Damside, Ayr, Scotland KA8 ER8. Tel: 0292 280096.

SOARES, João   Portugal PES (PS)

João Soares was elected in 1994. A member of the national Parliament since 1987. Deputy mayor of Lisbon. Lawyer. Born July 29 1953.

Address: Campo Grande 99-1, P1700 Lisboa.

SOLTWEDEL, Irene   Germany Verts (Grüne)

Irene Soltwedel was elected in 1994. Member of Hesse regional assembly. Teacher. Born January 28 1955.

Address: Frankfurterstrasse 48, D-Marburg. Tel: 06421 24 117. Fax: 06421 14 721.

SONNEVELD, Jan   Netherlands EPP (CDA)

Jan Sonneveld was first elected in 1989. Agricultural engineer and former adviser to the Dutch ambassador in Washington. Former agricultural attaché at the Dutch Embassies in Beirut, Cairo, Rome. Permanent representative at FAO and WFP in Rome. Born May 13 1933.

Address: Marktstraat 36, 7642 Am Wierden. Tel: (0546) 731 89. Fax: (0546) 57 31 89.

SORNOSA MARTINEZ, María   Spain EUL (IU-IC)

María Sornosa Martinez was elected in 1994. Former local councillor. Born June 15 1949.

Address: Gran Via Ramon y Cajal 55 2, E-46007 Valencia.

SOUCHET, Dominique   France EDN (l'autre Europe)

Dominique Souchet was elected in 1994. A diplomat with the foreign affairs ministry and at present with the Vendée Council. Born 1946.

Address: La Popelinière, F-85400 Saint-Gemme-la-Plaine.

SOULIER, André — France EPP (UDF/RPR)

André Soulier became an MEP in 1992. Member of the national bureau of the Republican Party. Former regional councillor. Born October 18 1933.

Address: 51 avenue Maréchal Foch, F-69006 Lyon. Tel: 78 89 49 64. Fax: 78 89 15 35. 9 rue Grolée, F-69002 Lyon. Tel: 78 37 68 70.

SPAAK, Antionette — Belgium LDR (PVV)

Antionette Spaak, a minister and member of the Chamber of Deputies, was re-elected in 1994. Member of the EP 1979-84.

Address: 35 Avenue d'Italie, B-1050 Bruxelles. Tel: 660 07 70.

SPECIALE, Roberto — Italy PES (PDS)

Roberto Speciale was elected in 1989. Appointed chairman of the regional committee after the 1994 elections. Former member of the bureau of European United Left group. Member of central committee and regional secretary of the PDS. Regional councillor in Ligurie and a former local councillor. Born August 3 1943.

Address: Via Cairoli, I-16100 Genova. Tel: (010) 247 00 44. Fax: (010) 274 03 85.

237

SPENCER, Tom · UK Surrey EPP (C)

Tom Spencer, who won this seat in 1994, became chairman of the Conservative MEPs after the election. MEP for Surrey West, 1989-94 and Derbyshire, 1979-84. Conservative spokesman on the social affairs, employment and working environment committee in the outgoing Parliament. Associate Dean, Templeton College, Oxford, 1984-9; founding executive director, European Centre for Public Affairs, Oxford, 1987-9. Member of the council of the European Movement, 1968-75; chairman, European Union of Conservative and Christian Democratic Students, 1971-3. Born April 10 1948.

Address: Thornfalcon House, Northchapel, West Sussex GU28 9HP. Tel: (0428) 707756. Fax: (0428) 707401.

SPIERS, Shaun · UK London South East PES (Lab)

Shaun Spiers won this seat in 1994. Political officer with the South East Co-operative Society. Trustee of the industrial common ownership fund, the national loan fund for worker co-operatives. Sponsored by the Co-operative Party. Member, Fabian Society and Friends of the Earth. Born April 1962; educated St John's College, Oxford, and King's College, London.

Address: South East Co-op, 132-152 Powis Street, London SE 18 6NL. Tel: 081 692 2453.

STASI, Bernard · France EPP (UDF/RPR)

Bernard Stasi was elected in 1994. Mayor of Epernay. Former member of the National Assembly; former minister and former president of regional council. Member of the UDF political bureau. Vice-president of Christian Democrats International. Born July 4 1930.

Address: 21 Avenue de Champagne, F-51200 Epernay.

STEVENS, John   UK Thames Valley EPP (C)

John Stevens was first elected in 1989. A banker and director of RIT Capital Partners Securities and adviser to J Rothschild Investment Management; a director of Morgan Grenfell International, merchant bankers, 1986-9; foreign exchange bond trader in France, Germany and Italy, 1977-1980, when he joined Morgan Grenfell. Formerly responsible for securities trading in European capital markets. Member, national council, European Movement, 1981-2. Contested Rotherham in 1987 Westminster election. Born May 23 1955.

Address: 15 St James's Place, London SW1A 1NW. Tel: 071 493 8111. Fax: 071 493 5765. 40 Smith Square, London SW1P 3HL. Tel: (071) 222 8804. Fax: (071) 976 7172 (home).

STEWART, Ken   UK Merseyside West PES (Lab)

Ken Stewart was first elected to EP in 1984. Former member, Liverpool City Council and Merseyside County Council. Joiner and member of Ucatt, the building trade union. Former chairman and secretary, Liverpool West Derby Labour Party and a former shop steward. World War Two veteran and an ex-sergeant in the Parachute Regiment. Born July 28 1925.

Address: 62 Ballantyne Road, Liverpool, L13 9AL. Tel and Fax: 051 256 7782.

STEWART-CLARK Sir Jack   UK East Sussex and Kent South, EPP

Sir Jack Stewart-Clark was elected for this seat in 1994. MEP for Sussex East, 1979-94. Re-elected a vice-president of the EP in July 1994. Co-founder, European parliamentarians and industrialists council. President of the conference of regions of North West Europe. Former managing director and member of the Institute of Directors. Contested Aberdeen North in 1959 Westminster election. Born September 17 1929.

Address: Puckstye House, Holtye Common, near Cowden, Kent, TN8 7EL. Tel: 0342 850285. Fax: 0342 850789.

STIRBOIS, Marie-France France Ind (FN)

Marie-France Stirbois, a former member of the National Assembly, was elected in 1994. Member of the Centre Regional Council. Local councillor.

Address: 35 rue de la Ferme, F-92200 Nueilly S/Seine. Tel and Fax: 46 40 72 30.

STOCKMANN, Ulrich Germany PES (SPD)

Ulrich Stockmann was elected in 1994. Former member of the Volkskammer and the Bundestag and a former East German observer at the EP. Leader of the local party. Pastor. Born January 1 1951.

Address: Medlerstrasse 30, D06618 Naumburg/Saale.

STRIBY, Frédéric France EDN (l'autre Europe)

Frédéric Striby was elected in 1994. Mayor of Michelbach-leBas and local councillor. Teacher. Born 1943.

Address: 3 Place de l'Europe, F-68300 Saint Louis. Mairie, F-F-68730 Michelback-le-Bas. Tel: 89 68 40 16. Fax: 89 68 92 29.

STURDY Robert — UK Cambridgeshire EPP (C)

Robert Sturdy won this seat in 1994. A farmer. Member of the Conservative Group for Europe and chairman, York European constituency council. Contested Lancashire East in the 1989 Euro election and Normanton in the 1992 Westminster election. Born June 22 1944; educated at Ashville College, Harrogate.

Address: 153 St Neots Road, Hardwick, Cambridge CB3 7Q5. Tel: 01954 211 790. Fax: 01954 211 786.

TAJANI, Antonio — Italy FE (FI)

Antonio Tajani was elected in 1994. He is Press spokesman for Mr Berlusconi, leader of the party and Italian Prime Minister. He is a journalist and doctor of law. Born August 4 1953.

Address: Via T Salvini 51, I-00197 Roma.

TANNERT, Christof — Germany PES (SPD)

Christof Tannert was a co-founder of *Neues Forum*, the opposition movement in East Germany and was a prisoner of the Stasi in East Germany. Elected to the EP in 1994. Member of the Berlin assembly. A biologist. Born April 4 1946.

Address: Mllerstrasse 163, D-13353 Berlin. tel 46 920. Fax: 46 92 166 (164).

TAPIE, Bernard — France PES (RE)

Bernard Tapie, a former minister and member of the National Assembly, was elected to the EP in 1994. Businessman and President of the Olympique Marseille football club. Regional councillor. Born January 26 1943.

Address: 24 Avenbue de Friedland, F-75008 Paris. Tel: (1) 47 63 09 84. Fax: (1) 43 80 99 68.

TAPPIN, Michael — UK Staffordshire West and Congleton PES (Lab)

Michael Tappin won this seat in 1994. A lecturer on American politics at Keele University and author. Staffordshire county councilor since 1981. Former chairman of the West Midlands forum of local authorities, 1993-4.

Address: 7 Albert Road, Trentham Road, Trentham, Stoke-on-Trent, ST4 8HE. Tel: 0782 659554.

TATARELLA, Salvatore — Italy Ind (AN)

Salvatore Tatarella was elected in 1994. Mayor of Cerignola. Born October 11 1947.

Address: Municipio di Cerignola, I-71042 Cerignola.

TAUBIRA-DELANNON, Christiane   France PES (RE)

Christiane Taubira-Delannon is a member of the National Assembly for Guyana. Leader of the Walwari creole movement. Elected to EP in 1994. Teacher. Born 1952.

Address: Assemblée Nationale, 126 rue de l'Universitié, F-75007 Paris. Tel: (1) 40 63 72 55. Fax: (1) 40 63 77 12.

TELKAMPER, Wilfried   Germany Verts (Grüne)

Wilfried Telkamper became an MEP during the 1984-89 Parliament and was re-elected 1989. A vice-president of EP, 1989-92. Entered politics through youth organisations including Evangelic Youth Movement and Young Socialists. Became a voluntary worker with information centre for Third World in Freiburg and editor of its journal; broadcaster with free radio station Dreyeckland. Born January 16 1953.

Address: Elsa-Brandströmstrasse 31, D-79111 Freiburg in Breisgau. Dreyecklandburo, Habsburger Strasse 9, D-79104 Freiburg. Tel: (0761) 579 80. Fax: (0761) 525 18. Bundestag, Europagruppe die Grunen, Hochhaus am Tulpenfeld HT ZI 219, D-53113 Bonn. Tel: (0228) 16 92 10.

TERRON I CUSI, Ana   Spain PES (PSOE)

Ana Terron i Cusi became an MEP in January 1994 and was re-elected in the June election. Founding member of the the EC's young socialists movement in Spain. Civil servant. Born October 6 1962.

Address: PSC/PSOE Oficina Parlamentaria Europea, c/Nicaràgua 75, E-08029 Barcelona. Tel (3) 321 01 00/410 39 54. Fax: (3) 419 06 02.

TEVERSON, Roger   UK Cornwall and Plymouth West LDR (LD)

Roger Teverson won this seat in 1994. He is managing director of a freight transport consultancy and a former manager with the National Frieght Corporation. Interests include transport and environmental issues. Member of the European Movement. He contested Cornwall South East in the 1992 Westminster election. Joined the Liberal Democrats when the party was formed in 1988. Born March 31 1952; ed Chigwell School; Waltham Forest Technical College; and Exeter University.

Address: Newton Farm, Metherell, Callington, Cornwall, PL17 8DQ. Tel: 0579 51234. Fax: 0579 51 321.

THEATO, Diemut   Germany EPP (CDU)

Diemut Theato became an MEP in October 1987. Appointed chairman of the budgetary control committee in 1994. Deputy chairman, Baden-Württemberg CDU since 1991. Chairman, Europa Union for Thein-Neckar district since 1985. District vice-chairman, Rhein-Neckar CDU. Member, executive committee, Baden-Württemberg CDU women's association, 1979. District chairman, Rhein-Neckar CDU women's association. Translator and conference organiser. Born April 13 1937.

Address: Wiesenweg 21, D-69151 Neckargemünd-Waldhilsbach. Tel: (06223) 34 77. Fax: (06223) 73 240.

THEONAS, Ioannis   Greece EUL (KKE)

Ioannis Theonas was elected in 1994. An economist with Greek telecommunications organisation. Secretary-general of the Confederation of Greek Workers.

Address: Leoforous Irakliou 145. GR-142 31 Nea Ionia. Tel: (01) 2522 591. Fax: (01) 25 11 998.

THOMAS, David   UK Suffolk and Norfolk South West PES (Lab)

David Thomas won this seat in 1994. A Suffolk county councillor. Served in the Royal Navy and Suffolk police force. Member of Greenpeace. Born January 1955; educated at University of East Anglia.

Address: 20 Kirkley Cliff, Lowestoft NR33 0BY. Tel: 0502 563133. Fax: 0502 563105. 3 Parl Walk, Holton, Halesworth, IP19 8NA. Tel: 0986 873817.

THYSSEN, Marianne   Belgium EPP (CVP)

Marianne Thyssen became an MEP in December 1991. Former legal adviser and research director of party movement. Chairman, Flemish women's consultative committee. Member, administrative board, Flemish institute of independent enterprises. Mmeber CVP national executive, 1989-92. General secretary, NCMV (Catholic self-employed and small businessmen's association), since 1991. On staff of deputy Minister of Public Health, 1986-8. Born July 24 1956.

Address: Oude Nethensebaan 24, B-3051 Sint-Joris-Weert.

TILLICH, Stanislaw   Germany EPP (CDU)

Stanislaw Tillich was elected in 1994. Former member of the Volkskammer and an East German observer at the EP. Civil engineer. Born April 10 1959.

Address: Friedensstrasse 13, D-01920 Bernbruch. Tel: 03578 83 167. Fax: 03578 83 169.

TINDEMANS, Leo — Belgium EPP (CVP)

Leo Tindemans, the Prime Minister of Belgium, 1974-8; was first elected to the Parliament in 1979, but resigned in 1981 and was re-elected in 1989. Minister for External Relations, 1981-9. He held other ministerial offices during the Seventies. Member, Belgian Chamber of Deputies, 1961-89. Chairman, EPP group in the outgoing Parliament. Former chairman and secretary-general, European Union of Christian Democrats (EUCD); chairman, Christelijke Volkspartij (CVP), 1979-81. Co-President, African, Caribbean, Pacific-EU Assembly, 1989-92. Born April 16 1922.

Address: Jan Verbertlei 24, B-2650 Edegem. Tel 03/455 66 58. Fax: 02/569 51 36.

TITLEY, Gary — UK Greater Manchester West PES (Lab)

Gary Titley was elected to the EP in 1989. He was a personal assistant to an MEP, 1984-9. Teacher, 1973-84. Contested Dudley West in 1987 Westminster election and Bromsgrove in 1983. Director, West Midlands Enterprise Board, 1982-9; chairman, West Midlands Co-operative Finance Company, 1982-9. Member, West Midlands Council, 1981-6; chairman, Black Country Co-operative Development Agency, 1982-8. Born January 19 1950.

Addresses: Euro Office, 16 Spring Lane, Radcliffe, Manchester, M26 9TQ. Tel: 061 724 4008. Fax: 061 724 4009. 15 Langside Drive, Bolton BL3 4US. Tel: (0204) 653144.

TODINI, Luisa — Italy FE (FI)

Luisa Todini was elected in 1994. Businessperson. Born October 22 1966.

Address: Biale America 93, I-00144 Roma.

TOMLINSON, John — UK Birmingham West PES (Lab)

John Tomlinson was first elected to EP in 1984. Westminster MP for Meriden, 1974-9. PPS to Harold Wilson, Prime Minister, 1975-6. Under secretary for foreign and Commonwealth affairs, 1976-9, and parliamentary secretary, Ministry of Overseas Development, 1977-9. Deputy Leader, EP Labour Group, 1987-8; chief whip, Socialist Group, 1985-9. Former Socialist Group and Labour spokesman on budgets and budgetary control committees and rapporteur on 1990 budget. Born August 1 1939.

Address: 42 Bridge Street, Walsall, West Midlands, WS1 1JQ. Tel: 0922 22586. Fax: 0922 724923.

TONGUE, Carole — UK London East PES (Lab)

Carole Tongue who was first elected to the EP in 1984. Board member, Westminster Foundation for Democracy. Member of the staff of EP Socialist Group, 1980-4. Robert Schuman scholarship for research in social affairs with EP, 1979-80. Courier/guide in France with Sunsites Ltd, 1978-9. Assistant editor, *Laboratory Practice*, 1977-8. Vice-President, Socialist environmental and resources association. Member, Quaker Council for European Affairs. Born October 14 1955.

Address: Euro Constituency Office, 97a Ilford Lane, Ilford, Essex IG1 2RJ.
Tel: 081 514 0198. Fax: 081 553 4764.

TORRES COUTO, Jose Manuel — Portugal PES (PS)

Jose Manuel Torres Couto, secretary-general of the trade union UGT since 1978, was first elected in 1989. Deputy in Portuguese Parliament since 1987. Member, executive committee, International Confederation of Free Trade Unions (CISL) and executive committee of European Confederation of Trade Unions (CES). Born February 1 1947.

Address: Rua Buenos Aires 11, P-Lisboa. Tel: (1) 60 00 11. Av. Afonso III 23-6 C, P-1900 Lisboa. Tel: (1) 82 51 12.

TORRES MARQUES, Helena   Portugal PES (Soc)

Helena Torres Marques was elected in 1994. A former secretary of state, she has been a member of the national Parliament since 1985. An economist. Born May 8 1941.

Address: Parque Oceano 13-5 Esq, P-2780 Oeiras. Tel: (01) 442 01 41.

TRAKATELLIS, Antonios   Greece EPP (ND)

Antonios Trakatellis was elected in 1994. Greek representative on European Union committee dealing with biomedical ethics. Doctor and university professor. Born 1931.

Address: Dim Gounari 1, GR 546 22 Thessaloniki. Tel: (031) 28 45 85.

TRAUTMANN, Catherine   France PES (ES)

Catherine Trautmann was born in Strasbourg and became Mayor of Strasbourg (Bas-Rhin) in March 1989. Member, municipal council since 1983; deputy for Bas-Rhin, 1986-8. In May 1988 became secretary of state for social affairs in Rocard government, with responsibility for the aged and handicapped. Chaired interdepartmental committee to counter drug addiction. First elected to EP in June 1989. Member of the National Assembly and Council of Europe. Theologian. Born January 15 1951.

Address: Hôtel de Ville, F-67000 Strasbourg. Tel: 88 60 90 90. Fax: 88 23 04 40.

TRIZZA, Antonello — Italy Ind (AN)

Antonello Trizza was elected in 1994. Mayor of S. Vito Dei Normanni. Former regional and local councillor. Born July 11 1956.

Address: Via Mesagne 145, I-72100 Brindisi.

TRUSCOTT, Peter — UK Hertfordshire PES (Lab)

Peter Truscott won this seat for Labour in the 1994 election. Formerly worked for the National Association for the Care and Resettlement of Offenders; former full-time agent for the Labour Party. Colchester borough councillor, 1988-92. Contested Torbay in the 1992 Westminster election. Born March 1959; ed Knowles Hill Comprehensive School and Exeter College, Oxford.

Address: 2A Oxford Street, Watford, WO1 8ES. Tel: 0923 800136. Fax: 0923 800136.

TSATSOS, Dimitrios — Greece PES (PASOK)

Dimitrios Tsatsos was elected in 1994. Former minister and member of the national parliament. University professor. Born 1933.

Address: Ipitou 3, GR 105 57 Athina.

ULLMANN, Wolfgang — Germany Verts (Grüne)

Wolfgang Ullman was elected in 1994. Co-founder of Democracy Now movement in East Germany. Member of the Bundestag and former vice-president of the Volkskammer. Former pastor and teacher. Born August 18 1929.

Address: Tieckstrasse 17, D-10115 Berlin.

VALDIVIESO DE CUE, Jaime — Spain EPP (PP)

Jaime Valdivielso De Cue was elected in 1994. President of the Alava chamber of commerce. Businessman. Born 1940.

Address: Altzarrate 10, E-01400 Llodio. Tel: (4) 672 66 50. Fax: (4) 672 29 99.

VALLVE I RIBERA, Joan — Spain LDR (CDC-CIU)

Joan Vallve i Ribera was elected in 1994. Civil servant with the Catalan regional ministry. Born 1940.

Address: Valencia 231, E-08007 Barcelona. Tel: (3) 487 01 11. Fax: (3) 487 12 09.

VALVERDE LOPEZ, Jose Luis   Spain EPP (PP)

Jose Luis Valverde Lopez was first elected in 1987. Pharmacist and university lecturer; vice-president of international pharmacists organisation; author of works on history of Spanish pharmacy. Member, Royal Academies of Pharmacy of Madrid and Barcelona. Born August 11 1940.

Address: Departamento de Farmacia y Tecnologia, Universidad de Granada, E-18001 Granada. Tel: (58) 27 25 89. Severa Ochoa 13 7 b, E-18001 Granada. Tel: (58) 27 23 54.

VANDEMEULEBROUCKE, Jaak   Belgium ERA (VU)

Jaak Vandemeulebroucke became an MEP in 1981. Member, Chamber of Deputies, 1974-7; deputy chef de cabinet to Secretary of State, Anciaux. Communal councillor at Ostend from 1970. A co-chairman of the former ARC Group. Member of his party's bureau since 1973. A vice-chairman, EP committee on regional policy and regional planning, 1987-9. Former teacher. Born May 27 1943.

Address: Anjelierenlaan 25, B-8400 Oostende. Tel: (059) 80 04 28. Fax: (059) 23 72 79.

VANHECKE, Frank   Belgium Ind (Far Right)

Frank Vanhecke, a party worker for the European Right group in the European Parliament, was elected in 1994. Born May 30 1959.

Address: Leitje 51, B-8310 Brugge. Tel: 050/36 14 26.

VAN LANCKER, Anne | Belgium PES (SP)

Anne Van Lancker, a former lecturer and party worker, was elected in 1994. Born March 4 1954.

Address: Prinses Clementinalaan 134, B-9000 Gent.

VARELA SUANCES-CARPEGNA, Daniel Luis | Spain EPP (PP)

Daniel Luis Varela Suances-Carpegna was elected in 1994. Adviser to the regional government of Galicia. Diplomat and lawyer. Born April 1 1950.

Address: Punxeiras Altas, Ortono Ames, E-15228 La Coruña. Tel: (981) 88 38 01.

VAZ DA SILVA, Helena | Portugal LDR (PSD)

Helena Vaz Da Silva was elected in 1994. President of the national committee of Unesco. President of the national centre for culture. Journalist. Born July 3 1939.

Address: Centro Nacional de Cultura, Rua Antonio Maria Cardoso 68, P-1200 Lisboa. Tel: (351 1) 34 66 722. fax: (351 1) 34 28 250.

VECCHI, Luciana — Italy PES (PDS)

Luciana Vecchi was first elected in 1989. Re-appointed a vice-chairman of the ACP/EU Assembly after the 1994 election. Member of the national committee of the Federation of Young Communists. Former civil servant. Born August 19 1961.

Address: Ufficio parlamentare PDS, Viale Fontanelli 11, I-41100 Modena. Tel: (059) 58 28 23. Fax: (059) 21 87 52.

VELZEN, Wim G van — Netherlands EPP (CDA)

Wim G van Velzen was elected in 1994. Senator and former civil servant. Former president of the Christian Democrats. Born January 15 1943.

Address: Maasland 8, 5144 en Waalwijk. Tel: (4160) 36 135. Fax: (4160) 41 690.

VELZEN, Wim J van — Netherlands PES (ESD)

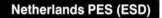

Willem J van Velzen was first elected in 1989. Former Mayor of Huizen. Former national secretary of his party. A teacher. Born May 13 1938.

Address: Botterwijnseweg 11, 1272 EG Huizen. Tel: (02152) 542 09. Fax (02152) 412 01.

VERDE I ALDEA, Josep — Spain PES (PSOE)

Josep Verde I Aldea has been an MEP since 1986. A vice-president of the outgoing Parliament. Former vice-chairman of the Socialist Group bureau. Former member of the Spanish Parliament and vice-president, Council of Europe. Lawyer. Born November 3 1928.

Address: Enric Granados 95 3 1a, E-08008 Barcelona. Tel: (3) 218 22 70. Oficina Parlamentaria Europea - PSC, Nicaragua 75, E-08029 Barcelona.

VERRIER, Odile — France PES (RE)

Odile Verrier was elected in 1994. President of the Paris branch of the *Mouvement des Radicaux de Gauche.* Psychologist and television consultant. Born October 18 1950.

Address: 4 rue Pierre Bonnard, F-75020 Paris. Tel: 43 56 67 43. Fax: 43 56 17 20.

VERWAERDE, Yves — France EPP (UDF/RPR)

Yves Verwaerde was first elected in 1989. Paris councillor and regional councillor for Ile-de-France. Appointed a vice-chairman of the ACP/EU Assembly in 1994. Born May 16 1947.

Address: 105 rue de l'Université, F-75007 Paris. 48 rue d'Eureux, F-27190 La Bonneville s/iton. Tel: 32 37 62 21.

VICECONTE, Walter — Italy FE (FI)

Walter Viceconte was elected in 1994. Doctor and university lecturer. Born October 16 1941.

Address: Presso Centro Studi Valitutti, Piazza Borghese 3, I-00187 Roma.

VILLALOBOS TALERO, Celia — Spain EPP (PP)

Celia Villalobos Talero, a member of the national Parliament, was elected to the EP in 1994. Appointed chairman of the temporary committee on employment in July 1994. An economist. Born 1950.

Address: Plaza Volador 32-0 D, E28007 Madrid. tel: 409 22 66.

VILLIERS, Philippe de — France EDN (l'autre Europe)

Philippe de Villiers was elected in 1994 as head of his own list opposed to closer integration across Europe. Former secretary of state. Member of the national Assembly and president of the Vendée General Council. Doctor of law. Born March 25 1949.

Photograph unavailable

Address: Conseil général de la Vendée, 40 rue Foch, F-85000 La Roche-sur-Yon. Tel: 51 34 48 02. fax: 51 34 49 72.

255

VINCI, Luigi — Italy EUL (RC)

Luigi Vinci was elected in 1994. A former senator. Member of the party national executive. Political scientist. Born May 16 1939.

Address: Direzione Nazionale Rifondazione Communista, Via Barberini 11, I-00187 Roma.

VITORINO, António — Portugal PES (PS)

António Vitorino was elected in 1994. A judge in the Portuguese Constitutional Tribune since 1989. Appointed chairman of the civil liberties and internal affairs committee in 1994. Former member of the national Parliament and secretary of state. Lawyer. Born January 3 1957.

Address: Rue Marlos Portugal 16-RIC, P-1200 Lisboa. Tel: 39 64 845.

von BLOTTNITZ, Undine — Germany Verts (Grüne)

Undine von Blottnitz was an MEP in 1984 and was re-elected in 1994. An architect. Born August 20 1936.

Address: D-29439 Grabow. Tel: 05864 349. Fax 05864 552.

VON HABSBURG, Otto | Germany EPP (CSU)

Otto von Habsburg, president of the International Pan-European Union, was elected in 1979. Member of the French Academy for Moral and Political Science, the Portuguese Cultural Academy and the Spanish Royal Academy for Moral and Political Science. Former group spokesman on political affairs committee. Born November 12 1912.

Address: Hindenburgstrasse 15, 8134 Pöcking. Tel: 08157 7015. Paneuropa Büro, Karlstrasse 57, 8000 München 2. Tel: 089 55 46 83.

VRIES, Gijs de | Netherlands LDR (VVD)

Gijs de Vries was unanimously elected president of the Liberal Group after the 1994 election. First elected to the EP in 1984. An academic and member of the staff of University of Leidnen. Former local councillor. Born February 22 1956.

Address: Postbus 11613, 2502 AP 's-Gravenhage. Tel: (070) 364 74 47. Fax: (070) 345 10 26.

WAAL VAN DER, Leen | Netherlands PES (SP)

Leen van der Waal was first elected in 1984. Engineer and former manager of a transport company and oil businesses. Former committee member, Reform Church in Holland. Born September 23 1928.

Address: Mansdalestr 108, 3067 Jt Rotterdam. Tel (010) 456 19 33. Fax: (010) 421 45 47. Lagendijk 60, 2981 EM Ridderberk. Tel: (01804) 250 64.

WADDINGTON, Sue   UK Leicester PES (Lab)

Sue Waddington won this seat in 1994. She is a former community project leader, lecturer in social policy and manager of community and tertiary education for the local education authorities in Derbyshire and Birmingham. Contested Leicestershire North West in the 1987 Westminster election. Member, Leicestershire County Council, 1973-91 and was former leader of Labour group and chair of education committee. Member, executive committee of UK Migrants Forum, a UK support group. B August 23 1944; educated at Leicester University.

Address: 5 Roundhill Road, Leicester LE5 5RJ. Tel: 0533 730066.

WALTER, Ralf   Germany PES (SPD)

Ralf Walter, a member of the Bundestag, was elected in 1994. Social worker and trade unionist. Born March 15 1958.

Photograph unavailable

Address: Schlaufstrasse 5, D-56812 Cochem. Tel: 02671) 13 10. Fax: (02671) 55 59.

WATSON, Graham,   UK Somerset and Devon North LDR (LD)

Graham Watson won this seat in 1994. Head of government affairs, Hong Kong and Shanghai Bank. He is a qualified French, German, and Italian interpreter. Founder member, EC Youth Forum; member, governing board of European Youth Centre, 1979-81. Former political adviser to Sir David Steel, former leader of the Liberal Party. Born March 23 1956; educated at Heriot Watt University.

Address: Benleigh House, Pilton, Somerset, BA4 4BS. Tel: 0749 890197. Fax: 0749 890198.

WATTS, Mark
UK Kent East, PES (Lab)

Mark Watts is leader of the Labour group on Maidstone Borough Council. Member of Compassion in World Farming. Born June 1964; educated at Maidstone Grammar School and London School of Economics.

Address: 16 Woodbridge Drive, Maidstone, Kent, ME15 6FU. Tel and Fax: 0622 679712.

WEBER, Jup
Luxembourg Verts (GLEI-GAP)

Jup Weber was elected in 1994. Member of the Chamber of Deputies. Local councillor. Forester specialising in work for non-governmental organisations. Born June 15 1950.

Address: 13 rue du Marché aux Herbes, L-2911, Luxembourg.

WEILER, Barbara
Germany PES (SPD)

Barbara Weiler, a member of the Bundestag, was elected to the EP in 1994. Member of Amnesty International. Trade unionist. Born September 17 1946.

Address: Arndstrasse 7, D36093 Künzell.

WEMHEUER, Rosemarie · Germany PES (SPD)

Rosemarie Wemheuer was elected in 1994. Leader of local party. Sociologist and historian and research assistant to member of the Bundestag. Born May 6 1950.

Address: Schloss Strasse 8, D38100 Braunschweig. Tel 0531/480 98 30.

WEST, Norman · UK Yorkshire South PES (Lab)

Norman West was first elected in 1984. Former member, South Yorkshire County Council (chairman, highways committee and anti-nuclear working party). Former vice-chairman of county Labour Party and chairman of Barnsley West and Penistone Labour Party. Former miner. Born November 26 1935.

Address: Treasurer' Department, Second Floor, 18 Regent Street, Barnsley, S70 2HG. Tel: 0226 200738. Fax: 0226 200791. 43 Coronation Drive, Birdwell, Barnsley S10 5RJ. Tel: (0226) 287464. Fax: 0226 200791.

WHITE, Ian · UK Bristol PES (Lab)

Ian White, a criminal lawyer with a Bristol practice, won this Euro seat in 1989; contested Wansdyke in 1987 Westminster election. Member, Society of Labour Lawyers; Labour Campaign for Criminal Justice; Campaign for Nuclear Disarmament; Legal Action Group; Avon Wildlife Trust; Co-operative Party. Born April 8 1945.

Address: 138 Gloucester Road North, Filton, Bristol, BS12 7BQ. Tel: 0272 236933. Fax: 0272 236966.

WHITEHEAD, Phillip   UK Staffordshire East and Derby PES (Lab)

Phillip Whitehead won this seat in 1994. He was Westminster MP for Derby North, 1970-83 and Labour spokesman on higher education and the arts. Member of the Council of Europe, 1974-9 and delegate to the Western European Union. He is a television producer who has won several awards; former columnist on *The Times*. Former executive member, the Howard League for Penal Reform, the Royal Society for the Prevention of Cruelty to Animals, and the Consumers' Association. Served in the Royal West African Frontier Force in Sierra Leone and The Gambia. B May 1937.

Address: 84 Patshull Road, London, NW5 2LD. Tel: 071 485 4884.

WIEBENGA, Jan Kees   Netherlands LDR (VVD)

Jan Kees Wiebenga was elected in 1994. Former member of both chambers of the national Parliament. Former mayor. Mawyer. Born April 6 1947.

Address: Sparrenlaan 17, 2111 AE Aerdenhout. Tel (23) 24 61 41.

WIERSMA, Jan Marinus   Netherlands PES (ESD)

Jan Marinus Wiersma was elected in 1994. A political adviser in the national Parliament. Born August 26 1951.

Address: Herengracht 72, 2312 Le Leiden. Tel (071) 12 58 83. Fax: (071) 12 58 83.

WIJSENBEEK, Florus — Netherlands LDR (VVD)

Florus Wijsenbeek was first elected in 1984. Former secretary general of the Federation of European Liberals. Head of personal cabinet of Cornelius Berkhouwer during his Presidency of the EP, 1973-5. Doctor of law and former member of the legal service of European Commission. Born June 16 1944.

Photograph unavailable

Address: Postbus 11581, 2502 AN 's-Graven-hage. Tel: (070) 364 74 47. Fax: (070) 345 10 26.

WILLOCKX, Freddy — Belgium PES (SP)

Freddy Willockx, a former minister and mayor, was elected in 1994. Member of the Chamber of Deputies since 1979. Former lecturer and party worker. Born, September 2 1947.

Address: Hoogstraat 211, B-9100 Sint-Niklaas. Tel: (03) 766 15 06.

WILSON, Joe — UK Wales North PES (Lab)

Joe Wilson won this Euro seat in 1989. Contested Montgomery in 1983 Westminster election. Lecturer in physical education at North Wales Institute of Higher Education, Wrexham. Chaired Wrexham/Maelor District Labour Party, 1973-88; vice-chairman, Committee of Welsh District Councils, 1987-9. Member, Wrexham/Maelor Council for 12 years; Wrexham Trades Council. Born July 6 1937.

Address: 14 Post Office Lane, Denbigh, Clwyd LL16 3UN. Tel and Fax: 0745 814434.

WOGAU, Karl von — Germany EPP (CDU)

Karl von Wogau was first elected to the EP in 1979. Appointed chairman of the economic, monetary affairs and industrial policy committee in 1994. Member, EPP group bureau. Chairman, EPP group working party on economic affairs. Political activitist in Junge Union since 1963 and CDU since 1969. Member, federal executive committee, CDU/CSU association of small and medium-sized undertakings; member, Bundestag subcommittee on Europe. Founder member of the Kangaroo Club. Commercial lawyer. Born July 18 1941.

Address: Leo-Wohleb-Strasse 6, Postfach 5540, D-79098 Freiburg. Tel: (0761) 218 08 41. Fax: (0761) 218 08 21.

WOLF, Frieder Otto — Germany Verts (Grüne)

Frieder Otto Wolf was elected in 1994; unelected substitute, 1984-9. Worked for the German Green MEPs 1990-2. University lecturer. Born February 1 1943.

Address: Hallesches Ufer 30, D-Berlin. Tel: 251 39 02. Fax: 251 44 25.

WURTH-POLFER, Lydie — Luxembourg LDR (DP)

Lydie Wurth-Polfer has been Mayor of Luxembourg since 1982. Member of the Chamber of Deputies. An MEP in 1985-9 and returned to the Parliament in 1990. Former vice-chairman of the Liberal and Democratic Reformist group (LDR). Former member of the Council of Europe and the Western European Union assemblies. Born November 22 1952.

Address: Mairie, Hotel de Ville, Place Guillaume, L-1648 Luxembourg. Tel: 259 39.

WURTZ, Francis   France EUL (PCF)

Francis Wurtz was first elected in 1979. Has served on central committee, French Communist Party. Former secretary, Bas-Rhin Federation of French Communist Party and of Strasbourg new university. Member, ACP/EU Assembly. Born January 3 1948.

Address: 2 Place du Colonel Fabien, F-75019 Paris. Tel: 40 40 12 91. Fax: 42 40 40 27.

WYNN, Terry   UK Merseyside East & Wigan PES (Lab)

Terry Wynn was elected in 1992. Elected chairman of the Labour group of MEPs (EPLP) in 1992. A training adviser in shipbuilding industry; formerly marine engineer in Merchant Navy. Former meber of Wigan council. Vice-chairman of Westhoughton Labour Party, 1975-80. Methodist local preacher. Born June 27 1946.

Addresses: European Office, 105 Corporation Street, St Helens, Merseyside WA10 1SX. Tel: 0744 451609. Fax: 0744 29832. 34 Holden Brook Close, Leigh WN7 2HL, Lancashire. Tel: (0942) 607327. Fax: 0942 607327.

ZIMMERMANN, Wilmya   Germany PES (SPD)

Wilmya Zimmermann was elected in 1994. Leader of the local party in Forchheim. Medical technician. Born July 30 1944.

Address: Eichenstrasse 9, D-91099 Poxdorf.

Vice-presidents and committee appointments

Vice-presidents

In July 1994 the Parliament elected the following as vice-presidents:
Nicole Fontaine (EPP); David Martin (PES); Nicole Péry (PES); Georgios Anastassopoulos (EPP); Paraskevas Avgerinos (PES); Poul Schulter (EPP); Ursula Schleicher (EPP); Antonio Capucho (LDR); José Maria Gil Robles (EPP); Sir Jack Stewart-Clark (EPP); Josep Verde i Aldea (PES); Renzo Imbeni (PES); Antonio Gutierrez Diaz (EUL); Alessandro Fontana (FE).

Joint assembly

The ACP-EU Joint Assembly was re-established with the following members:
Chairman: Lord Plumb (EPP)
Vice-chairmen: Glenys Kinnock (PES); Karin Junker (PES); Luciano Vecchi (PES); Yves Verwaerde (EPP); Nana Mouskouri (EPP); Pierluigi Castagnetti (EPP); Arlindo Cunha (LDR).
PES: Carniti; Cunningham; Darras; Dury; Ghilardotti; Gröner; Izquierdo Collado; Junker; Kinnock; Kokkola; Kouchner; Kuhn; Laignel; Morris; Péry; Pons Grau; Sauquillo Perez del Arco; Schmidbauer; Soares; Terron i Cusi; Torres Couto; van Putten; Vecchi; Waddington; Wynn.
EPP: Berend; Bernard-Reymond; Poggiolini; Castagnetti; Chanterie; Corrie; Dimitrakopoulos; Escudero; Fernandez Martin; Garcia-Margallo y Marfil; Gillis; Liese; Lucas Pires; Maij-Weggen; Mouskouri; Plumb; Schiedermeier; Schwaiger; Stasi; Verwaerde.
LDR: Bertens; Cunha; Dybkjaer; Galland; Neyts-Uyttebroeck; Wurth-Polfer.
EUL: Gutierrez Diaz; Pettinari; Wurtz. FE: Baldi; Baldini; Caccavale; EDA: Aldo; Andrews; Girao Pereira. Greens: Aelvoet; Lannoye; Telkämper. ERA: Castagnede; McCartney. EDN: Souchet; Sandbaek. Ind: Antony; Muscardini.

Committee membership

The following committees were established in July 1994:
Foreign affairs and security
Chairman: Abel Matutes (EPP). Vice-chairmen: Bernie Malone (PES); Hélène Carrere D'Encausse (EDA); José Mendiluce (PES).
PES: Balfe; Baron Crespo; Bladel; Colajanni; Hoff; Lang (Jack); Malone; Marinho; David; Mendiluce Pereiro; Newens; Occhetto; Papoutsis; Rocard; Roubatis; Sakellariou; Seal; Titley; Truscott.
EPP: Bernard-Reymond; Cassidy; Castagnetti; Fernandez-Albor; Gomolka; Graziani; von Habsburg; Kristoffersen; Lambrais; Lenz; Matutes; Oostlander; Poettering; Rinsche; Robles Piquer; Tindermans.
LDR: Bertens; De Melo; Gol; La Malfa. EUL: Alavanos; Carnero Gonzalez; Piquet. FE: Caligaris; Casini. EDA: Carrere d'Encausse; Daskalaki. Greens: Aelvoet; Langer. ERA: Lalumiere; Pannella. EDN: Souchet. Ind: Muscardini.
Agriculture and rural development
Chairman: Christian Jacob (EDA). Vice-chairmen: José Happart (PES); Friedrich-Wilhelm Graefe zu Baringdorf (Greens); Honor Funk (EPP).
PES: Baldarelli; Campos; Colino Salamanca; Fantuzzi; Görlach; Hallam; Happart; Hardstaff; Kindermann; Laignel; Lambraki; Rehder; Spiers; Thomas; Wilson.
EPP: Arias Cañete; Dimitrakopoulos; Ebner; Filippi; Fraga Estevez; Funk; Gillis; Goepel; Kepplehoff-Weichert; Mayer; Redondo; Sonneveld; Sturdy.
LDR: Cunha; Kofoed; Mulder. EUL: Ephremidis; Jové Peres. FE: De Luca; Santini. EDA: Hyland; Jacob; Rosado Fernandes. Greens: Graefe zu Baringdorf; Weber. ERA: Barthet-Mayer. END: Martin (Philippe); Poisson. Ind: Martinez; Parigi.

COMMITTEE APPOINTMENTS

Budgets
Chairman: Detlev Samland (PES). Vice-chairmen: Stanislaw Tillich (Greens) Manuel Porto (LDR); Frederik Willockx (PES).
PES: Avgerinos; Colom i Naval; Dankert; Dürkop Dürkop; Ghilardotti; Haug; Krehl; Samland; Tappin; Tomlinson; Trautman; Willockx; Wynn.
EPP: Bardong; Bébéar; Böge; Elles; Fabra Valles; McCartin; Nicholson; Raffarin; Tillich.
LDR: Brinkhorst; Moretti; Porto. EUL: Miranda. FE: Di Prima. EDA: Bazin. Greens: Müller. ERA: Dell'Alba. EDN: Fabre-Aubrespy. Ind: Le Gallou; Tartella.

Economic, monetary affairs and industrial policy
Chairman: Karl von Wogau (EPP). Vice-chairmen: Almen Metten (PES); Ioannis Tehonas (EUL); Georgios Katiforis (PES).
PES: Billingham; Caudron; Donnelly; Garcia; Glante; Harrison; Hendrick; Katiforis; Kucklekorn; Metten; Miller; Moscovici; Murphy; Perez-Royo; Randzio-Plath; Rapkay; Read; Ruffolo; Torres Marques.
EPP: Areitio Toledo; Bremond d'Ars; Christodoulou; Friedrich; Garcia-Margallo y Marfil; Herman; Hoppenstedt; Konrad; Langen; Lulling; McMillan-Scott; Peijs; Secchi; Thyssen; Wogau.
LDR: Gasoliba; Kestelijn-Sierens; Larive; Riis-Jorgensen; Watson. EUL: Theonas; Vinci. FE: Garosci; Mezzaroma. EDA: Gallagher; Greens: Soltwedel; Wolf. ERA: Dary. EDN: Rose. Ind: Mégret; Trizza.

Energy, research and technology
Chairman: Claude Desama (PES). Vice-chairman: Gordon Adam (PES); Godelieve Quisthoudt-Rowohl (EPP); Eryl McNally (PES).
PES: Adam; Desama; Izquiero Collado; Linkohr; McNally; Nencini; Rothe; Tannert; West.
EPP: Argyros; Chichester; Estevan Bolea; Ferber; Mombaur; Quisthoudt-Rowohl; Soulier; Velzen.
LDR: Formentini; Plooij-van Gorsel. EUL: Marset Campos. FE: Scapagnini. EDA: Pompidou. Greens: Ahern. ERA: Macartney. EDN: de Gaulle. Ind: Rauti.

External economic relations
Chairman: Willy de Clercq (LDR). Vice-chairman: Michael Hindley (PES); André Sainjon (ERA); Peter Pex (EPP).
PES: Beres; Falconer; Hindley; Imbeni; Mann; Miranda de Lage; Moniz; Smith; Stockmann.
EPP: Ferrer; Kittelmann; Moorhouse; Pex; Schwaiger; Valdivielso de Cué; Verwaerde.
LDR: Bossi; de Clercq. EUL: De Sa. FE: Malerba. EDA: Chesa. Greens: Kreissl-Dörfler. ERA: Sainjon. EDN: Goldsmith. Ind: Lang (Carl).

Legal affairs and citizens' rights
Chairman: Carlo Casini (EPP). Vice-chairmen: Willi Rothley (PES); Ana Palacio Vallelersundi (EPP); Roberto Barzanti (PES).
PES: Barzanti; Cot; Gebhardt; Green; Medina; Oddy; Rothley; Verdi i Aldea; Megahy.
EPP: Alber; Casini; Janssen van Raay; Malangré; Mosiek-Urbahn; Palacio Vallelersundi; Stevens.
LDR: de Vries. EUL Sierra Gonzalez; FE: Florio. EDA: Schaffner. Greens: Ullman. ERA: Pradier EDN: Krarup. Ind: Gollnisch; Musumeci.

Social affairs, employment and working environment
Chairman: Stephen Hughes (PES). Vice-chairmen: Winfried Menrad (EPP); Mireille Elmalan (EUL); Ombretta Colli (FE).
PES: Bredin; Cabezon; Carniti; Hughes; Joens; Kerr; McMahon; Morris; Papakyriazis; Peter; Skinner; Torres Couto; van Lancker; Velzen; Weiler.
EPP: Bourlanges; Chanterie; Glase; Imaz san Miguel; Mann; Mather; Menrad; Oomen Ruijten; Pronk; Schiedermeier; Villalobos Talero.
LDR: Boogerd-Quaak; Mendonca. EUL: Elmalan; Hermange. FE: Colli; Viceconte. EDA: Crowley; Hermange. Greens: Gyldenkilde. ERA: Vandemeulenboucke. EDN: Jensen. Ind: Angelilli; Stirbois; Vanhecke.

Regional policy and relations with local authorities

Chairman: Roberto Speciale (PES). Vice-chairmen: Francis Decourière; Konstantinos Klironomos (PES); Luis Campoy Zueco.

PES: Bernardini; Botz; Crampton; Darras; McCarthy; Frutos Gama; Howitt; Hume; Klironomos; Lage; Speciale; Walter.

EPP: Berend; Campoy Zueco; Corrie; de la Merced; Decourrière; Hatzidakis; Klass; Langenhagen; Schröder; Varela Suanzes-Carpegna.

LDR: Costa Neves; Teverson; Vallve Ribera. EUL: Ainardi; Gutiérrez. FE: Azzolini; Podesta. EDA: Baggioni; Collins (Gerard); Donnay. Greens: Schroedter. ERA: Castagnede; Sanchez Garcia. EDN: des Places. Ind: Cellai.

Transport and tourism

Chairman: Petrus Cornelissen (EPP). Vice-chairmen: Eolo Parodi (FE); Günter Lüttge (PES); Nikitas Kaklamanis (EDA).

PES: Castricum; Diez de Rivera Icaza; Lüttge; Panagopoulos; Piecyk; Schlechter; Simpson; Sindal; Stewart; Watts.

EPP: Cornelissen; Jarzembowski; Koch; McIntosh; Salafranca Sanchez-Neyra; Sarlis; Siso Cruellas.

LDR: Farassino; Wijsenbeek. EUL: Moreau. FE: Parodi. EDA: Kaklamanis; Killilea. Greens: Dijk. ERA: Tapie. EDN: Waal. Ind: Bellere; Le Rachinel.

Environment, public health and consumer protection

Chairman: Ken Collins (PES). Vice-chairmen: Caroline Jackson (EPP); Lone Dybkjaer (LDR); Kirsten Jensen (PES).

PES: Apolinario; Bowe; Collins; Gonzalez Trivino; Jensen; Kokkola; Kuhn; Marinucci; Pollack; Putten; Roth-Behrendt; Waddington; White; Whitehead.

EPP: Burtone; Florenz; Grossetête; Jackson; Oomen-Ruijten; Poggiolini; Rovsing; Schleicher; Schnellhardt; Trakatellis; Valverde Lopez.

LDR: Dybkjaer; Eisma; Pimenta. EUL: Bertinotti; Gonzalez Alvarez; Papayannakis. FE: Baldi; Leopardi; Viceconte. EDA: Cabrol; Fitzsimons. Greens: Bloch von Blottnitz; Breyer; Lannoye. ERA: Mamere. EDN: Blokland; Sandbaek. Ind: Amadeo; Feret.

Culture, youth and media

Chairman: Luciana Castellina (EUL). Vice-chairmen: Mary Banotti (EPP); Francisco Sanz Fernandez (PES); Daniel Cohn-Bendit (Greens).

PES: Aparicio Sanchez; Augias; De Coene; Elliott; Evans; Gröner; Kuhne; Montesano; Morgan; Sanz Fernandez; Tongue; Junker.

EPP: Banotti; Bianco; Escudero; Fontaine; Galeote Quecedo; Heinisch; Mouskouri; Pack; Perry.

LDR: André-Léonard; Marin; Vaz da Silva. EUL: Aramburu del Rio; Castellina. FE: Arroni; Boniperti; Todini. EDA: Aboville; Guinebertiere. Greens: Cohn-Bendit; Ripa di Mena. ERA: Verrier. EDN: Seillier. Ind: Dillen.

Development and co-operation

Chairman: Bernard Kouchner (PES). Vice-chairman: Francis Wurtz (EUL); Bernard Stasi (EPP); Raimondo Fassa (LDR).

PES: Cunningham; Junker; Kinnock; Kouchner; McGowan; Needle; Péry; Pons Grau; Sauquillo Perez del Arco; Schmid; Soares; Vecchi.

EPP: Añoveros Trias de Bes; Fernandez Martin; Grosch; Günther; Liese; Maij-Weggen; Oomen-Ruijten; Plumb; Stasi.

LDR: Fassa; Galland; Wurth-Polfer. EUL: Pettinari; Wurtz. FE: Baldi; Baldini. EDA: Aldo; Andrews. Greens: Telkämper. ERA: Hory; Taubira-Delannon. EDN: Stirby. Ind: Antony; Paisley.

Civil liberties and internal affairs

Chairman: Antonio Vitorino (PES). Vice-chairmen: Maria Paola Colombo Svevo (EPP); Rinaldo Bontempi (PES); Jan Wiebenga (LDR).

PES: d'Ancona; Barros Moura; Bontempi; Crawley; Ford; Lindeperg; Newman; Salisch; Schulz; Terron i Cusi; Vitorino; Zimmermann.

EPP: Colombo Svevo; d'Andrea; Deprez; Esteban Martin; Lehne; Nassauer; Posselt; Reding; Stewart-Clark.

LDR: Haarder; Wiebenga. EUL: Manisco. FE: Caccavale. EDA: Girão Pereira. Greens: Orlando; Roth. ERA: Fouque. EDN: de Villiers. Ind: Le Chevallier.

COMMITTEE APPOINTMENTS

Budgetary control
Chairman: Diemut Theato (EPP). Vice-chairmen: Freddy Blak (PES); Thierry Jean-Pierre (EDN); Joe McCartin (EPP).
PES: Blak; Lomas; Wemheuer; Lange; Schmidbauer.
EPP: Garriga Polledo; Hersant; Kellett-Bowman; McCartin; Theato.
LDR: Hansen. EUL: Pailler. FE: de Luca. EDA: Pasty. Greens: McKenna. ERA: Ewing. EDN: Jean-Pierre. Ind: Le Pen.

Institutional affairs
Chairman: Fernando Moran Lopez (PES). Vice-chairman: Inigo Mendez de Vigo (EPP); Georges Berthu (EDN) Elisabeth Guigou (PES).
PES: Barton; Coates; de Giovanni; Dury; Guigou; Izquierdo Rojo; Manzella; Martin; Moran Lopez; Schäfer; Tsatsos; Wiersma.
EPP: Anastassopoulos; Baudis; Brok; Cushnahan; Donnelly; Gil-Robles Gil-Delgado; Lucas Pires; Maij-Wegen; Martens; Mendez de Vigo; Segni.
LDR: Capucho; Cox; Neyts-Uyttebroeck; Spaak. EUL: Herzog; Puerta; Sornosa. FE: Danesin; Marra. EDA: Monteiro. Greens: Aglietta. ERA: Saint-Pierre. EDN: Berthu; Bonde. Ind: Blot; Ferri; Fini.

Fisheries
Chairman: Miguel Arias Canete (EPP). Vice-chairmen: Niels Kofoed (LDR); Heinz Kindermann (PES); Pat Gallagher (EDA).
PES: Adam; Baldarelli; Crampton; Izquierdo Rojo; Kindermann; Péry; Roubatis.
EPP: Arias Cañete; Bourlanges; Fraga Estevez; Langenhagen; Provan; Varela Suanzes-Carpegna.
LDR: Kofoed; Teverson. EUL: Jové Peres. FE: Marra. EDA: Aboville; Gallagher. Greens: McKenna. ERA: Macartney. Ind: Martinez.

Rules of procedure; verification of credentials and immunities
Chairman: Ben Fayot (PES). Vice-chairmen: Marlies Mosiek-Urbahn (EPP); Florus Wijsenbeek (LDR); Irini Lambraki (PES).
PES: Balfe; Fayot; Ford; Lambraki; Manzella; Marinho; Rothley; Verdi i Aldea.
EPP: d'Andrea; Donnelly; Galeote; Janssen van Raay; Malangré; Mosiek-Urbahn.
LDR: Capucho; Wijsenbeek. EUL: Ephremidis. FE: Florio. EDA: Crowley. Greens: Aglietta. ERA: Dell'Alba. EDN: Jean-Pierre. Ind: Tatarella.

Women's Rights
Chairman: Nel van Dijk (Greens). Vice-chairmen: Anne van Lancker; Francisca Bennasar Tous (EPP); Antoinette Fouque (ERA).
PES: d'Ancona; Crawley; Garcia Arias; Ghilardotti; Gröner; Kinnock; Kokkola; Pollack; Randzio-Plath; Read; Roth-Behrendt; Torres Marques; van Lancker; Waddington.
EPP: Banotti; Bennasar Tous; Colombo Svevo; Glase; Jackson; Lulling; Maij-Weggen; Menrad; Mouskouri; Peijs.
LDR: André-Léonard; Kestelijn-Sierens; Larive. EUL: Moreau; Sornosa Martinez. FE: Colli. EDA: Killilea. Greens: Dijk; Gyldenkilde. ERA: Fouque. EDN: Seiller. Ind: Stirbois.

Petitions
Chairman: Eddie Newman (PES). Vice-chairmen: Ingo Friedrich (EPP); Nuala Ahern (Greens); Georgios Dimitrakopoulos (EPP).
PES: Augias; Barros Moura; Blak; Kuhn; Lomas; Miranda de Lage; Newman; Papakyriazis; Schmidbauer; Stewart.
EPP: Banotti; Chanterie; Dimitrakopolous; Friedrich; Imaz san Miguel; Oomen-Ruijten; Palacio Vallelersundi; Perry.
LDR: Bertens; Dybkjaer. EUL: Gutiérrez Diaz. FE: Tajani. EDA: Schaffner. Greens: Ahern. ERA: Verrier. EDN Striby. Ind: Amadeo.

Temporary Committee on employment
Chairman: Daniel Villalobos Talero (EPP). Vice-chairmen: Wim G Van Velzen (PES); Giorgio La Malfa (LDR); Salvador Jové Peres (EUL).
PES: Barros Moura; Bontempi; Cabezon Alonso; Coates; Katiforis; McCarthy; Moscovici; Randzio-Plath; Ruffolo; Schmidbauer; Seal; Sindal; van Lancker; Velzen.
EPP: Areitio Toledo; Argyros; Bremond d'Ars; Burtone; Filippi; Friedrich; Mather; Pronk; Thyssen; Villalobos; Wogau.
LDR: Boogerd-Quaak; La Malfa; Porto. EUL: Jové Peres. FE: Fontana; EDA: Guinebertiere. Greens: Gyldenkilde. ERA: Sainjon. Ind: Martinez.

Quaestors
The following Quaestors, who are concerned with the internal management of the Parliament but not the control of its agenda, were elected:
Richard Balfe (PES); Otto Bardong (EPP); Jean-Pierre Raffarin (EPP); Sergio Ribeiro (EUL); João Soares (PES).

Presidents of the European Parliament

Common Assembly of the European Coal and Steel Community

Henri Spaak (Belgium, Soc)	Sep 11 1952 to May 11 1954
Alcide de Gasperi (Italy, CD)	May 11 1954 to Aug 18 1954

[On Mr De Gasperi's death, Jean Fohrman, (Luxembourg, Soc) assumed office — but not the title of president — from Aug 19 1954 to Nov 29 1954 until a successor could be elected.]

Giuseppe Pella (Italy, CD)	Nov 29 1954 to Nov 27 1956
Hans Furler (Germany, CD)	Nov 27 1954 to Mar 19 1958

European Parliament (Nominated MEPs)

Robert Schuman (France, CD)	Mar 19 1958 to Mar 28 1960
Hans Furler (Germany, CD)	Mar 28 1960 to Mar 27 1962
Gaetano Martino (Italy, LD)	Mar 27 1962 to Mar 21 1964
Jean Duvieusart (Belgium, CD)	Mar 21 1964 to Sep 24 1965
Victor Leemans (Belgium, CD)	Sep 24 1965 to Mar 7 1966
Alain Poher (France, CD)	Mar 6 1966 to Mar 12 1969
Mario Scelba (Italy, CD)	Mar 12 1969 to Mar 9 1971
Walter Behrendt (Germany, Soc)	Mar 9 1971 to Mar 13 1973
Cornelis Berkhouwer (Netherlands, LD)	Mar 13 1973 to Mar 11 1975
Georges Spenale (France, Soc)	Mar 11 1975 to Mar 8 1977
Emilio Columbo (Italy, EPP)	Mar 8 1977 to Jul 17 1979

European Parliament (Elected MEPs)

Simone Veil (France, LD)	Jul 17 1979 to Jan 18 1982
Pieter Dankert (Netherlands, Soc)	Jan 20 1982 to Jul 24 1984
Pierre Pflimlin (France, EPP)	Jul 24 1984 to Jan 20 1987
Lord Plumb (United Kingdom, ED)	Jan 20 1987 to Jul 25 1989
Enrique Barón Crespo (Spain, Soc)	Jul 25 1989 to Jan 13 1992
Ego Alfred Klepsch (Germany, Soc)	Jan 13 1992 to Jul 19 1994
Klaus Hänsch (Germany PES)	Jul 19 1994 to

The bureau of the Parliament consists of the President and Vice-Presidents and the enlarged bureau consists of those appointees plus the political group leaders. The five quaestors, elected to look after MEPs' interests and to manage the internal affairs of the Parliament, sit in on meetings of the enlarged bureau which arranges the Parliament's agenda and supervises all its activities.

European Parliament Information Offices

The European Parliament holds its plenary sessions at the Palais de l'Europe, Strasbourg (Tel: 88/374001). The Parliament's secretariat is based in the Centre Européen, Plateau Kirchberg, 2929 Luxembourg (Tel: 010 352 43001; Fax: 010 352 437261) and the Parliament has offices at 97-113, Rue Belliard, B-1047 Brussels (Tel: 010 32 2 284 2111; Fax: 010 32 2 230 7555).

The secretariats of the political groups and many EP staff are based in Brussels and MEPs can be contacted there, especially during committee sittings.

The President of the Parliament has offices in each of the three centres.

Information Offices of the Parliament:

Athens:	112A, Avenue Vassilissis Sophias, Athens 11527. Head: Georgios Papadopoulos	Tel: 010 30 1 771 88 33 Fax: 010 30 1 777 18 17
Bonn:	Bonn Center, Bundeskanzlerplatz, 5300 Bonn. Head: Klaus Loeffler Bonn Sub-office:	Tel: 010 49 2 2822 3091 Fax: 010 49 2 2821 8955 Tel: 010 49 30 893 0122 Fax: 010 49 30 892 1733
Brussels:	97 Rue Belliard, B-1047 Brussels. Head: Peter Thomas	Tel: 010 32 2 284 2111 Fax: 010 32 2 230 7555
Copenhagen:	Borsen, 1217 Copenhagen. Head: Mikael Bramsen.	Tel: 010 45 33 14 33 77 Fax: 010 45 33 15 08 05
Dublin:	43 Molesworth Street, Dublin 2. Head: James O'Brien	Tel: 010 353 1 71 91 00 Fax: 010 353 1 6795391
The Hague:	6 Korte Vyverberg, 2513 AB The Hague. Head: Eppo Jansen	Tel: 010 31 70 362 4941 Fax: 010 31 70 364 7001
Lisbon:	56 Rua do Salitre (sixth floor), 1200 Lisbon. Head: Nuno Campos	Tel: 010 35 1 157 8031 Fax: 010 35 1 154 0004
London:	2 Queen Anne's Gate, London, SW1H 9AA. Head: Martyn Bond	Tel: 071 222 0411 Fax: 071 222 2713
Luxembourg:	Europan Centre Kirchberg, 2929 Luxembourg. Head: Fernand Georges	Tel: 010 352 43001 Fax: 010 352 437261
Madrid:	4 Calle Fernanflor (Fourth Floor) 28014 Madrid. Head: Fernando Carbajo	Tel: 010 34 1 429 3352 Fax: 010 34 1 429 8349
Paris:	285 Boulevard St Germain, 75007 Paris. Head: Bernard Chevallier	Tel: 010 33 1 4063 4000 Fax: 010 33 1 4551 5253
Rome:	149 Via IV Novembre, 00187 Rome. Head: Giovanni Salimbeni	Tel: 010 39 6 69 95 01 Fax: 010 39 6 69 95 0200

☐ The offices of the European Conservatives (071 222 1720) and the British Labour Group (071 222 2719) are located in the London offices of the Parliament. Liberal Democract MEPs can be contacted throught the party's office at 4 Cowley Street, London, SW1P 3NB (071 222 7999) and the Scottish National Party MEPs can be contacted through their office at 6 North Charlotte Street, Edinburgh EH2 4JH (031 226 3661).

European Commission Offices

The European Commission can be contacted at the following addresses in the capitals and other large cities across the European Union.

United Kingdom
8 Storey's Gate, London SW1P 3AT. Tel: 071 973 1992. Fax 071 1900 and 1910. Sub-offices: Windsor House, 9/15 Bedford Street, Belfast BT2 7EG. Tel: 0232 240708. 4 Cathedral Road, Cardiff CF1 9SG. Tel: 0222 371631. 7 Elva Street, Edinburgh, EH2 4PH. Tel: 031 225 2058.

Belgium
Archimedesstraat 73, 1040 Brussels. Tel: 235 11 11

Denmark
Hojbrohus, Ostergade 61, Postbox 144, 1004 Kobenhaven, K. Tel: 14 41 40.

France
61 Rue des Belles-Feuilles, 75782 Paris Cedex 16. Tel: 45 01 58 85. CMCI/Bureau 320, 2 Rue Henri Barbusse, F-13241, Marseilles CEDEX 01. Tel: 91 46 00.

Germany
Zitelmannstrasse 22, 53000 Bonn. Tel: 23 80 41. Kurfurstebdamm 102, 1000 Berlin 31. Tel: 892 40 28. Erhardstrasse 27, 8000 Munich. Tel: 202 10 11.

Greece
2 Vassilissis Sofias, PO Box 11002, Athens 10674. Tel: 724 39 82.

Ireland
39 Molesworth Street, Dublin 2. Tel: 71 22 44.

Italy
Via Poli 29, 00187 Rome. Tel: 678 97 22. Corso Magenta 61, 20123 Milan. Tel: 80 15 05/6/7/8.

Luxembourg
Batiment Jean Monnet, Rue Alcide de Gasperi, 2920 Luxembourg. Tel: 430 11.

The Netherlands
Lange Voorhout 29, The Hague. Tel: 46 93 26.

Portugal
Centre Européen Jean Monnet, 56 Rua do Salitre, 1200 Lisbon. Tel: 154 11 44

Spain
Calle de Serrano 41, 5a Planta, Madrid 1. Tel: 435 17 00/435 15 28.

Switzerland
Case Postale 195, 37-39 Rue de Vermont, 1211 Geneva. Tel: 34 97 50.

The European Commission

The present Commission took office in January 1989. A new commission will take office in January 1995. It will include commissioners from the four new members, Austria, Finland, Norway and Sweden.

The portfolios of the existing commission are as follows:

Jacques Delors (French). President: Secretariat general; forward studies unit; inspectorate-general; legal service; monetary matters; spokesman's service; joint interpreting and conference service; security office.

Henning Christophersen (Danish). Vice-president: Economic and financial affairs; monetary matters (in conjuction with President Delors); credit and investments; statistical office.

Manuel Marin (Spanish). Vice-president: Co-operation and development; Lomé Convention; humanitarian aid.

Martin Bangemann (German). Industrial affairs; information and telecommunications technology.

Sir Leon Brittan (British). External economic affairs; commercial policy.

Antonio Ruberti (Italian). Science, research and development; joint research centre; human resources, education, training and youth.

Karel Van Miert (Belgian). Competition; personnel and administration policy; translation and informatics.

Peter Schmidhuber (German). Budgets; financial control; fraud prevention; cohesion fund.

Marcelino Oreja (Spanish). Energy and Euratom supply agency; transport.

Christiane Scrivener (French). Customs and indirect taxation; direct taxation; consumer policy.

Bruce Millan (British). Regional policy; relations with Committee of the Regions.

Hans van den Broek (Dutch). External political relations; common foreign and security policy; enlargement negotiations.

Joao de Deus Pinheiro (Portuguese). Relations with the European Parliament; internal relations with member states on openness, communication and information; culture and audiovisual; official publications.

Padraig Flynn (Irish). Social affairs and employment; relations with economic and social committee; immigration; justice and home affairs.

Rene Steichen (Luxembourger). Agriculture and rural development.

Ioannis Paleokrassas (Greek). Environment; nuclear safety and civil protection; fisheries.

Raniero Vanni d'Archirafi (Italian). Institutional questions; internal market; financial institutions; enterprise policy.